William Speirs Bruce

William Speirs Bruce
Forgotten Polar Hero

Isobel P. Williams
and
John Dudeney

AMBERLEY

First published 2018

Amberley Publishing
The Hill, Stroud
Gloucestershire, GL5 4EP

www.amberley-books.com

Copyright © Isobel P. Williams and John
Dudeney, 2018

The right of Isobel P. Williams and John
Dudeney to be identified as the Authors of this
work has been asserted in accordance with the
Copyrights, Designs and Patents Act 1988.

ISBN 978 1 4456 8081 1 (hardback)
ISBN 978 1 4456 8082 8 (ebook)

British Library Cataloguing in Publication Data.
A catalogue record for this book is available
from the British Library.

Map on page 7 by Laura Gerrish at the British
Antarctic Survey.
Typesetting and Origination by Amberley Publishing
Printed in the UK.

CONTENTS

Antarctica and the Southern Ocean

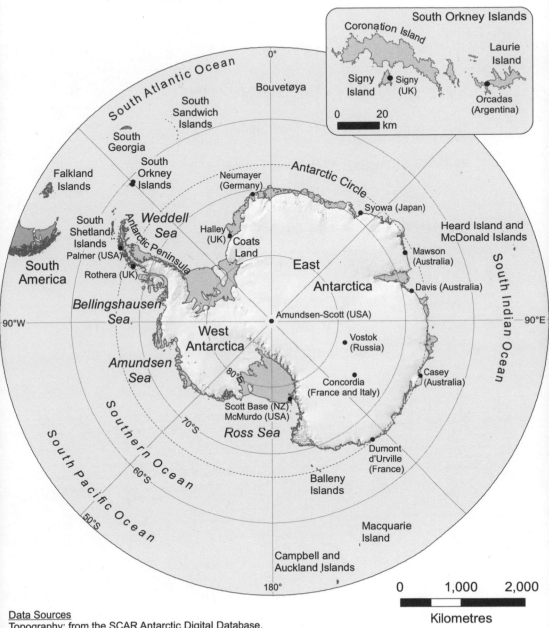

South Orkney Islands

Coronation Island

Laurie Island

Signy Island   Signy (UK)

Orcadas (Argentina)

0   20   km

0°

South Atlantic Ocean

Bouvetøya

South Sandwich Islands

South Georgia

South Orkney Islands

Antarctic Circle

Neumayer (Germany)

Falkland Islands

Syowa (Japan)

Weddell Sea

Heard Island and McDonald Islands

South Shetland Islands

Halley (UK)   Coats Land

Palmer (USA)

Antarctic Peninsula

Mawson (Australia)

South America

Rothera (UK)

East Antarctica

Davis (Australia)

90°W

Bellingshausen Sea

Amundsen-Scott (USA)

90°E

West Antarctica

Vostok (Russia)

Amundsen Sea

Casey (Australia)

80°S

Concordia (France and Italy)

Scott Base (NZ)
McMurdo (USA)

70°S   Ross Sea

Dumont d'Urville (France)

Southern Ocean

60°S

Balleny Islands

50°S

South Pacific Ocean

Macquarie Island

South Indian Ocean

Campbell and Auckland Islands

180°

0   1,000   2,000

Kilometres

Data Sources
Topography: from the SCAR Antarctic Digital Database.
Research stations: selected from the COMNAP list of facilities
(nationalities in parentheses).

PROLOGUE

William Speirs Bruce was born in 1867 when Queen Victoria was on the throne and the sun did not set on the British Empire. He was twenty-eight when scientific societies throughout the world were urged to promote the cause of Antarctic exploration, and he supported that call. He died, aged fifty-four, in 1921, just after the First World War, one of the great polar explorers of the 'Heroic Age'. His story has been neglected. In our estimation Bruce has had at least as great an impact on polar science and diplomacy as any of the other 'greats' of that period.

'Scotland is not a dependent country but an individual nation working hand in hand on at least an equal footing with her partners in the Great British Federation.'[1] An unexpected declaration from a man born and brought up in England, but one that has resonance today and one that he felt passionately until his dying day. This Scottish nationalism and his other passion, natural science, dominated his thoughts and actions.

A driven man then, not an easy-going character, one that a friend and admirer, William Gordon Burn Murdoch, said could be 'as prickly as the Scottish thistle itself'.[2] He was a poor communicator and a man of reticence, with a deep reserve that was difficult to penetrate – 'no man and certainly no woman ever crossed that barrier'.[3] Indeed, today, his reserve, his single minded focus, his apparent difficulty in sharing and communicating with others, might suggest that he could be considered as being on the autistic spectrum. He was nevertheless a man of integrity, honesty and determination, and achieved much in the advancement of exploration, geography and science in the name of his beloved Scotland.

Like other famous Heroic Age explorers he did not achieve all his ambitions, but he did make discoveries that are recognised today. Under the banner of Scotland he brought together a team of experienced scientists who contributed significantly to knowledge about the polar regions. On the *Scotia* expedition to the Antarctic in 1902 he discovered new land bordering the Weddell Sea, made an unrivalled number of meteorological and oceanographic records and built a meteorological station in the South Orkneys that still operates today. In addition he explored and charted the Arctic islands and was a pioneer in attempts to develop a viable mineral extraction industry on the Spitsbergen archipelago. He linked up with scientists in Europe and South America to make a model for international collaboration and advancement of knowledge. His contribution to science, particularly oceanography, was probably greater and more lasting than that of any of his contemporaries, and he might have achieved more had not his reticence, his reserve and his obstinate Scottish nationalism hobbled his ability to garner financial support from the British government.

This is his story.

I

THE EARLY LIFE OF A NATURALIST

Although born and educated in England, William Speirs Bruce had Scottish ancestry. His paternal grandfather, the Reverend William Bruce (1799–1882), came from Glasgow; his grandmother Charity Isbister (1794–1862) from the Orkneys. After their wedding, William and Charity lived in Edinburgh where William converted to the Swedenborgian Church[1] (the New Church), becoming first a member and subsequently assistant in the church. The couple moved to Dundee, where William's role was to revitalise the failing congregation. Here his energy and determination, his thrice-weekly hour-long sermons (with an hourglass placed on the pulpit so that the congregation could be sure that they were getting what they had come for), appear to have had the desired effect: the congregation got bigger, and aged thirty he was ordained as a minister. In 1851 the family moved to London, where the Reverend William ministered to the church in Cross Street, Hatton Gardens, a prosperous area famous for its diamond merchants.

William and Charity had two children, Samuel and Sarah. Samuel Noble Bruce,[2] the father of the subject of this book, was born in

Edinburgh in 1834 but spent his later youth in London, qualifying as a doctor at University College London and running a successful medical practice in London's West End.

In 1861 Samuel married Mary Lloyd, the daughter of a London architect. The family home was initially in Queensbury Terrace, London, and subsequently Kensington Gardens Square. This square, said to be the oldest garden square in London, had been home to some famous residents: philosopher and economist John Stuart Mill, Pre-Raphaelite painter Edward Burne-Jones and, unexpectedly, the 'Kensington School', the headquarters of one of the groups that founded the Football Association in 1863, its members taking a spirited part in the debates and agreements over common rules for the game.

Dr Samuel Bruce needed to be successful. The house in Kensington Gardens Square was a large property, and he and his wife had eight children between 1862 and 1878: William Bruce, his brother Samuel Noble Douglas, and six daughters.[3] In addition there was the usual retinue of servants, coachmen and nursemaids. After his mother's death, Dr Samuel also offered his home to his father, the Revd William, and his own sister, Sarah. These two family members would make a deep impression on the young William Speirs, each playing a major role in his early education.

William Speirs was born in Kensington Gardens on 1 August 1867. When he was four the family moved to an even more prestigious address, 18 Royal Crescent, Holland Park. Here, curved Nash terraces enclosed a garden enjoyed by the inhabitants of the crescent and their children. To his ménage Dr Bruce added footmen, horse-drawn carriages and several general servants.[4]

The house was large – six stories – and must have been bursting with activity. By the 1881 census (when Bruce was fourteen and not at home), there were fourteen residents: Bruce's parents; his eighty-one-year-old grandfather William, a widower from 1864; his aunt Sarah, aged forty-nine; three living-in servants; Bruce's brother, Samuel Noble Douglas, aged eight; and their six sisters, ranging in age from four to eighteen. By this time Bruce was a boarder at Norfolk County School, but when he came home he seems to have had a good relationship with his siblings.[5]

The family was a typical example of the successful middle class. Bruce's background was privileged but hardly exceptional, and the household must have been fairly chaotic at times. William's upbringing was also typical of his class, with one important exception: the young children did not have tutors or governesses. The boys were not sent away to school at an early age; instead their aunt Sarah and their grandfather, the Revd William Bruce, taught all eight children. During his childhood William gave no particular hint of fascination with the natural sciences, though Dr Samuel was later to suggest that, as his father and his sister had taken on the role of teachers when the children were young, and as this education had included visits to the nearby Kensington Gardens and the Natural History Museum,[6] such exposure might have lit the spark that was to burn so brightly.

The traditional education mode started when William was ten and was sent as a dayboy to the nearby University College School, a school founded by academics at University College London. These worthies had felt that the educational standard achieved by applicants to their university was poor, and to address this they established their own school in 1830. Bruce was there for a year, until in 1878 he was sent to Norfolk County School.[7] This institution was presumably chosen by his father to widen his son's educational base in the hopes that it would prepare him for entry into the medical profession.

Bruce seems to have been unhappy at Norfolk County School, at least initially. The system of uprooting children from their homes (often at a much younger age than eleven) to deposit them in a distant, alien environment was a particularly British tradition and must have felt brutal to a quiet, shy, thoughtful boy used to the feminine company of his aunt and sisters and his solicitous grandfather. Bruce did not shine at the school during his six years there, although he did show a particular interest in natural history in his teenage years.[8]

Dr Samuel Bruce had prospered in medicine and wanted his son to follow in his footsteps. The young man agreed, seemingly more from a lack of particular ambition than any feeling of vocation for medicine. He was obviously intelligent, as shown by his subsequent career, but preparatory work for his entrance to university does not seem to have commanded his full attention. He failed his matriculation exams twice,[9] though, it has to be said, the requirements were daunting: students had to show a proficiency in English, Latin, arithmetic, Euclid (Geometry), algebra, the elements of mechanics, plus an optional modern language (French, German, Greek or Italian), or logic, botany, zoology or elementary chemistry. To actually get into medical school, a student (who had to be seventeen years of age) had to pass a preliminary examination in physics, chemistry, botany and zoology.[10] Bruce was finally accepted at University College London in the autumn term of 1887, by which time he was three years older than some of his fellow students.

But Bruce never studied medicine in London. As a preliminary to medical school, Dr Samuel, probably in an attempt to encourage his son, arranged for him to attend two summer courses in the natural sciences in Edinburgh organised by Professor Patrick Geddes.[11] This experience was the turning point of Bruce's life.

He arrived at an opportune time. The late 1880s was a golden period of Scottish academic innovation and Edinburgh was a hotbed of scientific activity. Geddes arranged for the students to study botany in the Edinburgh Botanical Gardens and natural history at the recently established Scottish Marine Station on the shore of the Firth of Forth.

Here Bruce was taught in a floating laboratory, a converted canal barge named the *Elizabeth* ('The Ark'), moored in an old quarry. This cramped but productive environment seems to have immediately commanded Bruce's single-minded attention. Here he eagerly absorbed all aspects of what was to become his chosen career, growing particularly fascinated with the science of oceanography. Geddes was a remarkable man; apart from his expertise in geography and biology, he was committed to a holistic approach to the environment (later he became known widely as an ecologist and town planner) and was a pivotal influence on the young Bruce, who was not only captivated by the presentation of so much new scientific information, but inspired by Geddes' wider vision – Geddes was determined to encourage a Scottish Celtic revival in the arts and culture, along with a spirit of nationalism. This was a new idea and direction for Bruce. Geddes was the influence that stoked in the impressionable student the beginnings of a Celtic fire, a nascent nationalism nurtured by discussions, stories, verse and popular magazines (for example *The Evergreen*, a publication filled with poems and paintings that aimed to inspire a Celtic revival aesthetically, spiritually and politically).

In these few weeks in Edinburgh Bruce not only became immersed in the natural sciences but decided that Edinburgh, rather than London, was where he wanted to study. Geddes' inspirational group of instructors not only had a wealth of enthusiasm and knowledge for the sweep of philosophy, natural history, oceanography and anatomy, but crucially could also communicate their enthusiasm and bond with their students. Among the lecturers was Hugh Robert Mill,[12] a lecturer in Geography and Physiography at Heriot-Watt College. Mill was to be a loyal friend and supporter, and later facilitated several invaluable opportunities for Bruce to travel to the polar regions.

At this time, the results from the round the-world *Challenger* expedition of 1872–76 were still being examined by an international group of scientists chosen purely for their expertise. Much of the work was carried out in the floating laboratory, *The Elizabeth. Challenger* had paid a 'flying visit'[13] to the south polar regions in 1874, and the expedition had undertaken the most comprehensive marine research programme yet. This was the first expedition to focus primarily on the study of the oceans, and as such was a seminal step in the development of the modern scientific discipline of oceanography. Until this time, virtually everything known about the seas was limited to its upper layers (plus some sparse information about the seabed in some shallow areas). Nothing else was certain. The oceans fascinated scientists who were eager to learn their secrets and *Challenger*'s mission was to find answers to questions regarding their structure and dynamics: sea temperature, chemistry, currents, life beneath the waves and the geology of the sea floor. *Challenger* had laboratories, a dredging platform, dredges, trawls, microscopes, thermometers specially designed to take measurements at different depths, chemical apparatus, sampling bottles and miles of hemp for sounding the sea depth. The leaders of this uniquely innovative expedition were Professor Charles Wyville Thomson[14] and John Murray.[15] Murray was the chief editor of the *Challenger* reports and it was he who had persuaded the Scottish Meteorological Society and the Royal Society of Edinburgh to establish the marine station on the Firth of Forth. He was to play a very significant part in Bruce's development and in shaping his career.

Challenger had sailed to South Africa, crossed the Antarctic Circle (66°32' S), travelled on to Australia and New Zealand, and then navigated the Pacific to reach South America and home. She had zigzagged around the world for forty-two months, travelled, explored and surveyed 70,000 nautical miles and returned with an immense number of samples and data that took years to analyse and study. When Bruce arrived at *The*

Elizabeth, he became one of the keenest assistants in the continuing analysis of the results.

Bruce abandoned all thoughts of returning to London. He transferred his medical place to Edinburgh,[16] enrolling in 1887 (numbered signature 1379) and studying medicine until 1892. He seems to have been a conscientious student. There are records of his good attendance at practical chemistry (he attended virtually all the classes)[17] and classes in philosophy, botany, embryology, anatomy, histology, zoology, chemistry, physiology, natural history and philosophy. He was on the committee of the University Swimming Club.[18] He passed his first professional examination for the year 1887–8.[19] He worked as a demonstrator for John Arthur Thomson[20] (1861–1935), the Scottish naturalist and author. He wrote subsequently that he had also passed the preliminary scientific examination for London University in botany, zoology, chemistry and natural philosophy.

But medicine could not hold Bruce's complete interest. Whenever he could he assisted John Murray with the *Challenger* work. From Murray and John Young Buchanan (the chemist on the *Challenger* expedition) he received an unparalleled instruction in the theory and practice of the new field of oceanography, honing his analytical skills all the while.

As a young student he stayed originally in University Hall, 2, Mound Place, Edinburgh, but in 1891 he moved to the centre of Edinburgh into Riddle's Court (said to have been visited by James VI of Scotland and his wife Queen Anne). This 'student residence' was a fine-looking building that had been bought, restored and furnished by Geddes, who wanted to see how young men from different backgrounds and academic disciplines would live and cooperate in an unsupervised, self-governing small community. In fact when Bruce moved to Riddle's Court the only occupant was William Gordon Burn Murdoch,[21] an artist and piper, but another medical student, Riccardo Stephens, soon joined them. Burn

Murdoch wrote that the three would sit comfortably by the classical fireplace, Stephens playing his guitar, Burn Murdoch the bagpipes and Bruce just beaming.[22] The number of residents increased gradually until fourteen young men lived in Riddle's Court. Although Bruce made friends and associates, he appears to have been most happy in a small group, apparently becoming more withdrawn and self-contained as the group enlarged. A description of him hardly fits the picture of a typical medical student: he was serious and pale, rarely smiling and walking with a slight stoop, his clothes hanging loosely on him.[23] He had dark hair and dark eyes and weighed 10 stone 10 lbs,[24] but he was physically very fit. Burn Murdoch said (probably optimistically) that Bruce could walk 60 miles in a day without problems. He was a strong swimmer.

His settled, earnest life changed when, on Hugh Robert Mill's recommendation, he was offered the post of surgeon/naturalist on a Dundee whaler sailing to the Antarctic. Becoming a ship's surgeon was not an uncommon occupation for Edinburgh medical students; for example, Conan Doyle had gone on a whaling ship to the Arctic when he was a medical student, as had John Murray, and Bruce probably considered initially that the expedition would be a temporary pause in the studies that he was close to finishing.

In consideration of the career he was ultimately to follow, his time in Edinburgh had been very productive. He had worked with eminent men who could influence his career, gaining practical experience and learning to value international cooperation and to think of himself both as a scientist and a Scot.

2

THE FIRST VISIT TO ANTARCTICA, THE DUNDEE EXPEDITION ON BALAENA

At the end of the nineteenth century, the main whale species hunted from sailing ships were 'right' whales, or bowheads. Sperm whales were also hunted for spermaceti and ambergris. 'Right' whales have enormous heads, and baleen plates (flexible filters of up to 3 metres) in their jaws. The whales are about 50 feet long and were named 'right' because they move relatively slowly and, importantly, because their blubber content causes them to float on the surface of the sea when killed. These features meant that they could be hunted in the traditional method with rowing boats and hand-launched harpoons, and their blubber could be stripped away without the carcass having to be beached or hoisted onto the ship. Baleen was hugely sought after for fashion items, particularly corset stays and umbrella spokes. 'Right' whales had enormous value for their blubber (some whales produced up to 30 tons of whale oil), baleen plates, meat and bone; the baleen from the jaws of a single whale could be worth £2,000–£3,000.

But the global whaling industry was in serious decline by the 1890s. The reasons for this were complex. The 'right' whale population around the coasts had been greatly depleted, but also the market for whale oil was declining as gas and electricity replaced oil for heating and lighting. Prices for oil were depressed. Although technology was starting to provide the tools for hunting the faster whales (blue, fin and humpback), at this stage it was still experimental and too expensive to be profitable in a declining market. A decade or more would pass before technology would provide the means to turn oil into edible fat (margarine) and soap, creating a huge new market for whale oil. But although whaling was in decline, the whalers were nevertheless aware that James Clark Ross had reported that the Southern Ocean teemed with 'right' whales. Ross said that the whales were so tame that they allowed ships to almost touch them.[1] A report on 'The New Whaling Grounds in the Southern Sea'[2] had been widely circulated, and whaling entrepreneurs such as Robert Kinnes of Dundee and Norwegians Christen Christensen and Svend Foyn (who patented the exploding whaling harpoon and gun) turned their attention south. They launched several exploratory whaling expeditions using the traditional approach to hunting, thus effectively limiting them to 'right' whales. In 1892 Kinnes fitted out four ships for such an expedition, and it was on one of these ships that Bruce was to make his first scientific recordings in Antarctica as doctor/naturalist.

By this time the captains of whaling ships had been persuaded to sometimes take naturalists and artists on whalers. Taking medical students as doctors was also common practice. Whaling ships were not licensed to carry passengers, but as Bruce had had a considerable amount of medical and natural science training he was a very practical choice to fill the combined role as a crew member. This expedition gave him a unique opportunity to see that part of the world about which little was known and to put into practice the skills that he had learnt from his mentors on *The Elizabeth*. He already had a grasp of what data and specimens should be collected.

Dr Mill had by now been appointed librarian at the Royal Geographical Society (RGS) in London. He wrote later that one of his first duties was to make a list of instructions for naturalists visiting the Antarctic. When the Dundee enterprise was agreed, Mr Benjamin Leigh Smith, the veteran Arctic explorer,[3] chose the nautical instruments that the RGS was to supply and also persuaded Kinnes to take out young naturalists; he asked Mill to suggest suitable candidates, and Bruce's name was put forward. He accepted promptly.

Bruce seems to have surprised his friends in the students' hall when he announced that he was taking leave from his studies to go on a Dundee whaler to the Antarctic. He asked his friend William Gordon Burn Murdoch to go with him. In September 1892 the two signed on to sail on the *Balaena*, a barque whaler (number 99205, Captain Alexander Fairweather), one of the four Dundee ships. Bruce signed as surgeon and naturalist; he was to be paid £7 14s for the trip, which lasted from 6 September 1892 to 30 May 1893. Burn Murdoch, with no medical training, sailed as assistant surgeon and artist.

Robert Kinnes spent £28,000 on fitting out his four ships in Dundee. All had auxiliary steam engines. The four ships had 130 crewmembers in total, including Bruce and Burn Murdoch. Sailing with the *Balaena* was the *Active* (Captain Thomas Robertson, later to captain the *Scotia* during the Scottish National Antarctic Expedition; see Appendix 1 for more details of his life), the *Diana* (Captain Robert Davidson) and the *Polar Star* (Captain James Davidson). The Norwegians (Christensen) separately fitted out and dispatched a fifth ship, the *Jason*, which sailed from Sandefjord (Captain Carl Anton Larsen[4]) to the same general area in the Northern Weddell Sea. Bruce was honoured to spend the short time before departure on a voyage with John Murray and the German polymath Ernst Heinrich Haeckel.[5] He needed to practise and improve his handling of the oceanographic apparatus. He also collected the equipment donated to the expedition – the RGS spent £150 on instruments for the four vessels, which were also provided with deep-sea thermometers, a pocket aneroid barometer, a spectroscope and equipment for zoology and biology studies.

Mill made the journey from London to see *Balaena* off. He wrote that Bruce 'lounged up'[6] half an hour before the ship sailed, not aware that he was expected to supply his own bedding. Without any cash (not an unusual state for Bruce), he appealed to Mill, who was unable to help. So Andrew Coats, a member of the family that was to back Bruce for his Antarctic exploration, hurriedly produced £5 – a bystander gave instructions to the nearest ship's chandler!

Balaena sailed from Dundee on 6 September 1892. She was given an enthusiastic send-off for her expedition into the unknown. An early search for stowaways routed out twelve young boys. They were sent home, some crying with disappointment and, apparently, hunger[7] and *Balaena's* fifty-man crew were thrown together for a voyage of 'whisky, devilment and adventure'.[8] (Two other young stowaways eluded the search and signed on as crew when *Balaena* reached Port Stanley!)[9]

Wild weather kept the ships off the coast of Scotland for three weeks. On *Balaena* 'well-nigh everything was adrift from stem to stern'[10] and here Bruce had to use his surgical knowledge when he tended to a seaman who had been hit on the head by an iron bolt. The duties of Assistant Surgeon Burn Murdoch were limited to hanging on to Bruce to keep him steady as the ship rocked. Further on in the voyage Bruce was transported by whaleboat to a barque, the *Guy Mannering*, where the master was ill. After weeks at sea, shut off from the rest of the world by a seemingly endless horizon, the crew were delighted to come across evidence of civilisation. The master was dealt with, but Bruce's crewmates could not believe that he had hardly glanced at the master's daughter, a pretty girl in a lovely blue dress, whom they had been spying on eagerly from *Balaena*; Bruce, a focused young man and serious about his work, had apparently not noticed her. When his duties were finished, the ships dipped their ensigns and went their separate ways, 'the fair one waving us adieu with a tiny handkerchief'.[11] The crew quarrelled for the rest of the day as to whom the lovely young lady's salute was intended for.

They longed to see land.[12] Finally, after ninety-three days and 7,000 miles, *Balaena* reached the Falklands on 8 December 1892.[13] Here the men enjoyed their first proper wash for weeks and Bruce was delighted to hear the voices of Scottish shepherds and to smell the sweet peat smoke blowing off shore (peat was the primary fuel source in the Falklands until well into the twentieth century). The captain, officers and the 'surgical team' put on their 'mildewed finery'[14] to be met by the governor and his lady, Sir Roger and Lady Goldsworthy.

Bruce's first shooting outing is recorded with glee. After 'a fearful explosion … a cloud of feathers floated in the smoke-laden air and the goose lay in a soft white heap on the grass'.[15] Boyish happiness lit Bruce's face as he advanced, smiling with what remained of his first shot: Lady Goldsworthy's favourite white goose!

The expedition left the Falklands on Sunday 11 December, and ice was seen on the 16th (at the southern equivalent to the Orkneys in Scotland). *Balaena* encountered her first tabular iceberg, described by Burn Murdoch as 'about half a mile long and about 200 feet high; the top was as level as a billiard table and absolutely white'.[16] The ships sailed on to the Weddell Sea searching for 'right' whales. In his journal of the voyage,[17] Bruce describes the icebergs, cape pigeons, blue petrels, penguins and blue whales. The ships found themselves having to navigate cautiously though fog while surrounded by giant icebergs. They endured impressive gales; in one of these *Balaena* sheltered in the lee of a berg, estimated to be 30 miles long, having to use her auxiliary engines to keep her position.[18]

But whaling was a failure. No 'right' whales were seen, though plenty of finbacks, bottlenoses and grampuses were sighted in 'an almost incredible number'.[19] After several weeks of searching, since the expedition was commercial, whaling was abandoned and a decision made to fill the holds with seals.

Bruce worked with the crew in the mass killing. Each day, with muscles 'stiff as a board',[20] he and Burn Murdoch climbed wearily into a whaler, rowed to the pack ice where seals were resting and killed all day. The animals had never seen humans and lay passively as the whalers advanced. Over 2,000 sealskins lay across *Balaena*'s deck, the pile reaching the gunwale on each side. Blood was everywhere; the stench was appalling. This indiscriminate killing by the five ships (including the Norwegian ship, the *Jason*) of more than 20,000 seals, young and old, appalled Bruce. He thought that most of the females that had been killed were pregnant and he feared that this widespread slaughter would lead to the extinction of the species. His spirits only lifted when the ship's tanks were full and the decks piled with skins and the butchery ended.

In his account of the Dundee Whaling Expedition he wrote that whaling could be adopted commercially with modern whaling methods,[21] but more importantly he commented that the expedition 'demonstrated the immense results that would accrue from a purely scientific expedition to Antarctic waters'.[22] Although on the expedition he was frustrated that he could not collect as much scientific material as he wanted, the experience left him with a fascination with Antarctica and a determination to return. His official comments were restrained, though on his return in 1893 he wrote to the RGS to explain what he thought of as his meagre results, due, he said, to the hours spent working with the whalers on the boats. Burn Murdoch was not so reticent: he wrote that Bruce had 'lost irrecoverable opportunities for doing good natural history work in the ice, owing to his having been obliged to take more than his share in long spells at the wheel, killing and skinning seals and so on, not to mention his nightly attention to his principal patient, the old man'[23] (referring to Captain Alexander Fairweather, who apparently consumed a goodly supply of 'spiritual comfort'). Burn Murdoch complained that the scientific work was hindered and 'mocked and jeered'.[24] He wrote that he and Bruce idled away the return journey 'planning how to tip the old man overboard or slit his throat'.[25]

Bruce's frustration with Captain Fairweather, who had no time to waste for activities that could not be turned into money and whose commercial interests were diametrically opposed to Bruce's scientific ambitions, was real, lasting and unforgiving. His anxiety was that he had not achieved as much as he could have done. After the expedition he refused to cooperate with Fairweather on presentations. He wrote to Dr Mill saying that 'owing to present relationships I could not possibly cooperate with the skipper'.[26] Indeed, he never forgave Fairweather for what he thought of as his bitter experiences on *Balaena*. He said that he had signed on as a surgeon, but was told soon after the voyage began that there was to be no science on the ship when she was outside six fathoms. The bird specimens he had been promised were either sold or given to the captain's friends. Captain Fairweather had managed to get hold of Bruce's photographs, and he and his agents had taken advantage of Bruce and Burn Murdoch in every possible way. These were strong opinions for a novice sailor and naturalist. Whether he communicated these feelings while on board is not clear, but what is clear is his frustration and his inability to communicate this frustration effectively. It was obviously important to make the expedition a financial success, but Alexander Fairweather could have made the naturalists his allies if he had given them more support. Although Bruce was well supplied with equipment (supplies from the RGS, the Meteorological Office, Mr Leigh Smith and others), he was not allowed to consult navigation charts, chart the sun or use the sounding machine (other than occasionally). His special specimen bucket was swept away, tow netting was considered impracticable because it stopped the routine of the ship, and when catches were made they were often

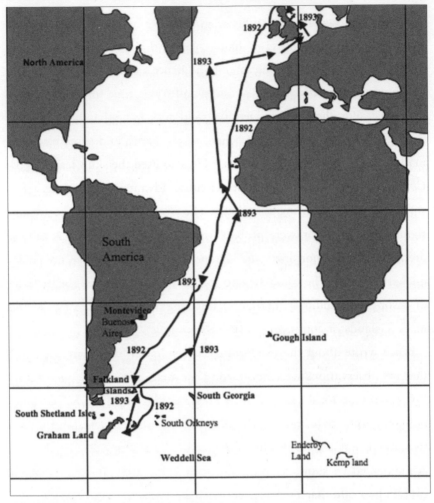

Map showing the track of the Balaena, *on which Bruce was the surgeon/ naturalist during the expedition of 1892–3 to find right whales in Antarctic waters. (D. J. Williams)*

contaminated by refuse. When *Balaena* returned to Dundee, Captain Fairweather attempted to sell Bruce's precious logs, some specimens and a stuffed penguin.[27] Commerce was, after all, the overriding concern. Bruce, conscious of the interest that Leigh Smith has taken in his contribution to the expedition, wrote that he was 'inclined to rest on his decision as to its disposal'.[28] It was because of these experiences that when he eventually organised his own expedition his scientists were not asked to sign ship's papers and officers and crew had to agree that observations, written reports, drawings, memos, etc. should be Bruce's property.[29]

The voyage on *Balaena* was a testing and trying time for the ambitious naturalist. But though his scientific yield was not what he hoped, he managed to keep specimens of lichen, rocks, fossils and some birds and made notes on four species of seals.[30] He also used the skills learnt in the *Challenger* office to considerable scientific advantage, managing a few soundings and measuring sea salinity. The two collections of the greatest significance, however, were probably his meteorological records and the dredging of metamorphic[31] and sedimentary[32] rock in these previously uncharted areas. The characteristics of the rocks supported the presence of a southern landmass, though at this stage the characteristics of this mass – islands or continent – remained unknown.

Bruce wrote about the meteorological results on his return. He noted that his observations were 'more complete than any others made before for general or local conditions'.[33] Observations were made, as far as possible, every two hours, with twelve observations each day for over two months. Gales and calm alternated: gales from the south were accompanied by snow, from the north by dense fog. He wrote that the captain had said that 13 February, when a gale was compounded by fog, was the hardest gale he had ever experienced (*Balaena* steamed as hard as she could for ten hours and made 1 knot).[34] Bruce wrote later that these meteorological results indicated, for the first time, 'the existence of a large anticyclone extending around the South Pole, and supporting the probability of the Hypothetical Antarctic continent of Murray'.[35] This was a most significant observation. These reports, and details of the sedimentary rocks, were given significant publicity when John Murray brought them to the society's attention in his pivotal address to the RGS in November 1893.[36]

In addition, Bruce brought back other new information from the south: records of soundings, sea colour and salinity, ambient temperatures, sea temperatures (maximum 37.2°F, minimum 28.5°F, the mean for the whole period 30.6°F). He wrote that the temperature was never above freezing except for the last two weeks of December, all of January and the first two weeks of February 1893. At a latitude and longitude that was roughly comparable with the Faroes north of Scotland, the freezing Antarctic temperature during the warmest month could be compared with the 23° above freezing in the Faroes. He described the icy, snow-clad distant land; only steep slopes and cliffs were free of snow.

His relationship with *Balaena* did not end with his return. He gave talks, wrote papers and narrowly avoided a court case. His friend, Burn Murdoch, wrote an account of the voyage titled *From Edinburgh to the Antarctic*.[37] A review of the work in 1895 in *Natural Science* by Thomas Southwell FZS drew Bruce's fury. Southwell wrote that the book was 'often flippant and subordinates fact to fancy even beyond the limit of poetic licence', claiming that if it had been about anywhere other than the Antarctic 'it would have been looked upon in the light of a very amusing production of no scientific interest'.[38] Southwell stated, incorrectly, that Burn Murdoch had 'accompanied' the *Balaena* by the kindness of the owner (Burn Murdoch, as assistant surgeon, was paid a shilling per month)[39] and that Burn Murdoch had used unscientific terms (for example varieties, rather than species). Bruce wrote to the editor of *Natural Science* saying that he agreed with Burn Murdoch that science should be for everyone and he supported his friend's comment that it was a hideous marvel that though Dundonians had shown enterprise in sending four ships to the Antarctic, they had shown a total disregard for the scientific possibilities of such a cruise[40] (as can be imagined, this had met with an 'anything but a friendly reception in Dundee seafaring circles').[41]

The editor of *Natural Science*, not unnaturally perplexed and probably a little alarmed by this onslaught, advised Bruce of his concern over possible legal action, but Bruce, though impecunious and very junior, would not give up. This incident gives early evidence of aspects of his character: dogged, stubborn, possibly unwise and unwilling to compromise. He sought legal advice; the matter was eventually settled when his lawyer opined that the petty tyrannies of a whaling skipper could never be realised by those who have not experienced them and the editor wrote an emollient note.

Much interest was shown in the expedition, not only in Dundee but also from scientific societies in Scotland (where Bruce was elected as an Ordinary Fellow of the Royal Physical Society of Edinburgh in March 1894)[42] and more broadly throughout Britain. Importantly, Bruce's work drew attention to the need for, and possibilities of, further Antarctic scientific work. He started to dream of leading such an expedition and made the momentous decision to alter his career path fundamentally. He decided to abandon medicine and become a naturalist. Why he made this decision after five years of medical training (which he could have finished, no doubt satisfying his father) before embarking on a more uncertain scientific career is open to speculation. On the one hand, the decision took courage. He would have known that, having annoyed and upset his father, he could not hope for any further parental support – his father had, in any case, many other domestic responsibilities – and also that a medical career would have been lucrative and secure; he might well have joined his father's practice in London had he continued on his original path. On the other hand it could be that the Dundee whaling experience was a lifeline and *Balaena* crystallised a decision that had been forming for years.

Bruce has been described variously as single-minded, reserved and serious, difficult to divert from any project and with little time for trivial social interactions.[43] He may have realised that his 'prickly' nature was not well suited to the rumbustious strains of a medical career. Once he had experienced the possibilities of science in the South Atlantic, he probably decided that laboratory work and research was more suited to his abilities and that there was no point in delaying his decision. He undoubtedly had a passion to 'lift the veil from the unknown', and so he took a gamble and turned his face towards the potentially stony financial future of science – a future for which he had no formal qualifications. But he never looked back. He was to become a driven, single-minded naturalist. Exploration in the Antarctic became his goal. Nowadays it would be almost impossible to make a career in science without graduate and postgraduate qualifications, but in the Victorian era there still was a place for the 'gentleman scientist' – both Murray and Geddes rose to their eminent positions without a degree – although this was a rapidly dying breed.

Dr Samuel Bruce's feelings are not recorded, but it is fair to say that he is likely to have been unhappy at his son's decision, having supported him through several attempts at the matriculation examination before he was accepted at medical school, and having accepted his son's decision to study in Edinburgh rather than London and paid for his medical training for five years. No wonder Speak writes that Bruce seems to have had a distant relationship with his father.[44] This rejection of his father's hopes and plans is likely to have confirmed Dr Samuel's apprehensions and put a permanent strain on the relationship; when Dr Samuel died in 1926, five years after William's death, he left nothing in his will to William's wife or children: all of his estate (net value a little over £1,000, or around £55,000 in 2016) was inherited by his daughter Evelyn Rose.[45]

3

THE BEN NEVIS OBSERVATORY

Bruce was virtually penniless on his return to Edinburgh, with little income and no prospect of employment. To raise cash he gave tutorials to students studying for the first professional examination in physics, chemistry, botany and zoology (fees reduced if three or four subjects were taken and special rates offered for private tuition). He went on lecture tours with his friend Burn Murdoch, often using lime-light illustrations.[1] They talked to big and small societies, in 'big towns and in little towns',[2] describing their Antarctic experiences – Bruce 'did' the science while Burn Murdoch spoke on the aesthetic aspects of the voyage and Antarctic ice effects. Bruce was not a natural lecturer, and in an attempt to boost his confidence he followed the style adopted by one of the medical school lecturers, who, when holding up a skull would intone: 'GENT – LE – MEN — THIS – IS – THE – BONE – OF – THE – OC – CI – PUT — OTHERWISE — THE – OC – CIP – IT – AL — BONE'.[3]

But he wanted to return to Antarctica, eager to draw attention to its huge potential for scientific study. He started canvassing immediately. Within a week of his return he wrote to Dr Mill at the RGS, saying that he was 'burning to be off again, anywhere, but particularly to the far south where I believe there is a vast sphere for research'.[4] He sent an article detailing the expedition's activities to Mill. This was published in *The Times*, and generated interest in spite of the fact that it just recorded the work done; no hair's-breadth escapes or exciting adventures.[5] He wrote again a little later to say that he was actively planning an expedition to South Georgia (one of several schemes he had in mind). He contacted the Governor of the Falklands, Sir Roger Goldsworthy, in August 1893, with a proposal 'to test the capacity of the island for sheep farming, and to ascertain how far the seal fisheries might be prosecuted there', he wanted also to complete the geographical survey as far as possible, 'to report on the meteorological condition and on the geology, fauna and flora'.[6]

Clearly, although he remained distressed about the 'butchery' on *Balaena*, he understood now that incorporating commercial proposals into a plan was the most realistic way of getting a project taken up. He wanted to be in South Georgia for a year and requested assistance for transport to get him and an assistant to and from the island. The letter was passed to the Colonial Office, who consulted the Admiralty, who decided that it 'was inexpedient' to commit a ship. A Colonial Office official helpfully pointed out that even if a ship was made available there was no guarantee of Bruce being retrieved and no prospect of sufficient revenue being raised from the island to justify the outlay. On this basis the Colonial Office refused assistance.[7]

But Bruce persisted in arguing the case. At the British Association (BA) meeting in Nottingham in August 1893, a committee was set up to report on the value of 'geographical, meteorological and natural history observations in South Georgia or other Antarctic island (*sic*)'. Chaired by Sir Clements Markham,[8] with Mill as secretary, it met twice before reporting at the 1894 meeting of the association in Oxford. The committee's aim seems to have been to obtain funding for Bruce; it had already obtained a grant of £50 from the BA towards the £400 needed.

In the event it concluded that the risk of Bruce becoming stranded for want of a vessel to bring him home was too great, but it urged the association to lobby government on the desirability of supporting Antarctic exploration.[9] Mill summarised the report of the committee in the *Scottish Geographical Magazine*. He wrote, in what must have been a positive and consoling comment, that 'the Committee in the circumstances could not take the risk of causing the death of an eminent scientist'.[10]

Even so, Bruce travelled to London to present the scheme to Sir John Scott Keltie[11] at the RGS in an attempt to gain his scientific backing. He said the British Museum would supply seeds and the Meteorological Office would provide instruments. By this time Bruce was so short of funds that Burn Murdoch had to lend him cash to allow him to 'get his evening clothes out of pawn, and appear before the Great Old Scientists, of whom he was rather in awe, at their dinners and meetings, and make some show'.[12] But lack of personal cash did not dent his confident demands for an assistant, passage from the Falklands to South Georgia and the provision of personal and scientific outfits. The grant was refused.

At a colonial office meeting a quarter-century later, when Bruce was asked to advise on post-war preparations in the Southern Ocean, he recalled this episode as a missed opportunity which could have seen British rather than Norwegian companies leading the way on Southern Ocean whaling.[13] In this he had been prescient in recognising, long before anybody else, that the island of South Georgia might become economically important.

He worked on presentations, and in November 1893 he spoke on the Dundee Expedition to the sixty-third meeting of the British Association for the Advancement of Science, reporting on his findings and canvassing for funds for his planned expedition to South Georgia. He attended the Royal Physical Society of Edinburgh and commented on a paper on 'Animal Life Observed during a Voyage to Antarctica'.[14] He had one offer of an Antarctic journey in 1893, this time to travel as the naturalist on a sealing and whaling expedition organised by the Norwegian businessman and entrepreneur Henrik Johan Bull (1844–1930). But again fate was against him, and he could not get to Norway before Bull's ship left.

It seemed that a further expedition would never materialise, and since he desperately needed employment he applied in 1895 for the post of curator of the Raffles Library and Museum in Singapore. He wrote that he was twenty-eight, unmarried and in perfect health. He listed his university experiences (the first part BSc in Botany, Chemistry and Zoology in 1889, and in the same year the preliminary scientific examination of the University of London in Botany, Zoology, Chemistry and Natural Philosophy) and his post-student work, which included anatomy demonstration and tutoring undergraduates. He described his time as naturalist on *Balaena*, his Fellowship of the Royal Physical Society of Edinburgh, membership of the Royal Scottish Geographical Society and a grant from the British Association towards his scientific work.[15] But he did not have a degree, and although both Geddes and Murray had succeeded without higher qualifications it is quite possible that this was the reason that, in spite of excellent testimonials and fifteen referees (including Geddes), the post was awarded to another candidate. Perhaps it was as well, because in 1895 he applied for and was offered a locum post on the Ben Nevis Observatory.

The High Level Meteorological Observatory, on the summit of Ben Nevis at 4,406 feet, was opened in October 1893. It was completed a year later with the addition of a tower and an enlarged observatory room. A Low Level Observatory, close to sea level, was built at Fort William in 1886 and synchronous recordings made from high and low levels. Such information had not been recorded previously in Britain. It was of very great value in understanding the weather in mountainous regions.

Robert Traill Omond (1856–1914) was appointed as supervisor when the observatory opened and Bruce became an assistant in 1895. The observer at the low-level station was Robert Cockburn Mossman,[16] who was to become a valued long-term colleague. Observations had to be made in rapidly changing conditions and, when possible, hourly. In winter (when the station was isolated enough even for Bruce), the snowdrifts were so high that the men often had to reach their instruments through snow tunnels, or even via the tower, and the variability in winds, fog and snow gave excellent training for Antarctic meteorology. When the conditions were warmer, true to his wide-ranging, holistic instincts, Bruce extended his observations to make a collection of the mountain's flora and fauna and to record bird migration.

New findings included the observation that fog was present on the summit for 80% of the time in November, December and January 1895/6, it was common for the summit to be capped in fog when surrounding summits were clear [17] (later Bruce was to tell his companions in Antarctica that they did not know what fog was unless they had experienced it on Ben Nevis). Temperature comparisons between the stations showed that the average fall in temperature between Fort William and the Summit was 15.3°F, with a mean annual temperature at the summit of 31.5°F and at the base of 46.8°F. The annual rainfall at the summit was approximately double that at Fort William.

Sir Alexander Buchan, the founder of the British Meteorological Service, was the scientist who appointed and instructed the observers, drew up their schedules and analysed the data. Four months after Bruce's appointment, Omond had to stop working at the summit for health reasons (though he continued his work as supervisor in Edinburgh) and Bruce understood that Sir Alexander had offered him the permanent position in Omond's place. He accepted this with alacrity, but confusion soon emerged about his official status, a distinction that was important to him in relation to further appointments. In his letters Bruce stated doggedly that he was Omond's replacement, in charge of the upper observatory. This seems unlikely; he was a relative tyro in comparison to Omond and Omond's replacement, Angus Rankin.[18]

Nevertheless, Bruce seems to have considered himself in charge. Writing to Rankin in February 1896, he said 'there seems to have been a misunderstanding as to my position on the observatory staff'; again, on 28 February he wrote that he was 'surprised when Mr Miller came up to me and told me he was in charge'.[19] Bruce wrote that the matter must be settled. He said he had a letter from Buchan asking him to take complete charge from May to October 1895; he was one of the permanent staff, standing in the same relationship to Rankin as Rankin himself had with Omond. Rankin said eventually that he had not considered Bruce as being a member of the permanent staff, rather being there to carry out meteorological work and the management of observatory work. Bruce could call himself whatever he wished, but Mr Miller had been appointed to work as his (Rankin's) first assistant;[20] therefore Bruce may have had day-to-day charge of logging observations, but he had no managerial responsibility. It is typical of Bruce that he never accepted this, and in his 1911 book *Polar Exploration* he still described himself as 'having been in charge of the summit observatory for more than a year'.[21]

Bruce visited Edinburgh during his Ben Nevis appointment. He had not lost sight of his ambitions to take charge of an Antarctic Meteorological Station and wrote to Mill that he hoped that 'the royal Geographical Society and the British Association would not think it is through lack of interest that I have not attended the late Congress ... I am still an enthusiastic though a poor man'.[22] His efforts to promote himself continued, as did his applications for funding and support – for example, he wrote to the publisher Edward Arnold in November 1895, saying that he was hopeful of leaving for the Antarctic the following year when he would make an attempt to reach the South Magnetic Pole. He offered Arnold the book rights (and asked Arnold, unsuccessfully, if he would make a prepayment!).[23] He became involved in plans to work with the Norwegian/English explorer Carsten Borchgrevink (1864–1932), and with the whaler Henrik Johan Bull, a Norwegian business and shipping magnate, for yet another exploratory whaling voyage to Antarctica. Borchgrevink and Bull planned to establish a whaling station on South Georgia in a venture that would combine science and commerce. But friction developed between the two men, likely to have been caused by Borchgrevink's claim that in 1895 he had been the first man to set foot on the Antarctic mainland.[24] This was the expedition that Bruce had failed to reach in 1893, when he could not get to Norway before Bull's ship left; he had been replaced by Borchgrevink. In making his claim, Borchgrevink effectively ignored the roles played by Bull and the other crewmembers.

Initially Borchgrevink was enthusiastic about an expedition with Bruce, writing in December 1895 that he wanted to meet Bruce to discuss plans. However, by 15 January 1896 enthusiasm had waned. Borchgrevink wrote that he understood that Bruce had agreed to go south with Mr H. J. Bull and said that if this was so he would not intrude; however, if Bruce would like to sail to Victoria Island in September 1897, he would be happy to cooperate. Bruce replied that if Bull could get backing, he was prepared to sail with him. Borchgrevink then ended the correspondence, writing on 24 January that as Bruce had made arrangements with Mr Bull he would withdraw. South Georgia plans were discussed with Murray, the Royal Scottish Geographical Society and the whalers Christian Salvesen & Co., but these also failed to get backing and were abandoned.

Ben Nevis was an important episode for Bruce. He had continued his apprenticeship in scientific investigations and scientific discipline. He had made regular meteorological observations in all types of weather for a year, recorded bird migration and compiled an insect collection. He had also made links with scientists of the greatest importance who could be of benefit to him; Peter Speak writes[25] that apart from Mill, eminent men who visited the observatory included Sir Archibald Geikie,[26] then Director-General of the Geological Survey of the United Kingdom and Director of the Museum of Practical Geology; Professor C. T. R. Wilson,[27] a physicist and meteorologist who would later be awarded the Nobel Prize; and the Harvard Professor of Physical Geography William Morris Davis,[28] who was called the father of American geography. It is difficult to imagine a more distinguished group.

In June 1896, while Bruce was working on the Ben Nevis summit, he received a telegram from the inestimable Hugh Robert Mill, asking if he could be prepared to sail to Franz Josef Land to join the Jackson–Harmsworth expedition. He was given five days to prepare. He accepted the offer instantly.

4

THE JACKSON–HARMSWORTH
EXPEDITION TO FRANZ JOSEF LAND

The stated aims of the expedition, which ran from 1894 to 1897, were to survey Franz Josef Land, carry out scientific studies and explore a route to the North Pole. At that time the hope of reaching the Pole overland by sledge was strong; an Austro-Hungarian expedition of 1875 had reported land to the far north and it was hoped that this land might be a route to the Pole or, at least, provide an advanced land base. The search for a North Pole route made for wide public and press interest.

Alfred Harmsworth,[1] the publishing magnate and pioneer of tabloid journalism, financed the expedition. As the owner of *The Evening News and Post* and periodicals whose combined circulation reached nearly 2 million, he was a man of significant influence. Harmsworth had visited the United States when the American explorer Robert Edwin Peary[2] was preparing for an expedition to northern Greenland, and he was inspired to promote a similar British expedition. Sponsorship of potentially hazardous ventures was a guaranteed method of increasing readership; for instance, James Gordon Bennett, the owner of the *New York Herald*, had sponsored Stanley in his successful expedition to find David Livingstone in 1871, an expedition avidly followed by thousands of readers. Harmsworth contacted Frederick George Jackson (1860–1939), a young adventurer and big game hunter, and the plan for the Jackson–Harmsworth polar expedition to Franz Josef Land was laid.

Harmsworth retained exclusive rights to Jackson's expedition (this included any written reports, memoranda, photographs, drawings, plans, sketches, etc. that Bruce had made and all records and new finds).[3] Obviously the more daring the expedition the greater the interest, and there were high hopes that Jackson's expedition would answer expectations, but Harmsworth wrote that he would be 'entirely satisfied if he and his companions add to our knowledge of the geography and the flora and fauna of Franz Josef Land and the area lying immediately to the north of it'.[4] Expedition leader Jackson, described in the papers as a modern-day Ulysses,[5] was certainly of the type to catch the public's imagination – during the three years of the expedition he shot over 100 polar bears, plus walruses, seals, foxes and birds and any other available wildlife. His passion for hunting infected the crew; one Sunday service was read by the mate, who, desperate to get the formalities over, finished his reading, 'For-ever-and-ever-Amen-there's-a bear.'[6]

The expedition had left London in June 1894 and established its base at Cape Flora on Franz Josef Land. Franz Josef Land is an archipelago of nearly two hundred islands in the Arctic Ocean between 79°57' and 82°52'N. The land is ice-bound for most of the year but can be approached by sea from the south in summer. It was discovered in 1873, but by 1894 it was still largely unknown and, importantly, potentially unclaimed territory. Little was known of its natural history.

Dr Mill acted on behalf of the Jackson–Harmsworth expedition when he offered Bruce the post of naturalist in 1896, two years into the expedition.[7] This was another tailor-made opportunity for the trainee to increase his apprenticeship skills. However, he was disorganised about

his personal preparations; when he arrived in London with eight hours
to spare before his ship, the *Windward*, sailed off, he was asked about
his luggage, much like he had been before the whaling expedition. When
he admitted that he had not brought any, his friends had to rally round
to find some basic equipment and an Ulster (a greatcoat). Bruce provided
a few bottles and notebooks and sailed off. Rudmose Brown[8] wrote that
Bruce loved to work at high pressure,[9] though it could be said he created
his own pressure by being disorganised.

Jackson took four scientists on his expedition. For the first two years
the team included the botanist Henry Fisher,[10] along with two men who
were to go later on Scott's 1901 Antarctic expedition: Albert Armitage,[11]
who was in charge of magnetic, meteorological, and astronomical work,
and Reginald Koettlitz,[12] a doctor and geologist. There was also a
mineralogist, J. F. Child, and the expedition had a cook and three general
hands. Jackson had landed at the south-west of Northwood Island,[13]
an island in the south of Franz Josef Land. His base was on Cape Flora
and was named 'Elmwood'. Cape Flora was a historically significant
area where the explorer Benjamin Leigh Smith (the man who had been
indirectly responsible for Bruce's first expedition on *Balaena*) had been
shipwrecked in 1881.

The *Windward* called at Vardo in Norway and at Archangel. On the
way northwards Bruce indulged his passion for science in full, taking sea
temperatures, recording birds (gulls, skuas, kittiwakes, guillemots) and
throwing floats on to the sea to test the currents (many were picked up
years later in various sites, including one in New Zealand). In Archangel
Bruce met David Wilton[14] who was to be his long-term associate and
friend. Bruce described him as 'a young English fellow 23 years who has
lived in Russia a long time and is experienced with ski & sleigh & I think
we shall get on first rate'.[15] Wilton joined the expedition as assistant
zoologist. Bruce wrote to Mill from Vardo saying he had collected many

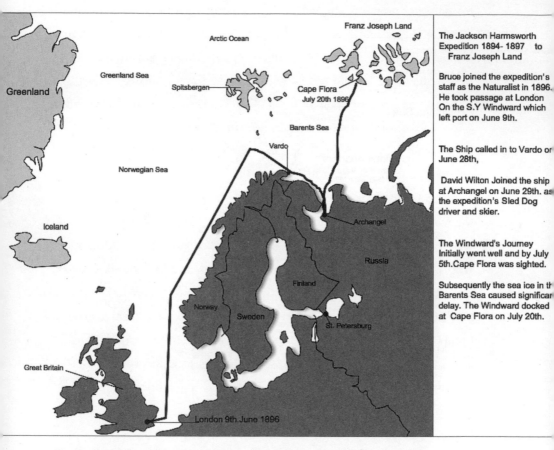

The Jackson Harmsworth Expedition 1894- 1897   to   Franz Joseph Land

Bruce joined the expedition's staff as the Naturalist in 1896. He took passage at London On the S.Y Windward which left port on June 9th.

The Ship called in to Vardo on June 28th,

David Wilton Joined the ship at Archangel on June 29th. as the expedition's Sled Dog driver and skier.

The Windward's Journey Initially went well and by July 5th.Cape Flora was sighted.

Subsequently the sea ice in the Barents Sea caused significant delay. The Windward docked at Cape Flora on July 20th.

Track of Windward *from London to Cape Flora, Franz Josef Land. Bruce joined the Jackson–Harmsworth expedition in 1896 as the naturalist and took passage in London on 9 June. (D. J. Williams)*

plant species. He thanked Mill and his wife for the interest they had taken in him. He wrote that he was 'eager for work and will especially value the experience of northern ice', but also that he was 'eager to return to the South soon'.[16]

Sea ice was first sighted on 6 July over 200 miles from Franz Josef Land at 76°31′N, 53°10'E.[17] *Windward* took twenty days to reach Cape Flora. Here a surprise awaited, a scoop that must have exceeded

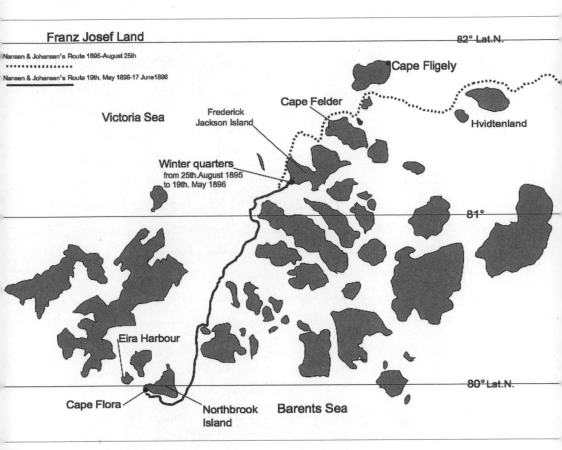

Map of the Archipelago of Franz Josef Land showing the path that Nansen and Johansen took to meet up with Jackson and his party at Cape Flora. (Taken in modified form from a map in Nansen's book Farthest North Vol. II, 1897 edition)

Harmsworth's most sanguine expectations: Fridtjof Nansen[18] and his companion Hjalmar Johansen[19] were at the base; they had been living at Elmwood for over a month. Nansen's attempt to reach the North Pole in his ship the *Fram*[20] – designed especially to be frozen into the pack ice and to ride on the ice, with the plan to start from Norway and be carried to north Greenland by drift, passing the North Pole en route – had been abandoned the previous year when it became obvious that she would not reach the Pole but pass miles from it. He and Johansen had finally left the ship on 14 March 1895[21] and attempted to reach their goal with dog sledges and kayaks. They were forced to turn south at 86°14'N and aimed at Franz Josef Land.

Jackson wrote that on 17 June 1896 a member of the team (Albert Armitage, his second-in-command)[22] had come rushing in to the base excitedly announcing that there was a man on the ice. Jackson thought initially that this must be either a member of the team or even a walrus. Having satisfied himself that it was indeed an unknown person, he 'picked up a gun, and followed by one of the dogs, set off to investigate this extraordinary apparition'.[23] By the summer of 1896 there had been no communication with Nansen and Johansen for almost three years, and it was assumed that they had perished. The meeting of Jackson and the initially unrecognisable Nansen was therefore one of the most dramatic events in Arctic history, rivalling that of Livingstone and Stanley in Africa: 'Aren't you Nansen? Yes, I am Nansen. By Jove I'm damned glad to see you.'[24]

Meeting the explorer was another wonderful opportunity for Bruce. Nansen was already famous for having made the first crossing of Greenland in 1888, and Bruce admired him greatly. He wrote: 'I believe in him so thoroughly, who could help doing so?'[25] Nansen, for his part, was to prove friendly and supportive to the younger man and would continue to be so in the long term – he advised Bruce in the outfitting of the Scottish National Antarctic Expedition five years later.

About a year after Bruce had arrived in the archipelago, Harmsworth sent copies of newspapers and magazines to the men on Franz Josef Land which described the sensational meeting. The reports were, of course, of fascinating interest to everyone at Elmwood, but particularly to Jackson, who devoured them – Bruce wrote sarcastically that Jackson 'does nothing but read the *Sketch, Daily Mail, Illustrated*

London News & Weekly Times. Yesterday evening he again spent about 2 hours admiring his own photos with a look of satisfaction on his face. The only time I have seen him beam more is when he is reading his own book.'[26]

There were plenty of opportunities for science, but Bruce felt thwarted once more considering the amount of work he achieved. As on the *Balaena*, his time and energy were taken up with what he considered to be superfluous duties. He had to check and prepare the sledging equipment, dig out snow and skin the bears, birds or other animals that Jackson had shot. He disliked this, although it might be thought perfectly reasonable that everyone at the base should contribute to the general duties. Indeed, Dr Koettlitz felt that the fresh meat that Bruce helped to prepare had one great advantage: the prevention of scurvy. There were no problems with scurvy at the expedition base, but men on board the *Windward* suffered from the disease in spite of having taken the advised cure, lemon juice, regularly. Bruce was familiar with scurvy, and he accepted Dr Koettlitz's erroneous conclusion that citrus fruits were not the cure[27] but rather that the disease was due to ptomaine poisoning, which, it was thought, was caused by bacteria present in preserved meats. It was considered that eating fresh meat regularly was the best cure. Jackson too wrote that he 'had no faith in lime juice having any effect against scurvy'.[28]

In fact, citrus fruits do cure scurvy. The reason that the bottled juice given to the crew of *Windward* was ineffective was that by this time the Navy was importing lime juice (less vitamin C than in lemons) from the West Indies rather than lemons from the Mediterranean, and the juices were transported in copper vats that further lessened their anti-scorbutic properties. Fresh meat in fact has only weak anti-scurvy effects, though offal, seal liver[29] and heart are effective. It is possible that men on the expedition were eating offal as well as meat. Certainly on the

Jackson–Harmsworth expedition daily 'meat' seems to have kept scurvy at bay.[30] Koettlitz was to continue with his opinions when he went as senior doctor on Scott's first expedition in 1902; scurvy was to blight this expedition.[31]

Bruce, as mentioned, had left in a rush and was without some essential equipment. He grumbled privately that he had to make rope out of loose-spun yarn and nets out of handkerchiefs; everything had been on a makeshift scale.[32] He asked Mr Montifiore Brice (Harmsworth's secretary for the expedition) to forward the necessary items, but Brice failed to do this and Bruce felt this deficiency keenly. He believed his scientific work has been compromised. After the expedition he wrote to Harmsworth in October 1997 (at length, with some courage and self-belief, but apparently without consideration that his letters might be merely irritating) in a prickly, complaining letter saying that Montifiore Brice had taken no notice of the lists that had been sent to him requesting formalin, tow net material, dredging and trawling apparatus, deep-sea thermometers and seawater bottles. He complained that zoological specimens had been destroyed because of the lack of formalin. Also, neither specimens of seawater that had been sent back to Montifiore Brice, nor the meteorological log prepared by his colleague Wilton, had been acknowledged. This sort of communication was likely to antagonise, and revealed a side to Bruce's character that undoubtedly worked against him in his search for backers for his various projects throughout his life.

Remarkably, Harmsworth, eager to milk public interest aroused by Nansen's appearance, suggested that at the end of the expedition Jackson and Bruce should return to Britain in kayaks rather than on the *Windward*. Bruce dismissed the idea contemptuously: 'Personally I would never have dreamt of undertaking such an absolutely foolhardy thing as to risk coming home in a Kyak (*sic*), unless it were a dire necessity, and even then I should have started never expecting to come through. An Esquimaux[33] in his Kyak, and a man who has never been in one in his life have two very different chances, and I should not even hold out much hope for an Esquimaux undertaking such a voyage.'[34]

Although Bruce's results were not as comprehensive as he hoped, he did manage to collect a significant amount of data. As the expedition's zoologist he recorded the multifarious animal life: bears (both males and females wandered about all the winter, contrary to previous reports), blue foxes, reindeer, seals, whales including the narwhal, walruses, and many birds. In all eleven classes of mammals were noted and nineteen species of birds,[35] five being unexpected visitors to Franz Josef Land. He listed the Lapland bunting, the shorelark, the snowy owl, the purple sandpiper and Bonaparte's sandpiper, as well as auks, guillemot, gulls, snow bunting, brent geese and eider ducks. He trapped seven species of springtails (small insects) – the first recorded in Franz Josef Land – and tow netted, catching some fish (thirteen specimens, six of which were alive), also bringing back unidentified bones for further examination.

He was a man who could become completely absorbed in his work. On one occasion he was working on the sea ice collecting marine samples, too focused to realise that he was being stalked by a polar bear. When Jackson saw the situation he set off from base with his rifle. When Bruce eventually noticed the animal he made so much noise that the bear took to the water before Jackson could get a shot in. Jackson lamented in his diary: 'We need the bear meat.'[36]

But Bruce was proud of what he had achieved. In a later letter to Mill he made a comparison of his specimen numbers with other expeditions. He wrote that on his own he had collected 611 species in a year, whereas, for example, an American expedition (the United States

International, 1881–1883), which boasted two naturalists, had collected 295 species in two years.[37]

In the summer of 1897, the *Balaena*, a ship familiar to Bruce from the Dundee expedition to the Antarctic, arrived in Franz Josef Land. Captain Thomas Robertson, who had captained the *Diana* on that previous expedition, was skipper. The renewal of this acquaintance would result in Captain Robertson being appointed as master of the *Scotia* in 1902.

In relation to the aims of the expedition, a survey was made of Franz Josef Land.[38] It was found that the land was, in fact, an archipelago. No serious attempt was made to reach the North Pole. Jackson had discovered open sea to the north of Franz Josef Land, which made overland sledging to high latitudes impossible, and *Windward* did not have the engine power to force a way through the ice. The archipelago, however, became peppered with names familiar to the readers of Harmsworth's papers: Queen Victoria Sea, Alfred Harmsworth Island, Nightingale Sound, the British Channel, Hooker Island, Markham Sound. One of the islands was named 'Bruce Island'.[39] A cape at 80°55'N, on the northern edge of Northbrook Island, was called 'Cape Bruce'.

Windward arrived to take the expedition home in July 1897. On the way home Bruce saw Bear Island, the southernmost island on the Spitsbergen archipelago, an island group that was to occupy much of Bruce's time and attention in later years. *Windward* reached London in September 1897.

After the expedition Bruce returned to Edinburgh. He worked on his specimens, writing papers like 'The Mammals of Franz Josef Land by William S. Bruce, FRSGS' describing his zoological and botanical findings on the expedition.[40] He received £60 for his work for the expedition in May 1897[41] and returned to work as a demonstrator in John Arthur Thomson's zoology classes and gave talks such as 'Life in the Polar Regions, A lecture by W. S. Bruce Esq.' (prices ranging from 2s for front seats to 1/6d for seats under the gallery) and 'Recent Voyages in the Antarctic', held in the Royal Scottish Geographical Society's Hall, chaired by Sir John Murray KCB (with members invited to introduce guests either personally or by visiting card).

Bruce continued to show what could be considered rather unwise, self-confident independence. While Jackson wanted the expedition's scientific collection to be amalgamated, Bruce did not intend that his collection should be combined with Dr Koettlitz's specimens but instead collaborated with Dr William Eagle Clarke,[42] an expert on bird migration and Arctic birds. This decision irritated Jackson, although he did appreciate Bruce's commitment: 'It is no pleasant job to dabble in icy-cold water, with the thermometer some degrees below zero, or to plod in the summer through snow, slush and mud many miles in search of animal life as I have known Mr Bruce frequently do.'[43] Bruce sent other specimens to his chosen experts (some bone samples were identified in the anatomy department of the University of Edinburgh as being from a 'right' whale, others the tibia of a seal; antlers were also identified) and Bruce was truly inexhaustible with his reports: biology specimens, plants, zoological specimens, lists of animals including mammals, fauna, microscopic work, fishes, birds, oceanography reports, survey maps of the area.

Mr Harmsworth kept in touch. He wrote in June 1897, asking how Bruce had enjoyed his year in the north – one that had started with the eventful meeting with Nansen – mentioning that there had been rumours that Nansen *had* reached the North Pole. He sent Bruce cigars and newspaper and magazine reports on the expedition. He asked Bruce, Jackson and Armitage to come for dinner and for Bruce to stay the night – Bruce does not appear to have gone. He entirely lacked those social attributes and communication skills that might have smoothed his progress.

Bruce could, however, reflect on new achievements: his meeting with Nansen and his collaboration with Mr Eagle Clark, the numerous reports he made on his findings and observations, not to mention his collections. The experience had strengthened his ambition for a purely scientific expedition to Antarctica, its aims undiluted by commerce or sensational activities. But he was now thirty, and this 'narrow' intention can only have reduced its general appeal. With no prospect of regular work he somehow kept faith that he would eventually achieve renown as a naturalist. He must have had some encouragement when the Royal Scottish Geographical Society elected him as a Free Life Ordinary Member.[44]

Having visited the Arctic, Bruce was to develop a passionate involvement with the islands in later years. He must have been outraged when Russia annexed Franz Josef Land in 1914. The schooner *Gherta* left Christiania on 29 July 1914, reached Cape Flora on 18 August and hoisted the Russian flag.

5

NOVAYA ZEMLYA, THE BARENTS SEA
AND SPITSBERGEN

In 1898, Major Andrew Coats,[1] a wealthy member of the Coats family of Paisley, the family that was to finance Bruce's Antarctic expedition of 1902, planned a hunting and sporting trip to Spitsbergen and the Barents Sea. He asked Mill to act as scientific observer, an occupation that Dr Mill would have relished. Unfortunately for Mill, Sir Clements Markham, as president of the Royal Geographical Society in London, refused to grant leave to the society's librarian, arguing that the proper place for a librarian was in the library.[2] Mill generously gave the opportunity to Bruce, who was taken on for £15 per month.[3] This expedition was to be a turning point in Bruce's life. During the tour with Coats he sailed the Barents Sea, saw the Svalbard archipelago (which was to become a major obsession in his life) and met the Coats family and Albert, Prince of Monaco,[4] who was to become a valued benefactor and friend.

Bruce was in charge of scientific observations; he did not want the responsibility of medical work, and recommended a colleague – in the event Major Coats took on a retired army surgeon.[5] Coats' yacht, the *Blencathra*, was well equipped for scientific research: sounding equipment, trawls, tow nets, sea traps, seawater bottles and thermometers were available, and part of the saloon was furnished with a table, shelves, hooks and racks, etc., to be used as a laboratory.[6] Andrew Coats was also prepared to provide any scientific instruments that Bruce needed – and he did. Bills of over £169 were issued to Coats and Bruce in April 1898.[7]

Bruce joined *Blencathra*, which had left the Clyde in early May 1898, at Tromsø, Norway, having waited for the delivery of sounding equipment. He travelled by mail steamer, calling on forty-four settlements on the way. When he caught up with *Blencathra* a fortnight was spent in the Norwegian fjords, and Bruce relished the opportunity to record the teeming bird life. In a letter to Dr Mill he wrote that he had emphasised to Major Coats that there was important work to be done around Franz Josef Land, but he asked Mill to underline these points as ' it might come better from you than too emphatically from me as I don't wish to assume the position of "Boss"'.[8] Coats always planned to visit the Arctic Islands, though not necessarily as far north as Franz Josef Land, and he sailed first towards Novaya Zemlya, an archipelago at 70°N. On the voyage Bruce at once took to his favourite occupations of sounding, trawling and throwing out floats.

Attempts to land on Novaya Zemlya were thwarted by heavy pack ice, so *Blencathra* headed to Kolguev Island, south of Novaya Zemlya at 69°3′N. The island had been explored in 1894 but was only visited briefly by Coats at this time, though the visit had its excitements. A heavy gale tossed *Blencathra* around and upset everything not fastened securely, including Bruce's 'spirit, formalin and all kinds of precious things'.[9] The brief landing was disappointing. Bruce did not get to the island proper; miles of wet sand, leads of water and ice blocks cut him off. However, he noted that ivory gulls were present in such large numbers that he thought they must be nesting – this was a new observation as the gulls had previously been thought to visit only in wintertime. He also collected more specimens before Coats attempted another, this time successful, attempt to visit Novaya Zemlya.

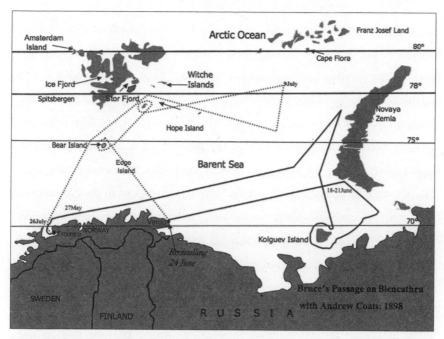

Bruce's voyages on Blencathra *in 1898, on which he was the naturalist on a hunting/pleasure cruise with Major Andrew Coats. (D. J. Williams)*

Novaya Zemlya is part of the Novaya Zemlya district of Russia. It has been known for over ten centuries, and by the fourteenth century was visited regularly by expeditions hunting for walrus tusks and hides and polar bear furs. The first European sighting was made in the 1500s, but it was not until the early 1800s that attempts were made to chart the coastline and the island was circumnavigated in 1870s when a permanent settlement was established. The coastline was finally mapped in 1913, so when Bruce visited much of the coast was still uncharted.

Bruce luxuriated in the plant and bird life. He was delighted to add a new bird, the grey phalarope (an Arctic-breeding wader),[10] to the list of the archipelago's visitors. After visiting Novaya Zemlya, Major Coats hoped to make more geographical discoveries; there was considerable doubt about details of some of the islands east of the Svalbard archipelago.[11] But the sea ice in the Barents Sea during the first half of 1898 proved an impassable obstruction in many places. Bear Island,[12] the southernmost island in the archipelago, was seen but could not be landed upon, so a course was made for Hope Island, another of the small islands in the archipelago, lying north of Bear Island. Here difficulties were encountered with heavy surf and a steeply sloping beach, which frustratingly prevented a landing. Wiche Island[13] was next. This island had been visited the previous year, but once again luck was not with the Coats expedition; the pack ice surrounding the island was impossible to penetrate, and the island could only be viewed from a distance. The expedition members thus contented themselves with the primary objective of the trip, shooting birds and walruses and hunting bears on the pack ice, while Bruce continued to make as many observations as was practicable: four-hourly meteorological observations, recording of sea temperatures, samples of seawater from the surface and below and measurement of sea salinity. He took photographs although, 'having had so little experience and no opportunity on the voyage to develop one of two so as to see what I was doing', he was uncertain how they would come out.[14] He kept the tow nets going almost continuously, made a few trawls, threw out 147 floats to record currents and made a careful examination of the fish of the region (after the expedition he wrote a report on these fish with financial support from Andrew Coats and a George Heriot Research Fellowship; in it he identified, measured and described sixty fish, some of which had rarely, if ever, been identified).[15]

Blencathra returned to Tromsø in July 1898. Bruce only received one letter; from Dr Mill, and he replied immediately, telling Mill of his achievements and, incidentally, commenting on his pleasure that his Edinburgh mentor, John Murray, had been awarded a knighthood[16] – an honour, Bruce wrote, that was 'not conferred too soon'.[17]

This trip had given Bruce valuable information about the remarkable vagaries of pack ice in Spitsbergen waters – his own hand-drawn track of the sail was originally headed '*Blencathra's* BLETHERINGS'. But for him, a major disadvantage of the experience was that the expedition was primarily for pleasure. He wrote to Mill that he longed for a purely scientific trip. In this, he was soon to get his wish.

In Tromsø, Bruce saw the yacht *Princesse Alice* for the first time. She was a beautiful sailing ship belonging to Prince Albert of Monaco, and was said to be the best-equipped ship for oceanographic work since *Challenger*. The prince planned oceanographic research in the Arctic – Albert had been fascinated by the Arctic regions for years, and was to make four expeditions there between 1898 and 1907. Major Coats introduced Bruce to the prince, and Bruce was delighted when the prince invited him to join what, in 1898, was planned as a reconnaissance expedition (the prince intended to return in 1899 to continue the exploration). A few days after returning to Tromsø, then, Bruce was sailing north again. The prince's priority on this voyage was to add specimens to the collection he had already begun for his Musée Oceanographic de Monaco.[18]

This was another wonderful opportunity for a relatively junior scientist eager to make his mark. Bruce was in the company of some of the best oceanographers in Europe on *Princesse Alice,* and they taught him how to unravel the mysteries of the ocean. Dr Jules Richard[19] was a French biologist and John Young Buchanan[20] was the chemist whom Bruce had met previously in relation to his *Challenger* work. Also on board was Karl Brandt,[21] a physical oceanographer. When, as arranged, Brandt and Buchanan left *Princesse Alice* midway through the expedition, Bruce took charge of many of the scientific observations.

As Bruce had noted earlier in the year, the variability of pack ice in different seasons was remarkable. By the summer of 1898 the seas were open and the Arctic Islands could be approached. Bear Island was finally visited on 30 July. Bruce climbed the well-named Mount Misery as far as the cloud base at 600 feet. He shot birds, as did the prince. He and the prince went fishing. Satisfactorily, the prince caught the bigger fish

(18 inches to Bruce's 8 inches). *Princesse Alice* then made a course for Hope Island, where, on 1 August, Prince Albert anchored on the eastern shores. Hope Island has a flat-topped plateau split by snow-capped gullies and is glaciated at higher altitudes. Bruce was surprised at the amount of vegetation in this unlikely environment, mostly saxifrages, but even at the summit little Icelandic poppies bloomed. Skuas' nests were observed and counted.

The ship sailed then for Spitsbergen, the largest island in the Svalbard archipelago. It covers more than 15,000 square miles and has a permanent population following the establishment of coalmining in the late 1800s. By 3 August *Princesse Alice* was sailing through Stor Fjord (the Great Fjord), a 68-mile fjord on the eastern coast. The fjord was free of ice and *Princesse Alice* (unusually for a vessel not protected for ice work), was able to sail to the head of the fjord at Ginevra Bay, incidentally sailing over what had been marked on the Admiralty chart as a 'low flat island'.[22] Bruce marvelled at the magnificent mountains and the glaciers flowing between them, and here in Stor Fjord the first oceanographic recordings of the area were made. The prince then made a cruise along the west coast of Spitsbergen, visiting its principal locations: in Ice Fjord, *Princesse Alice* called at Advent Bay (the site of a mining camp where Brandt and Buchanan left the ship) and two further bays at the furthest end of the fjord, Sassen Bay (*sas* means sluice or basin) and Klaas Billen Bay. *Princesse Alice* then returned to the west coast and journeyed to the north-west of Spitsbergen, visiting the old whaling centre of Smeerenburg, on the north of the island, and Danes Island, which lies in the Arctic Ocean to the north-west of Spitsbergen.

This expedition confirmed Bruce's interests in oceanography, already stimulated by his work on the *Challenger* and *Balaena* expeditions. He was, after all, in the most expert company, and here he perfected his techniques in sounding, sea records, examining specimens, making notes and, particularly, dredging. By this time oceanographic equipment was available that could collect samples of sea, marine life and bacteria from measured levels between the sea surface and the sea floor. Bruce fully understood the huge potential of such a rich scientific yield. On *Princesse Alice*, the laboratory claimed most of his time and attention. Oceanography became his predominant passion – although he described himself on the census and his marriage certificate in 1901 as a naturalist or zoologist, by the 1911 census he was an oceanographer.

Bruce achieved a great deal on this trip. He not only saw and visited many places in Spitsbergen, an island that was to become almost a fixation, but also, with the help of the experts on the *Princesse Alice*, was able to build upon the training he had received while working both on the *Challenger* data and in the Ben Nevis Observatory, completing a valuable series of oceanographic, meteorological and zoological observations which contributed useful information to existing knowledge about the region. In this way he cemented his apprenticeship for polar work.

After the expedition Bruce returned to Edinburgh, but was pleased to receive an invitation from Prince Albert to winter in the palace at Monaco and to cruise in the Mediterranean. During the winter Bruce worked on his Arctic specimens, and in the summer of 1899 he eagerly accepted the prince's invitation to return to Spitsbergen. Albert aimed to make a detailed hydrographical survey of one of the larger fjords: the venue chosen was Wiche Sound (Liefde Bay) on the north-west of Spitsbergen, previously visited by Russian trappers but still largely unexplored in 1899.

The outward voyage must have been enormously exhilarating, even for someone of Bruce's reserved character. *Princesse Alice* sailed from Le Havre in June 1899, and Kiel was the first port of call. Kaiser Wilhelm II[23] had invited the prince to attend the Kiel regatta and Bruce was not only to witness the pomp and ceremony of the formalities but was also to meet the kaiser himself and, later, the empress.[24] Bruce wrote that the Kaiser had arranged for a naval officer to be attached to *Princesse Alice* for the duration of the Prince Albert's visit, and he recorded in his journal that 'the *Princesse Alice* sailed between lines of battleships and cruisers that stretched the length of Kiel harbour'.[25] He attended a soiree arranged by the emperor. *Princesse Alice* then called at Tromsø, and the empress herself entertained the prince's company on her yacht *Thistle* as she cruised along the Norwegian Lyngen Fjord. This was dazzling stuff for the grave, reserved naturalist.

Princesse Alice steamed north to Spitsbergen. On the voyage she passed Prince Charles Foreland;[26] Bruce was to return here in 1906 to make the first systematic survey and map of the island. The foreland's southern extremity 'stood out like a separate island from the northern end'.[27] Wiche Sound could not be entered because of heavy ice that was then considered impossible for a steel yacht to navigate, so *Princesse Alice* carefully steamed west along the coast to reach Red Bay (80°N). Here the entrance was open, and it was obvious that the bay, marked on the clearly inaccurate Admiralty map as a shallow inlet, was actually a long, narrow fjord. Since the bay had not been charted properly and was a perfect site for oceanographic work, the prince decided to spend the summer season there; Bruce wrote later that this was an example of the coastline being charted 'in entire where it ought to be in dotted outline where it is practically unsurveyed'.[28]

Cautious sounding was continuously done before *Princesse Alice* anchored in eight fathoms in the shelter of a point that was later named Point Bruce. Bruce explored the eastern side of the bay with the biologist Dr Jules Richard. He commented that they crammed every available pocket with bottles and tubes for their specimens. The men found an unexpected high-altitude freshwater lake populated by salmon, which they caught in a method that Bruce advised others to follow, employing

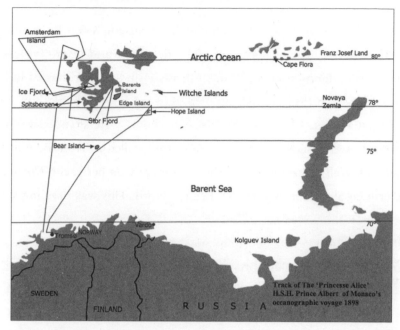

Above: Map showing the voyage of HSH Prince Albert's steam yacht
Princesse Alice *to Spitsbergen in 1898, in which Bruce assisted in a*
hydrographic survey. (D. J. Williams)

Below: A map showing the tracks of Princesse Alice *on which Bruce*
accompanied Prince Albert of Monaco in 1899. (D. J. Williams)

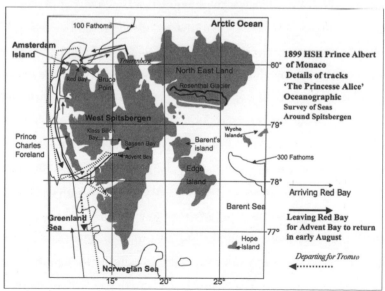

a stick, a piece of string, a hook and beef for bait. He noted glacier-filled valleys with intervening bare ridges; there was no true ice cap. He climbed to the highest peak, at 2,995 feet, which the prince named 'Ben Nevis' in his honour. He wrote that there were signs of the glaciers advancing 'with irresistible power ... One can imagine that he actually sees them creeping down like a river'.[29] Red Bay was confirmed to be a fjord 12 miles long. Bruce described seven glaciers on its western side, each filling the valleys between the peaked mountains. At the feet of the mountains and between the glaciers, there were raised beaches rich in vegetation. The eastern side was free of glaciers.

While the hydrographical work was proceeding, *Princesse Alice* sailed the 300 miles to visit Advent Bay and other places on the west coast. On her return she made for her previous anchorage. Soundings to port and starboard were made carefully as she went, but, in spite of all precautions, at high tide she grounded. There was no hope of immediate escape, and it was possible that the ship would be stuck in the bay for the winter. The prince sent his steam launch with the two women who had sailed on the *Princesse Alice* to Advent Bay. He asked Bruce to organise a shore camp for the sixty-man crew. Coal, movable gear and boats were taken off the ship and Bruce organised a camp with enough food for three months and enough coal for the winter. Crew morale was understandably low, and Bruce tried to buoy their spirits by keeping them fully occupied while attempts to release the *Princesse Alice* were made at every high tide. Rudmose Brown writes that Bruce enjoyed himself immensely. Finally after five days, and at the ninth tide, the ship was re-floated, though leaking. The men on the shore 'raised a cheer, hoisted a piece of canvas for a flag and fired a salute with five shot guns'.[30]

Remarkably a vessel appeared. The steam launch had left a notice in Advent Bay describing *Princesse Alice*'s predicament, and a Swedish gunboat on her way to Treurenburg[31] diverted to offer to escort the vessel on a trial run. This offer was accepted gratefully, but help from a German tourist ship that had also appeared, hoping to give its passengers the thrill of seeing a shipwreck, was not needed. *Princesse Alice* sailed to Treurenburg Bay where she was re-coaled before sailing to Advent Bay for a full inspection. After that it was on to Tromsø for temporary repairs to damage below the water line before she finally sailed to Le Havre for a complete overhaul.

Bruce published his account of the voyages in the *Scottish Geographical Magazine* in September 1900. He felt the work that he had achieved was worthwhile. He praised the Prince of Monaco, writing that in 'facilitating the thorough survey of Red Bay, hydrographically, biologically and otherwise, in addition to the oceanographic research round Spitsbergen, His Highness has rendered most valuable services to science and to navigation'.[32] Incidentally, the crew made 2,400 soundings in their survey of Red Bay. The rock on which *Princesse Alice* grounded was the only one recorded.

After this voyage, Bruce, as one of Britain's most experienced and expertly trained polar workers, was confident, eager and ready for an Antarctic voyage. He wrote papers and gave talks, and his report on 'The Exploration of Spitsbergen and Soundings in Seas Adjacent' was read in the Royal Society of Scotland's 1900–01 session. Bruce was keen to draw attention to his scientific findings and to gain support for a return to the Antarctic. But in spite of his determination to return to the south, he could never stoop to obsequiousness; he was always completely confident of his worth and the value of his work, and, seemingly unaware that his comments could be counterproductive, he never hesitated to criticise.

There were tensions between Bruce and some of his colleagues in London. He wrote to Mill on 3 March 1899 about his irritation with John Scott Keltie, the eminent Secretary of the Royal Geographical Society, saying that though Keltie was not pleased that he (Bruce) had lectured to the Royal Scottish Geographical Society, 'I don't see what harm I have done especially as he could not tell me what the RGS wanted'. Bruce was willing to give the RGS something, 'but I can't spend time writing things and then have them put on shelves for two or three years and possibly even have them lost. I did not know that there was this rivalry between the London and Scottish Societies, which caused them either to try or prevent the other getting geographical information. It is scarcely in the scientific spirit.'[33] By October of that year he was relieved that the society thought his report worth publishing, but, as he wrote bluntly, 'I am not inclined to conjure the confidence of the RGS or any other society. My work must stand on its own merits.'[34] Even at this stage of his career, although Bruce was prepared to work with his English colleagues, concern over English 'domination' – imbibed originally during his time in the *Challenger* office – combined with his prickly pride, unwillingness to compromise and confidence in his work made cooperation difficult and created problems for him in achieving the recognition he undoubtedly deserved.

6

PREPARATIONS FOR THE SCOTIA EXPEDITION

In the latter part of the 1800s, groups in the United Kingdom and in Europe showed great interest in the Antarctic. Information was needed as to whether there actually was a seventh continent – separate land sightings had been made, but it was not known if these were in fact islands or part of the mythical continent. In addition, there was much demand for more information about the scientific parameters of the area, particularly regarding the current location of the South Magnetic Pole, which had moved continuously since Sir James Clark Ross had established its approximate position over fifty years previously. Knowledge of the positions of the magnetic poles was essential for navigation as they bear a variable relationship to the Geographical North and South Poles. Failure to correct a ship's compass accurately for the magnetic declination (the angle between the bearings of Magnetic and Geographic Poles at any point on the Earth) could, and often did, result in a ship navigating a course miles from its intended land destination, sometimes with perilous – and infamous – consequences.[1]

Groups such as the British Association for the Advancement of Science, the Royal Societies of London and Edinburgh, a joint Scottish and Australian committee (partially funded by the British government) and the International Geographic Union were all aware of the potential for exploration and scientific advance. What was lacking was not enthusiasm or expertise but financial backing; neither commercial companies or scientific societies – nor, in Great Britain, the government – would commit to adequate funding. Expeditions needed support from all three.

In November 1893, Sir Clements Markham, the newly elected President of the Royal Geographical Society and the man who was to become the prime mover in organising Scott's *Discovery* expedition of 1901, determined to make Antarctic exploration a cornerstone of his presidency. His inaugural presidential address expounded upon the importance of Antarctic exploration and its opportunities for geographic and scientific work. Fourteen days later, John Murray, widely respected for his oceanographic work on the *Challenger* expedition,[2] gave the keynote speech on Antarctica at a special meeting organised by Markham at the RGS. Murray again highlighted the benefits to be gained from southern exploration, but emphasised that oceanography was key to understanding climatic conditions. In relationship to the nature of the southern lands, he drew attention to Bruce's work on the *Balaena* expedition, stating that Bruce had dredged up rock samples of continental origin (the metamorphic and sedimentary rock) and mentioning Bruce's meteorological work on *Balaena*.

Murray stressed the need for work in all scientific branches, but was against 'a dash to the South Pole'. British science, he said, needed 'a steady, continuous, laborious and systematic exploration of the whole southern region',[3] work that would provide information as to where the continent could be explored with the greatest likelihood of success. In his diary entry for that day Sir Clements commented that 'Dr Murray gave us an admirable paper setting forth the argument for a renewal of Antarctic discovery with telling force'.[4] But although at this juncture the two collaborated closely, Sir Clements, as a geographer, put greater emphasis on geographical exploration and survey than on systematic scientific research, and they were subsequently to disagree fundamentally about the purpose of the expedition and therefore about its leadership. Murray favoured a scientist as director of scientific staff whereas Sir Clements was determined that a Royal Navy commander should be both ship's captain and expedition leader.

Bruce wholeheartedly agreed with Murray's general premise. He was in the audience when Murray made his address, and he spoke up to say that he agreed that the expedition should be of a national character, immediately volunteering himself for scientific work. By this time he had already failed to join the *Antarctic* on her voyage to Victoria Land, having been unable get to Melbourne in time to join the ship (when Carsten Borchgrevink took his place). Sir Clements, in his diary entry for the day, mentioned Bruce as 'young Bruce who went South in a whaler last season'.[5]

Any thought of Bruce being in charge of a sortie to the Antarctic was, at this point, a chimera, but he supported the British expedition strongly – after Murray's address he read a paper to the Royal Scottish Geographical Society (RSGS) on the attractions of a national Antarctic expedition. Following this presentation, the society's chairman, Professor James Geikie, stated that the RSGS had resolved to give its support to the promotion of further exploration in the Antarctic. An Edinburgh-based Antarctic Committee was appointed consisting of John Murray, Professor Geikie himself, Dr Alexander Buchan[6] and Mr J. G. Bartholomew.[7] There was no thought of a Scottish expedition; the committee planned to support a British expedition and to back Bruce in his attempts to join it. Although appeals for funds (even with the added enticement of the possibility of valuable whale oil) failed,[8] this committee was significant; it included delegates from ten Scottish scientific societies and would be important later in supporting Bruce's own Scottish National Antarctic Expedition.[9]

Although the scientific significance of Antarctica was understood, little national attention or progress followed until the Sixth International Geographical Congress of 1895. This was held in London. Sir Clements, in the chair, used this Congress to build international support for Antarctic exploration. Professor Georg Newmayer[10] was the opening speaker. The congress attracted delegates from forty countries, was reported in four languages and covered a range of topics, but prioritised Antarctica. It was at this meeting that Borchgrevink, having dashed halfway around the world to attend, claimed, to a receptive audience, that he had been the first man to set foot on the Antarctic in January 1895.

Sir Clements' triumph for the congress was achieving unanimous agreement to a crucial resolution that would be used to pressure the government for money. It read:

> The Congress concluded that the exploration of the Antarctic regions is the greatest piece of geographical exploration still to be undertaken. That in view of the additions to knowledge in almost every branch of science which would result from such a scientific exploration, the Congress recommends that the scientific societies throughout the world should urge, in whatever way seems to them most effective, that the work should be undertaken before the close of the century.[11]

For Bruce to continue his chosen path required courage. He was without funds, and although friends were supportive not one of the people or organisations he approached was prepared to produce the finances for southern work. He gave talks, wrote to people of influence and planned with colleagues. He wrote to the Secretary of the Meteorological Office, Sir Roger Scott, in September 1895, again seeking help for himself and an assistant to go to South Georgia to make a scientific exploration. In November 1895, he wrote a paper: 'The Proposed Scientific and Commercial Expedition to the Antarctic 1896–1898 by W. S. Bruce, Naturalist to the Antarctic Expedition 1892–1893'.[12] His plan was that he would be left in Antarctica for a year. The suggestion (with Sven

Foyn,[13] the Norwegian whaler, and Henrik Johan Bull)[14] failed to get backing, but Bruce's ideas, which included a fixed base for meteorological and geomagnetic observations (which would add to information about the location of the South Magnetic Pole), were ahead of their time when the southernmost observatories were at the Cape of Good Hope, Cape Horn and Melbourne.

The RGS did offer what help it could. A letter in April 1896 from the explorer and whaler Captain Carl Anton Larsen to J. S. Keltie, the secretary of the society, states that Keltie had informed Larsen that Bruce wanted to winter somewhere at Graham Land. Larsen wrote that he wanted to start a fishery in the south and would provide all the help he could, although, at the time of writing, he also lacked finance.[15] Bruce knew Larsen; the two had met on the Dundee whaling expedition of 1893 when Larsen was captain of *Jason* and Bruce was on the *Balaena*. Burn Murdoch wrote of Larsen in his book on the expedition: 'We had jolly evening in the cabin, smoking and yarning. We gave them a parting salute on the pipes as their two boats rowed away to the *Jason* in the early morning.'[16]

In 1898 the Royal Society (RS) and the RGS set up a Joint Antarctic Committee in London. Sir Clements was chair and Sir John Murray was a member. Hugh Robert Mill, as secretary of the RGS, reported on the committee's deliberations and he wrote that the work resulted in a confusion of jealousies, arguments, and misunderstandings. John Buchanan wrote to Bruce to say that at one meeting there had been 'a great row' and that he had 'lost his temper with Markham, who wishes to keep everything up his sleeve'.[17] It was to prove difficult, or impossible, to reconcile the diverging aims of the subcommittees, which consisted, in 1899, of twelve representatives from the RS and twelve from the RGS, which included experts on oceanography, magnetism, meteorology, geology, physical geography and biology.[18] The inevitable factions, in addition to Murray and Sir Clements' fundamentally different views on the primary aims of the expedition, resulted in Murray beginning to withdraw from discussions and to look favourably on a separate Scottish expedition.

For years Bruce would have been aware of the resentment in Scotland of a perceived 'dictatorial' attitude from London. His mentor Murray wanted any expedition to be equipped on a scientific scale that was worthy of Great Britain, and although Murray gave his support for co-operation in Antarctic expeditions in a plea circulated in the RSGS magazine in 1898, he eventually resigned from the joint venture. His resignation could have been cemented by a letter (14 November 1899) signed by the secretary of the Royal Society, Sir Michael Foster, on behalf of his society and the RGS, turning down the request of the Royal *Scottish* Geographical Society to have a representative on the Joint Antarctic Committee.[19] It may have been considered difficult to include a RSGS member into the numerous groupings that made up the Joint Antarctic Committee, but the decision suggests hubris.

The personal fracture in relations between Bruce and Sir Clements started in 1899 when Bruce applied to join the *Discovery* expedition. He wrote to Sir Clements on 15 April saying that having seen an announcement about the proposed British National Antarctic Expedition, he wished to be considered for a scientific post. By this time he was one of the most experienced polar scientists or explorers in Britain, if not *the* most experienced. He listed his considerable qualifications for the post – a summer in the Antarctic, three summers and one winter in the Arctic, and a year on the summit of Ben Nevis. He said he would be happy to send a formal application with testimonials if required. He wrote that he would be in London the following week. Clearly he did not harbour an overwhelming animus against the *Discovery* expedition at this juncture; his wish to do work in the Antarctic overcame any nationalistic prejudice. Sir Clements replied promptly, writing that no decisions had been made as to staff but that he would be glad to meet in London. However, Bruce did not meet Sir Clements. The reason for this is unknown, but a message was sent to him, probably in early 1900, via Dr Reginald Koettlitz (who knew Bruce from the Jackson–Harmsworth expedition of 1897) telling Bruce to apply for an assistant's place on *Discovery*.

Bruce wrote again to Sir Clements on 21 March 1900 (by this time nearly a year after his original letter) giving the names of seven impressive referees: HSH The Prince of Monaco, Sir John Murray KCB FRS, Dr Alexander Buchan FRS, Dr Fridtjof Nansen, Mr Andrew Coats, Mr Alfred Harmsworth and John Young Buchanan MA FRS. This was a remarkable list. Bruce wrote that he had already lodged his application, which Sir Clements had acknowledged on 17 April 1899,[20] and he may well have thought this enough, though as mentioned in his original letter of 15 April he had written that he would send a formal application, plus referees, if required.

In 1899, while awaiting further communication from Sir Clements, Bruce was not idle. He gave further serious consideration to leading his own Antarctic expedition. He discussed plans again with John Young Buchanan, the chemistry expert who had been on the *Challenger*, and also with his friend Burn Murdoch, Sir John Murray and the meteorologist Robert Omond. Murray at this time was unconvinced, but the three other men were persuaded that Bruce could push his plans through and contributed enough money to allow him to begin to prepare a programme for 'the exploration of the Weddell Sea'.[21] Andrew Coats, Bruce's employer on the *Blencathra*, was supportive and made an initial contribution of £500.

When Bruce wrote to Sir Clements on 21 March 1900, he ended with a paragraph that was to sour relations. He said he was 'not without hopes of being myself able to raise sufficient capital whereby I could take out a second British ship to explore in the Antarctic regions'.[22]

The RSGS met in the National Portrait Gallery in Edinburgh the following day (22 March), where Bruce gave an account of his recent voyages in the Arctic. Sir John Murray was in the chair and he announced plans for a Scottish expedition to the Weddell Sea – an expedition to be led by Bruce. Murray commented that although he had thought that funds would not be secured, 'within the past few months people have given liberally towards many objects in which the nation is interested'. Bruce had received 'much encouragement'.[23] Murray spoke, to loud applause, of the possibility of raising £35,000 to £40,000.

Since this was only a day after Bruce had written to Sir Clements Markham he clearly felt the need to keep his options open, but in response to this stirring announcement the RSGS changed its allegiance and agreed to direct its patronage and assistance away from a British expedition towards this specifically Scottish endeavour.

A detailed report of the RSGS meeting and the plans appeared in *The Scotsman* on 23 March 1900. It was also on that day, when Mill and Markham were at the RGS, that the RGS became fully aware of a Scottish expedition; this was probably the first time that Sir Clements completely understood that the 'second British ship' was to be a separate Scottish venture. Mill's personal journal for that day states: 'Heard Bruce had got up expedition.'[24] It is likely that *The Scotsman* article was also available to them, as suggested by Markham's angry letter to Bruce of the same day: 'I am very sorry to hear that an attempt is to be made at Edinburgh to divert funds from the Antarctic expedition in order to get up a rival enterprise ... I do not understand why this mischievous rivalry should have been started, but I trust you will not connect yourself with it.'[25] This provocative communication did not reach Bruce until 26 March, by which point he had unknowingly stoked up more irritation by writing to Markham on 24 March that funding was assured for a second ship, which he said would be complementary to and co-operative with the German and British expeditions. When he actually received Sir Clements' letter, Bruce responded by return: 'I am very sorry that you should look upon my efforts as mischievous rivalry. Perhaps my letter of the 24th inst., which has crossed with yours, will show I am not working as a rival.'[26] Bruce shared Sir Clements' letters with Sir John

Murray, and was careful to seek Murray's advice about his replies. Murray 'advised me in, and approved of, my answers to them'.[27]

It is difficult not to have sympathy with Sir Clements. He had spent years canvassing and negotiating for the British Antarctic venture. He needed more finance; he thought that Bruce's monies should have been added to *Discovery*'s coffers. But his prickly response was bound to excite antipathy, and the crossover of the letters did little to help the situation. Further correspondence did nothing to reduce the ill feeling. Bruce could not understand why his expedition was considered a rival to *Discovery*. His plan was to sail to the Weddell Sea (*Discovery* went to the Ross Sea). He wrote on 26 March 1900 that there were at least five expeditions wintering in the 'much explored Arctic Regions ... I do not understand why you should look upon my expedition as a rival. If my friends are prepared to give me money to carry out my plans I do not see why I should not accept it ... I do not see how there cannot be room for my small expedition in addition to the German and British [in the Antarctic].'[28]

Also, Sir Clements' arrogant and proprietary attitude must have offended Bruce and his supporters. Sir Clements wrote that the expedition had been sprung on him without consultation about its advisability or route, a comment that annoyed the Scots since Markham 'had no particular knowledge of the Antarctic' and was 'presuming to be in a position to give useful advice to Bruce to say nothing of John Murray and other authorities who supported Bruce'.[29] Sir Clements wrote that Bruce had volunteered to join *Discovery* and that he had the right to prior consultation. He stated that the Weddell Sea was fully provided for; if Germany did not explore it, the British would.[30] In fact no instructions had been given to Scott in relation to the Weddell quadrant, the British expedition never intended to go anywhere near it and the German exploration leader welcomed Bruce's plans.

And Bruce reflected his Edinburgh teachers' ethos. He always envisaged cooperation between the expeditions that went to Antarctica in the early

1900s. In spite of national priorities, Bruce's *Scotia*, Scott's *Discovery*, the German expedition ship *Gauss*, led by Drygalski, and the Swedish ship *Antarctic*, led by Nordenskjöld, all aimed to cooperate over their scientific observations. Bruce actually met Dr Nordenskjöld and Dr Drygalski, and cooperation was emphasised when Bruce outlined his plans, firstly in a privately circulated communication and subsequently in the *Scottish Geographical Magazine* when the complementary nature of the expeditions was stressed. He wrote also that the Scots had no money for a relief ship. There was no room for bungling.

Sir Clements and Bruce did meet subsequently. Hugh Robert Mill wrote that he had, at Bruce's request, secured the post of naturalist for him on *Discovery*: 'And I was present when Markham proposed very pleasantly that he [Bruce] should join the ship. It was with a shock of surprise that we heard Bruce reply, "No thank you, I have arranged an expedition of my own."'[31] This meeting probably took place on 28 March 1900, since Mill's diary for that day contains the terse comment, 'W. S. Bruce calling discussing his Antarctic Expedition.'[32] Perhaps Bruce had travelled to London to try to reconcile himself with Markham, but given the contents of the conversation and Bruce's single-minded character this seems unlikely. A more likely explanation is that Bruce came to visit his long-standing fiancée, Jessie Mackenzie,[33] a nurse in his father's practice, to arrange a date for their marriage. Now, as leader of the Scottish National Expedition, he felt he could support a wife.

But even on the subject of his engagement Bruce's difficulty in communication was apparent, as illustrated by this remarkable letter to Mill, a man to whom Bruce owed a great deal, having been nominated by him for the *Balaena* expedition, the Jackson–Harmsworth expedition and the Arctic voyage with Andrew Coats:

I was intending to tell Mrs Mill and yourself the other day that I was intending to marry, but when the time came it seemed even more difficult to say so than to reach the South Pole. Such is the case however & I should not like the event to take place without having told you.[34]

He did write to Prince Albert of Monaco on 31 December 1900, saying that from the kindly interest that Albert had shown him he thought that the prince might be interested to know that he was intending to marry in January 1901 after an 'engagement of long standing'.[35] But although he told his mentor John Buchanan of his plans, he spoke in such a reserved and roundabout way that Buchanan felt he had to write that Bruce must have thought him '*peu sympathetique* when you told me of your approaching marriage but I was rather taken aback'.[36]

The couple married on 26 January 1901 at the Chapelhill United Free Church in the Parish of Nigg (Ross and Cromarty) – Jessie's birthplace.[37] They set up home at William's house at 17 Joppa Street, Portobello,[38] on the east side of Edinburgh. Bruce wrote to Jules Richard, the biologist on the *Princesse Alice*, in late January 1901, saying that he had abandoned the ranks of bachelors and become a respectable married man like Richard, and that he liked the new state very much.

On 10 February 1901, Markham wrote to Bruce in a conciliatory manner:

I am afraid I replied rather angrily when you announced your expedition to me: for I feared that your proceedings would divert funds from the national expedition which was and is much in need. But I can now see things from your point of view; and wish you success. Mr Armitage tells me that you have been married, and I send my congratulations on the happy event. I shall be at Dundee in March for the launching of the *Discovery*, and I hope to see you then.[39]

Markham also sent the *Scotia* expedition a telegram conveying his best wishes for success, which Bruce received when the ship arrived in

Funchal on its way south, and to which Bruce replied in writing from the ship.[40] It seems likely that once the *Discovery* expedition was funded and underway, Markham ceased to consider Bruce's expedition as important or as a rival to his own activities. He appears to have maintained that position for the next decade.[41]

Despite Markham, or perhaps stimulated by his original negative correspondence, the treasurers of the Scottish National Antarctic Expedition managed to raise support for an expedition that was to have a strongly nationalistic flavour. Societies and individuals throughout Scotland contributed, knowing that in Bruce Scotland had a scientist/explorer with more experience of polar research than anyone in Britain. The expedition was launched!

Jessie became pregnant six months after her marriage to Bruce. At thirty-one she was considerably older than was customary at the time for a *prima gravida*. Their son Eillium (Gaelic for William) Alastair was born in April 1902, seven months before the Scottish National Expedition sailed, at a time when Bruce was totally caught up in the logistical preparations. Jessie must have felt isolated. Victorian men expected their women to be in charge of the house and children, but although Jessie must have been well aware of Bruce's plans when they married, she was probably unprepared for the relative isolation in which she found herself. She had been the youngest child in a tight-knit Scottish family of ten children and had worked in London in a busy medical practice; she was used to company and activity. Yet after her marriage, she found herself without much support from her husband, caring for a baby but otherwise alone for much of the time, and perpetually short of money (Bruce's friends often sent cheques to help out)[42] and it seems that, unusually for someone of William's social class, she even had to manage without domestic help. [43] Jessie had a stern start to a marriage that would struggle on for fourteen years.

7

THE SCOTIA EXPEDITION, 1902–1904

The *Scotia* expedition was a success; discoveries were made that changed the way the geography of Antarctica was understood. New land was discovered to the east of the Weddell Sea – the coast was found to be 500 miles further north than had been expected. The Weddell Sea and South Atlantic were extensively explored by sounding, dredging and trawling, with the discovery of a major new subsea feature now known as the Scotia Ridge which bounds the Scotia Sea. A scientific base was set up on Laurie Island in the South Orkney Islands (this continues today as the Orcades Station, operated by Argentina). Thousands of meteorological recordings were made which gave rise to our current understanding of how the behaviour of sea ice in the Weddell Sea is coupled to the amount of rainfall in Southern South America. Finally, 1,100 species of animal were catalogued, of which 212 were previously unknown.

If Sir Clements Markham had been in a position to offer Bruce a place on the *Discovery* expedition in 1899, plans for a Scottish expedition are likely to have been put on hold. But Bruce's request was premature and the background strain between Scotland and London, coupled with Bruce's ambition, ability and enthusiasm to lead an Antarctic expedition, led to the formation of a purely Scottish enterprise.

The bulk of the financial backing came from the Coats family. James Coats (brother of Andrew Coats, the owner of *Blencathra*) was the principal donor, and the Coats family together contributed £30,000 in total (an amount larger than the donation of £25,000 that had launched Sir Clements Markham's *Discovery* expedition). Scottish societies and individuals[1] contributed £6,405, including 'some little orphans who had saved up their pennies to help the expedition'.[2] Scientists and enthusiasts gave specialised equipment.[3] The British Admiralty gave hydrographic instruments and charts. The Treasury gave the *Challenger* reports, but not cash; there is no evidence in the official National Archives files that Bruce asked for financial support from the government. But with backing of nearly £40,000 assured, he was in a confident position to turn down Sir Clements' offer in 1900. Plans were made for a ship of 250 to 300 tons register, equipped with the most modern oceanographic equipment and able to work in depths of 2,000–3,000 fathoms.

The aims and structure of British and Scottish expeditions differed. The British National Antarctic Expedition planned both geographical and scientific discoveries; the Scottish National Antarctic Expedition emphasised methodical scientific research, in keeping with Bruce's philosophy on polar exploration. He articulated his opinions succinctly some years later: 'Polar explorers might be categorised as those whose sole aim was to reach the Pole, and the more modern Polar exploration where, say, six to eight men were equipped in every way for the scientific survey of a definite sector of land or water, as might encompass astronomy, meteorology, magnetism, ocean physics, bathymetry, geology, and the investigation of terrestrial and marine life.'[4] This was his ambition. Also, whereas the *Discovery* coffers received a £40.000 injection of government monies, all the finance for Bruce's expedition was raised in Scotland. It was therefore considered to be a private expedition.

By March 1901, *The Scotsman* was able to announce that preparations were well advanced for an entirely Scottish expedition, backed by

Scottish capital and led by a man with more ice experience than any other explorer of his age in Britain. Bruce's plan, as described in the *Geographical Journal* of 1902, was to sail to the Falklands, and then head south-east towards the South Sandwich Islands as far as 30°W. He then planned to strike south, proposing to go as far south 'as is compatible with the attainments of the best results for science'.[5] He had insufficient money to realise his original plan of establishing a wintering party, and did not intend to allow *Scotia* to be frozen in the ice. His intention was to spend the summer and autumn in the south and then, during the winter, to retreat north of the ice edge. All the while he intended to continue his meteorological and oceanographic observations. This plan would exhaust his funds; to remain in the Southern Ocean for a second summer would necessitate a further injection of resources. He estimated that he would strike land between 70° and 80°S as the season closed in.

True to his belief in international scientific cooperation, he planned to coordinate his results with British, German and Swedish expeditions, which, following the conclusions of the Sixth International Congress of 1895, all went to Antarctica in the early 1900s. He showed this in a map drawn for his expedition prospectus which identified the route he planned, the position he wanted to reach and how that position related to the locations planned for the British and German expeditions. On this map he actually identified a 'Scottish Station', rather fancifully located at approximately 85°S and 30°W.[6] But Bruce makes it clear in the *Geographical Journal* that this would only be possible if more funds became available. In the event, he ended up wintering on *Scotia* in the South Orkney Islands, having first reached above 70°S. He was eventually able to obtain the extra funds needed for a second summer, but not for his southern wintering station.

Scotia sounded, dredged and trawled extensively in what is now known as the Scotia Sea and the Weddell Sea, collected new information about seals, penguins and other birds, and made regular meteorological and geomagnetic recordings. The shore observatory on the South Orkney Islands has continuously collected records ever since. These have greatly informed our appreciation of the far-reaching effects of Antarctic meteorological conditions. The extensive new land that he discovered helped to establish that the continent was larger than previously thought. *Scotia* returned to Scotland with a wealth of new information that would take years to analyse, plus large collections of fish, plankton and marine sediment and animals.

With funds assured, Bruce was able to choose a vessel for his expedition. *Balaena* was too expensive, and with the help of Mr Colin Archer, who had designed the *Fram* for Nansen, he bought the Norwegian whaler *Hekla* for £2,620. *Hekla* was in a bad state of repair. Two-thirds of her timber needed replacing, at considerable expense. At this point subscriptions had only reached £16,000, so the repairs were undertaken on shaky financial grounds; it was an act of faith, but to give up at this stage was unthinkable. The naval architect George Lennox Watson[7] (who by 1901 had designed King Edward VII's yacht *Britannia* and four of the challengers for the America's Cup) supervised *Hekla*'s refit. This included new engines and boilers. Mr Watson gave his services free of charge, and *Hekla* was transformed into a sleek and graceful oceanographic ship. Bruce renamed her *Scotia*.

Meanwhile, the expedition's Edinburgh-based secretary, Mr James Ferrier, collected gifts of stores and equipment from 150 firms and Bruce travelled unendingly to raise support and funds. Rudmose Brown wrote that 'many a week he barely received enough to cover his travelling expenses'[8] as he addressed organisations and small and large societies (for example, the Royal Society of Scotland, with the Astronomer Royal in the chair, on 'Explorations in Spitsbergen and Soundings in Seas Adjacent in 1898 and 1899').[9] He also personally visited possible subscribers. It was exhausting work, and his family must have been low on his list of priorities. Responses to appeals for support varied; for example, Andrew Carnegie refused to supply a library, writing that he did not support such expeditions,[10] but local Scottish interest snowballed as newspapers emphasised the Scottish nature of the expedition. The press influence was mostly positive; the reports encouraged nationalistic backing and supported appeals for further monies to fund a second year in the south. The papers also stimulated general interest in the expedition; for instance, there were reports on the testing of the meteorological kites, which recorded details such as wind speed and temperature, along with eager coverage of how the expedition's dog had competed in a dog show at Edinburgh Waverley Market, taking second place.[11] This strongly Scottish emphasis must have coloured, and been reflected in, the British government's responses to Bruce at a later date.

As mentioned, however, in spite of the generous financial backing from the Coats family and others, finances were only sufficient for a year in Antarctica (the expenses for the *Scotia* and her refit, at £16,730 12s 10d,[12] had been more than planned). Rudmose Brown wrote that Bruce, short of money at the best of times, agreed to go without any salary, as did his scientific staff. This proposal provoked a significant reaction; J. Y. Buchanan wrote to the press that 'we must be proud that Scotland continues to produce such men' but that 'we other Scotsmen cannot without humiliation consent to take advantage of the staff's offer'. He contributed £100 towards salaries. Coats promptly sent another contribution earmarked for salaries.[13] The final salary bill came to £3,242 18s 2d, as recorded in an abstract of the Scottish National Antarctic Expedition,[14] and of this Bruce received £500 per annum and the master £360. This £500 – a very comfortable salary for the time – must have come as a significant relief to Jessie and would have supported her and Eillium whilst Bruce was away. But the fact that he had seemed prepared to set off on the expedition without making proper financial provision for his family is an indication of his single-mindedness.

Preparations for the voyage received unwelcome attention in February 1902 when a Mr Campbell Brown brought a case against the Scottish National Antarctic Expedition claiming £1,340. Campbell Brown stated that he had been asked to apply for the post of geologist at £250 per annum (more when the expedition sailed) and that he had already incurred expenses. He incorrectly stated that he had turned down a post on Scott's expedition. It appears that Campbell Brown could not work with other members planning the expedition, returned his key to the office and did not attend an arranged meeting. Bruce formally dismissed him in February. This case was a distraction and an embarrassment; Campbell Brown brought his action against the important members of the *Scotia* committee, and Bruce was concerned that his funding could be withdrawn. The matter was finally settled with a payment of £80. Funding was not withdrawn, and the pursuer (Campbell Brown) was found liable for expenses.

After sea trials and a celebratory dinner hosted by Sir John Murray, with toasts to the royal family, *Scotia*, captained by Thomas Robertson, left Troon for her historic voyage to the Weddell Sea on 2 November 1902, eight days later than planned. She flew the flag of the Scottish National Antarctic Expedition proudly. Some newspapers were unaware of the delay, and the veracity of their reporting standards must have been called into doubt when they reported that on 25 October the *Scotia* 'steamed majestically down the Clyde surrounded by a fleet of gaily-bedecked yachts and other craft'.[15] The ship looked like 'a midshipman's bag, everything on top and nothing handy'.[16] All the officers and crew were from Scotland and had home addresses north of the border; just one of the scientists, David Wilton, did not have a Scottish home base. The officers were all experienced in polar conditions.

Scottish newspapers were supportive, proud of an expedition that aimed at a patient, economic voyage of investigation and discovery that would add to the world's store of scientific knowledge. Many focused on the Scottish identity of the expedition, perhaps implicitly supporting hopes for financial support under this guise: 'Though the venture is the result of private organisation and enthusiasm, it partakes largely of a national character, for the money has been raised in Scotland, the ship had been all but rebuilt in Scotland, the scientific staff and crew, with perhaps one or two exceptions, are Scotsmen. Scotland has thus done her share in the work which is going forward in the Antarctic.'[17] The only discordant note was scandalised criticism that *Scotia* had sailed on the Sabbath with bagpipes playing.

There were thirty-three men on *Scotia*. Apart from Bruce, there were four other key scientists. One was David Wilton, a man experienced with dogs and sledging, and Bruce's friend from the Jackson–Harmsworth expedition; Wilton was responsible for vertebrate zoology and helped with meteorological work. Another was Robert Mossman from the Ben Nevis Observatory, who served as meteorologist and magnetic expert, along with Dr J. H. Harvey Pirie, the medical officer and geologist, and Robert N. Rudmose Brown, the botanist and invertebrate zoologist. There were two assistants, Mr W. Cuthbertson and Mr A Ross. In addition, Gilbert Kerr worked in the laboratory; he became the taxidermist for the expedition and was an expert bagpipe player.

The expedition was given beer by Guinness of Dublin and tobacco and spirits by James Coats, who had sailed on his yacht to Ireland with *Scotia*. Dublin offered a warm reception, and at a final dinner on 9 November, when Bruce proposed a birthday toast to King Edward VII, the national anthem 'so dear to every Briton' was sung with enthusiasm. The ship was to call at Madeira, Cape Verde, Saint Paul's Rocks and Port Stanley in the Falklands before proceeding to the Weddell Sea. Here Bruce was to make his base on Laurie Island in the South Orkney Islands. *Scotia* would then sail to South America and refit in Buenos Aires before sailing again to the Weddell Sea to pick up those scientists who had continued to work in the South Orkneys, afterwards sailing home via Gough Island, Cape Town, St Helena, Ascension Island and Ireland – a journey of over 30,000 miles.

After Madeira, where there was some misunderstanding when the Royal Standard of Scotland was mistaken for a quarantine flag, *Scotia* sailed to Cape Verde and then coaled at St Vincent, where coal was cheaper than in the Falklands. An attempt to land at St Paul's Rocks failed because of a large swell that broke over the rocks, and here Dr Pirie narrowly escaped an early departure from the expedition (and life) as he attempted to jump on to the rocks, failed, and fell into the sea and a turmoil of angry sharks – he was hoisted out by the scruff of his neck. The ship then sailed on to the Falklands, making landfall on 6 January 1903. Rudmose Brown wrote of the strangeness of eating a Christmas dinner in subtropical heat on a ship rolling 25° to either side. On the voyage to the Falklands (7,000 miles), meteorological observations were made and preliminary work was done with the trawl and the scientific instruments. The crew became particularly fascinated by microscopic work, a science new to many of them.

The Falkland Islands were reached in fifty-nine days.[18] Here, at Port Stanley, the men received letters from home and sent their final goodbyes in return. Bruce made a final appeal to the Scottish public for continued support – it was to be successful. The ship was provisioned and the scientists busied themselves with bird collections, sea samples and equipping a meteorological station at Cape Pembroke Lighthouse a few miles east of Port Stanley. Bruce wrote that 'many synchronous and comparative readings were made by us at Port Stanley along with the lighthouse & they agreed very satisfactorily'. There was thus 'a very complete station at Cape Pembroke and Port Stanley which may be of great value'.[19] These stations were to be base meteorological stations during the Antarctic campaign.

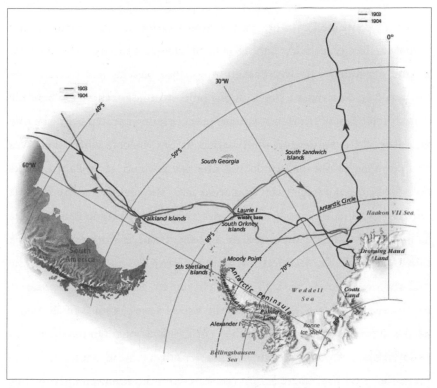

Map showing the tracks of the Scotia *in the South Atlantic for 1903 and 1904.
(From* Antarctica, The Complete Story, *2003, Francis Lincoln, Ed., McGonigal,
D. & Woodworth, L.)*

Scotia set sail for Antarctica on 26 January. The first icebergs were
seen on 29 January 1903 (flat-topped, later peaked) at 60°28'S. This was
further north than Bruce had expected;[20] he knew that Ross had reached
the pack ice at 65°S and d'Urville, the French explorer, at 63°30'S, and
he had hoped he would meet similar conditions. At this time there was
almost no database of information for him to consult; the whaling
industry was yet to get underway here.

Captain Robertson carefully advanced as great blocks of ice rolled,
tossed and crashed against each other and the ship. By 3 February the
South Orkney Islands were sighted and reached after skirting the heavy
pack. Bruce and his scientists made the first ever collections of birds and

rocks from the islands. The captain then steered the ship back to open water as dredging and sounding continued. But February is late in the southern summer – the temperature was falling steadily and visibility was restricted by an overcast sky and mist, and by mid-February the ice pack was so tight that passage to the south-east became impracticable. The ship was still at the entrance of the Weddell Sea. At 61°06'S, 45°40'W, Bruce and Captain Robertson decided to steer northwards, clear the pack and then make a big sweep east,[21] gambling that the prevailing south-easterly winds would drive the ice westward and allow them passage south. This was an inspired idea, and to this day theirs is the route generally taken to reach the Southern Weddell.[22] At 26°W, *Scotia* turned south and reached as far as 70°25'S, 17°12'W. But by now it was early March; extensive new ice was forming and the nights were getting long and dark as the Antarctic winter approached. Bruce decided to change from his original plan of wintering north of the ice edge, instead opting to search for a sheltered bay where *Scotia* could become ice-bound for the winter. Captain Robertson therefore headed back to the South Orkneys, and on 21 March land was sighted.

The South Orkneys were, at the time, only mapped in a very rudimentary way. They had been visited and roughly delineated by the British sealers Powell and Weddell in the 1820s, and by Dumont d'Urville in 1838. The only map available suggested an anchorage named Spence Harbour in the Lewthwaite Strait, which lies between Powell and Coronation Islands. After a stressful few days of steering through heavy squalls, thick cloud and driving snow, Bruce and Robertson found Spence Harbour to be 'a fraud'.[23] Eventually they found a safe, well-protected harbour on the south side of Laurie Island (60.73°S, 44.52°W). Bruce called this Scotia Bay. Robertson, who thought the Orkneys 'an ugly-looking group',[24] was delighted with the magnificent anchorage. Scotia Bay was to be their winter quarters from 25 March to 27 November 1903.

Bruce started his station log[25] on 13 November 1902. A 'station' is defined as a position at which a ship is steadied at a specific geophysical point whilst observations are being made. Confirmation that this status has been achieved and maintained is that the sounding line stays vertical until all the necessary readings have been collected.[26] Records were made of the time, date, ship's position (latitude and longitude), wind direction, ambient temperature and sea temperature in Fahrenheit.[27] Sea conditions, currents and total depth were recorded and seawater samples were taken, at known sea depths, from the sea surface to the seabed – the salinity, density, colour and bacteriology of each sample was noted. Nets and Monegasque trawls[28] were used and the sea floor dragged.

One of the many new findings was that the soundings suggested a ridge connecting the South Orkneys and the South Sandwich group of islands; this was subsequently proved to be correct, and the ridge is now known as the South Scotia Ridge. Several records were made each day, and ultimately over 500 numbered stations were established and sampled in the course of the expedition.

By early 1903, the tow-net was being used regularly. The trawl deposit was rock, mineral debris and diatom ooze, later glacial mud and boulders. In March 1903, at Station 290, the depth was recorded as 1,850 fathoms, and at Station 291 it was 2,500. Here, twenty-five species were recovered in the trawl along with the glacial mud. Floats were dropped regularly (over 850), to gain information about tidal flows. Meteorological records were made every hour from 17 November 1902 to 17 July 1904, in spite of the most trying conditions. Mossman, the meteorologist, wrote that 'never before had hourly observations been made at sea in such heavy weather'.[29]

Bruce wanted the *Scotia* records to complement results obtained by Britain, Germany and Sweden and thereby create a network of new information from the Antarctic. His dream was the development of a regional network of observatories covering the South Atlantic.

These ambitions get to the essence of Bruce the scientist; it can be argued that he was the father of the modern network of coordinated work and observations in Antarctica. Mossman published *The Present Position of Antarctic Meteorology* in 1910, and this report took up Bruce's vision of coordinating observations to give a continent-wide perspective of the climate.[30] It synthesised the observations made by all the major expeditions to the South, starting with the Belgian expedition of 1899, thus providing the first broad picture of Antarctic climatology.

Bruce's written journal (the *Log of the* Scotia; see appendix 2), which accompanied the station log, was started as *Scotia* was steaming along the pack on 2 February 1903. The written journal gave a narrative to the expedition. Bruce filled over 200 pages to record daily events large and small, whether scientific, social or personal, until the ship reached Ascension Island on 10 June 1904. He writes of the initial seasickness of the scientific staff, the icebergs, the work of the ship, the 'hands' playing poker for matches. He describes finding a serious shortage of winter clothes, 'possibly stolen by someone who ought to be flayed alive for this dastardly act',[31] and writes of the skiing, and the difficulties on land of judging surfaces in a glaring light which cast no shadows[32] – it was 'impossible to see the rises and falls of the ice-floe till one stumbled or fell over, or in, them'.[33] He said that alcohol was not popular; the 'chocolate league' thought it was better to avoid alcohol in active, open-air lives, and a bottle of whisky lasted the men three days, though alcohol was enjoyed for celebrations. He wrote of 'ice floes large enough to damage *Scotia*, blinding snow, furious squalls, Fin whales and seals'.[34]

In the South Orkneys, *Scotia* was soon ice bound. Sails were stored, the topmasts taken down, the boats lowered onto the floe, and the boiler emptied. In these winter months Bruce understood the importance of keeping all hands busy and maintaining a routine through the often freezing, sunless, stormy and monotonous days. At 7.30 a.m. the crew went

out on the floe to quarry ice for their daily water needs.[35] Breakfast was
at 8 a.m.: porridge, often followed by fresh fish. Although Bruce had
originally hoped to be in open water during the winter, he recognised that
the South Orkneys were virtually unknown from a scientific point of view
and that, located as they were at the northern edge of the Antarctic pack
ice and between Cape Horn and the Cape of Good Hope, they provided
a uniquely valuable location for a meteorological station. Because of this,
fairly early in the winter he decided to establish a shore station that he
hoped Argentina would continue to operate in the future.[36]

Bruce also devised a rigorous scientific programme to take advantage
of the fixed location. Meteorological records were made throughout the
night and day, but the daily working routine started promptly at 8.30
a.m. A dredge collection was made, initially along a narrow lane of water,
subsequently via a fire-hole (to provide a source of water in case of a
fire on the ship), kept permanently open near the bow of the ship, and
a second hole in the ice. A 60-foot whale line dredged between the two,
and although the same ground was often gone over repeatedly the men
never failed to get a comprehensive haul, 'so prolific is the animal life in
Antarctic waters'.[37] One find of great interest was a previously unknown
massive ten-legged sea spider.[38] Traps were sunk in various parts of
the bay and a routine of biological work and trap baiting was soon
established. If the men ventured any distance from the ship they used
snowshoes or skis – the snow surface was often not hard enough to bear
a man's weight. Outside activities finished after 3 p.m., tea was at 4 p.m.
and dinner (seal or penguin) at 6 p.m. Those men not on watch enjoyed
singsongs, debates, reading, poker, chess, listening to the gramophone,
and sometimes short ski runs (there was a gently sloping glacier nearby).

Celebrations such as birthdays were marked with alcohol and tobacco
(some crew members had more than one birthday that year!), as were
events such as Waterloo, the birth of Tennyson and the opening of the

Suez Canal. Bruce was probably at his best at this time; he was stimulated, involved, excited, conscientious, careful of his men's well-being and participating fully in the scientific duties. He made the daily meteorological recordings between 4 and 8 a.m. and was happy to be on the sounding platform in sleet or snow. This thoughtful approach was in contrast to the negative, argumentative (possibly autistic), aspects of his personality that he showed (and was to show) frequently in other situations, characteristics that are not normally associated with a natural leader. But on Laurie Island he was with a group of interested colleagues, and with the *Scotia* expedition he had achieved what must have seemed impossible for years. He was invigorated. He thought that the winter had passed singularly free of incident and wrote that hoped that his men would think of the ship 'as their university, as their alma mater in the highest possible sense'.[39]

There was one death over the winter months. Bruce had taken a strong contingent of officers on *Scotia*, including two engineers, Allen G. Ramsay and H. Gravill. Allen Ramsay is likely to have had heart problems before *Scotia* sailed, and it is unclear whether he (or any other member of the expedition) had a medical examination before being signed on. During the voyage Ramsay deteriorated dramatically. On examination a heart murmur was heard and during the final days of his life on Laurie Island he became so breathless that he could only lie propped up on a deck chair. He knew he was dying and said goodbye to all, thanking Bruce for his kindness.[40] On 6 August 1903 he died, almost certainly of heart failure. His burial took place on the beach facing Uruguay Cove in a coffin draped in a Scottish standard, while piper Kerr played 'The Flowers of the Forest' and 'The Old Hundredth'. Ramsay's grave was the first in the island cemetery. It can still be visited today, carefully maintained by the Argentine residents.

Preparatory work for a permanent base began before midwinter. The main requirement was to house those scientists who were to remain on the island the following summer when *Scotia* went north for her refit.

In addition, it could act as an emergency base if *Scotia* met with an accident. Bruce had no building materials as no base had been planned originally, so he embarked on a dry stone building familiar to his Scottish crew. Difficulties in quarrying the stones, compounded by consistently bad weather, meant that it took until October before the building was completed and habitable. It consisted of a single room 14 feet by 14 feet, with 4–5-foot walls, built of stone and packed with gravel, sand and snow (which froze). The walls and door were lined with canvas,[41] the floors were made from the ship's hatches, the roof was canvas and felt saturated with oil and grease, old boxes were made into shelves and tables, and a window was made from glass found on board *Scotia*. For cooking, a spare stove from the ship was called into action. The hut was named Omond House after the director of the Edinburgh Observatory and provisioned with food and coal for twelve months. The meteorological observations were transferred from *Scotia* to Omond House on 1 November 1903.[42]

The construction of the hut did not finish the building work – a wooden magnetic laboratory was also built. This was called the Copeland Observatory after Ralph Copeland, the Scottish Astronomer Royal and a strong supporter of the SNAE. Here Mossman attended to his magnetometer, making recordings that were impossible on the ship. Finally, a 9-foot cairn was built and a flagstaff was placed on its top. The Union Jack and the Royal Standard of Scotland flew when *Scotia* was in the South Orkneys.

Attempts were made to explore some of the island. Three men visited Delta Island (on the eastern extremity of Scotia Bay), with difficulty and noted the animal life (a few seals and birds), some birds were shot and their details carefully recorded: total weight, weight of each organ, length of intestine, length of beak, length of tail, etc.[43] All the specimens obtained were similarly recorded. Soundings were documented, and the strata of the cliffs observed. Later Wilton Bay to the west of Scotia Bay was surveyed. Finally, in October, when thousands of penguins plus gulls, skuas, petrels, Weddell seals and the occasional sea leopard returned, the men were able to explore Laurie Island more fully.

Notably they did not see any fur seals – these had been brought close to extinction by over-harvesting in the nineteenth century (this is in sharp contrast to the current situation, where the beaches are overrun with fur seals in the summer months). On the sortie the men slept in three-man tents and three-man bags ('when Pa says turn, we all turn').[44] They conducted a trigonometric survey and made a map of the island, and Bruce made a photographic record. Microscopic pollen grains from the conifer *Podocarpus* were discovered. This discovery was seen at the time as new proof of wind carriage of pollen from southern South America, where the tree is common, to Antarctica.[45]

Finally, in the last week of November, the pack ice broke up, *Scotia* was released from her winter prison and on 27 November Captain Robertson headed for the Falklands, leaving five men, led by Robert Mossman, to remain at Omond House. Bruce's determination that his ground-breaking scientific work should continue after his time on Laurie Island, coupled with his imaginative ambition to develop a regional network of observatories covering the South Atlantic, remained as strong as ever. To further this strategy he planned to offer the stations on Laurie Island to the Argentine authorities.

On the voyage north the men celebrated Queen Alexandra's birthday. When *Scotia* arrived at Port Stanley, the crew received their mail and the latest news of the *Discovery* (frozen in), the *Gauss* and the *Antarctic*. Bruce had the welcome news that James Coats had agreed to fund a further summer and that the subscription lists in Edinburgh included a £50 donation from the author J. M. Barrie.[46] As coal was too expensive in the Falklands, at 49/9d per ton (the expedition funds were virtually used up), *Scotia* sailed on to Argentina for refuelling, as coal here was half the price. Bruce 'regretted very much that owing to this I was driven out of a British Colony and forced to refit in a foreign country'.[47] The Falklands were not at that time equipped with telegraph facilities, so Bruce left the ship to travel by mail ship to Montevideo and Buenos Aires in order to cable the up-to-date news of the expedition and its progress to Edinburgh.

His cable was to the point:

Buenos Aires, *Scotia*, Stanley, December 2, refitting here. Hydrograph surveyed 4,000 miles unexplored ocean, 70°25' S.17°to 45°W. 2.700 fathoms trawled there: wintered Orkneys; detailed survey. Mossman and five men continue first-class meteorological, magnetical, biological station. Ramsay died August 6. All others robust. *Scotia* splendid. Bruce.[48]

This extraordinarily terse telegram, though containing more than enough words about his scientific programme, was probably crafted to be short on personal detail because telegrams were priced by the word and funds were low, but the announcement of Ramsay's death is brutally short of sentiment or detail.

Scotia endured a difficult journey to Buenos Aires. The Argentine coastline was dangerous, and the ship was becalmed off Medano Point before she was grounded at high tide when sailing along the Rio de la Plata, eventually clearing the following day. Messages were sent to Bruce informing him of the position, and finally *Scotia* entered Buenos Aires docks on Christmas Eve. The expedition was enthusiastically welcomed by the Argentine communities and was covered extensively in the press. *El Gladiator* published a dashing cartoon of 'Doctor Roberto Bruce',[49] and Bruce was grateful to the Buenos Aires authorities for providing 200 tons of coal and for repairing *Scotia* free of charge.

When he arrived at Buenos Aires, Bruce pursued his plans for the future of the laboratories immediately. Cooperation with the Argentine

Meteorological Service would be of great value to South America, and the director of the Meteorological Service, Walter G. Davis, an American by birth,[50] was supportive. Bruce wrote to the British First Minister, Mr W. H. D. Haggard,[51] emphasising the importance of maintaining the observatory and suggesting that the Argentine Meteorological Office should be invited to continue the work. He offered to give passage to four scientists and to hand over Omond House, the magnetic observatory and eighteen months' food supply to the Argentine Meteorological Office. Haggard put the offer to the Argentine government before seeking Whitehall's opinion and the former responded with remarkable alacrity. It published a presidential decree on 2 January 1903, authorising Davis 'to take over the installation offered by Mr William S. Bruce in the South Orkney Islands and to establish a meteorological and magnetic observatory thereon'.[52]

Haggard was notified of the Argentine decree only three days after he had raised the proposal with the British Foreign Secretary, and long before he had received instructions from London; in fact, the Foreign Office and the Lords of the Admiralty had little interest in small islands in the South Atlantic that were of little strategic significance (incidentally described by the Admiralty to the Foreign Office as a desolate group of rocky islands lying about 600 miles south-east of the Falkland Islands, ice-bound for the greater part of the year, and not likely to ever be of any value unless gold or other valuable minerals were discovered, or fur seals were to become numerous again).[53] Thus Bruce and Haggard effectively gave the facilities away, motivated primarily by Bruce's vision of setting up a coordinated meteorological network in the South Atlantic but also by his gratitude to Argentina for supporting his expedition by overhauling, provisioning and fuelling the *Scotia* free of charge. He met with the British consul in Argentina, a Mr Carnegie Ross, with Dr Davis and the president and vice-president of the republic to agree on the transfer of the Laurie Island facilities to the Argentine government. Dr Davis wrote to Bruce to thank him. Haggard finally learnt that the British Foreign Secretary, the Marquess of Lansdowne, had approved the decision on 26 April.

Bruce only intended to hand Argentina the scientific station, not the entire archipelago. This can be inferred from a letter from Dr Davis to Bruce dated 19 January 1904 in which he writes of his 'sincere acknowledgement of your kindness and generosity in placing at the disposal of this department the buildings you erected at Scotia Bay, as well as the conveyance of our staff and materials to that place; and it gives me great pleasure to consider we may be able to carry on the scientific work so gloriously initiated and carried on, under your direction during the past year'.[54] But there was no affirmation of British sovereignty over Laurie Island at this time, and although Argentina did not publicly proclaim sovereignty, neither did they acknowledge British control. This handover was to have profound and lasting consequences for the relationship between Britain and Argentina. Britain's decision in January 1943 (enacted in 1944) to finally establish a permanent presence in Antarctica can be traced back to this fateful judgement.

Bruce's choice illustrates his dedication to science and his ready acceptance of international cooperation, but from the British point of view, the 1903 handover of the scientific base highlights a lack of forward thinking and planning by the authorities. It is now known that part of the problem was due to the intervention of a principal clerk at the Colonial Office, a Mr Round, who took it upon himself to hand the base to Argentina without seeking the views of his colleagues. Only two years later did the appropriate department become cognisant of Round's decision, by which time it was too late – a plaintive note on a Colonial Office file records that 'Mr Round's chickens are now coming home.'[55] British acceptance that an error had been made continued; forty years later an official in the Colonial Office remarked, 'It is no good crying over spilt milk now, but that this arrangement was a great mistake is abundantly clear.'[56]

Because of the arrangement, the door was thrown open for more than a century of claim and counter-claim. The British claim to the South Orkneys rests on prior discovery by the British sealer George Powell in December 1821.[57] The claim was 'perfected'[58] by the publication of letters patent of 1908 (as amended in 1917), which created the Falkland Islands Dependency (containing South Orkneys, South Shetlands, South Georgia, the South Sandwich Islands and Graham Land, all contained in a geographic sector between 20 and 80 degrees W longitude and from 50°S latitude to the South Pole) and the regulation by Britain of the whaling industry therein.

The current British claim, now called the British Antarctic Territory, stems directly from these letters patent, but has been amended to extend from 60°S to align it with the boundary of the Antarctic Treaty area. Argentina's overlapping claim is made on the basis of proximity and the fact that she has continuously occupied a scientific base, a permanent settlement, since 1904. It is clear that the Argentines had this claim in mind from the outset, since one of the new members of staff who went to the South Orkney Islands (Hugo Acuña), was designated as postmaster – a postal service is one of the internationally recognised tools for demonstrating effective administration of a territory over which a claim has been made.[59] And the stamp that was used in the Orkneys was the stamp of the Argentine Republic; the postmark was Orcades del Sud, Distrito Rio Gallegos, District 24. Mail with this postmark was carried on *Scotia* to South Africa, after she left the south, for onward posting.

Bruce's visit to Buenos Aires culminated in a gala banquet (nine courses), when Bruce and his officers were joined by Argentine dignitaries and entertained by the expedition's piper, Gilbert Kerr, to jigs and reels. Mr Haggard, speaking on behalf of the British community of Buenos Aires, said he hoped that the warm reception the men had received would contrast with the cold of the regions they had recently visited. The press reported the event with remarkable fervour. The English-language *Buenos Aires Herald* described Bruce on 16 December 1903 as 'a gentleman highly educated, having great experience in the work with which he is connected, is dark complexioned, tall, robust, in perfect health and apparently 40 years of age'. A reporter in the *Standard* of 30 December 1903 wrote that 'rarely had there been a more enthusiastic gathering witnessed than that which assembled ... to do honour to Dr Bruce and his brave officers'.[60] Mr Haggard's speech said the expedition reflected honour on the name of Scotland.

Scotia sailed south on 21 January 1904, calling at the Falklands on her way to Laurie Island, which she reached on 14 February. Sorely needed provisions were unloaded, as was the new staff from Argentina. The Argentine flag was hoisted on the cairn. The party who had spent the summer there were picked up save for Robert Mossman, who remained in charge, and William Smith (second steward); both men stayed for the next winter to continue the station's work with their Argentinean colleagues. At the handover both the Argentine national anthem and 'God Save the King' were sung.[61]

On 22 February, *Scotia* headed for her second journey into the Weddell Sea. Bruce aimed to push as far south as possible, and *Scotia* had a good run until 68°40'S, when she was temporarily stopped by pack ice, before being again able to manoeuvre through the berg-infested region.

A little later, on 3 March 1904, there was a momentous find: new land was seen to the east. A sounding of 1,131 fathoms was made[62] (compared with soundings of over 2,000 fathoms, which had been general up to that date), suggesting that the ship was approaching land.

An extensive ice barrier appeared, behind which snow-covered heights could be glimpsed. The mate's log recorded: '10 a.m. Sighted land glacier lying E.N.E and W.S.W in lat.72°24'S. 17°30'W'.[63] A sounding 2.5 miles from the barrier edge, Bruce wrote, 'struck a rocky bottom with 159 fathoms ... I did not expect less than 300 fathoms.'[64] This signalled the presence of a continental shelf and was the first positive sighting of the south-eastern margin of the Weddell Sea, showing that the continental coast was several hundred miles further north than had been previously thought. Bruce named his new land Coats Land, after James and Andrew Coats, the expedition's principal supporters. Modern maps show it to extend from 0 to 30°W and 70 to 80°S, but without specific geographical boundaries. No photographs were possible because of the weather.

Bruce reasoned that the existence of this land meant that the base of the Weddell Sea narrowed and that ice pressures would be great, but he made a running survey of the coast south-westwards for four days after the first sighting on 3 March until *Scotia* became trapped in the pack and stranded in a gale and blinding drift snow at 74°01'S, 22°00'W[65]. Here she remained for seven long days, her crew filled with the fearful anticipation that the ship would be trapped for the winter. To raise spirits, football was attempted and here photographs were possible; Gilbert Kerr was captured in full Highland dress serenading an emperor penguin – although the penguin looks attentive to the call of the pipes, it was actually tethered to Kerr's ankle!

To the crew's relief the wind changed, dispersing the pack ice sufficiently for *Scotia* to sail free. Exploration of the land was impossible, and any further delay would put the ship and crew in danger. Pragmatically, Bruce decided on champagne and cigars to celebrate the expedition's 'furthest south'. He called for toasts to wives, sweethearts and, most importantly, the Coats family.

Scotia then headed home, taking rich hauls from trawls at the high southern latitudes. A point of great interest was the geographical position at which James Clark Ross had recorded a sounding of 4,000 fathoms, no bottom, in his 1840 expedition.[66] This depth had seemed to exclude the possibility of any continental landmass in the vicinity. Bruce had questioned the accuracy of this sounding for years, and found that within 2 miles of Ross' position the depth was, in reality, 2,660 fathoms. He wrote later to Bartholomew, the RSGS chairman, confirming this point and saying that soundings on all sides of it were at much the same depth. So ended the mythical 'Ross Deep'. It was in this letter Bruce described the Mid Atlantic Ridge that stretched from south of Gough Island to the South Sandwich Islands.[67] He also wrote that 'Coats has done magnificently. Scotland is greatly indebted to him and his brother for in spite of so many enthusiastic subscribers the expedition would never have started without their help.'[68] He suggested that the Coats family should be thanked by the RSGS for their contribution to geophysical science and their service in Scotland, by the Society offering the brothers honorary fellowships and perhaps a vice-presidency of the society.[69] In fact, this suggestion had already been taken up; Andrew Coats was made an honorary FRSGS in 1899 and was elected a council member in the same year.[70]

After ploughing through heavy seas, the ship reached Gough Island on 22 April, where a landing party collected plants, observed birds – including two previously unknown species – and surveyed the island. *Scotia* then sailed to Cape Town where Bruce gave a talk on the expedition's history and findings to a large and interested audience. After calling at St Helena, Ascension Island and Ireland, she finished her voyage of 33,000 miles on 4 July 1904 at the Marine Biological Station on the Firth of Forth. Here a congratulatory telegram from King Edward VII awaited them:

I am commanded by the King to congratulate you and the officers and crew of the *Scotia* on your and their safe return, and on the completion of your important additions to the scientific knowledge and discoveries in the south-eastern part of the Weddell Sea.[71]

This was accompanied by a more prosaic greeting from Sir John Murray, who said that the ship was half an hour late, but that he was glad to see her. The press presence was large and enthusiastic. Ernest Shackleton, then secretary of the RSGS, arranged a reception. The officers and scientific staff of *Scotia*, together with some 400 guests, attended a celebratory lunch.

Surprisingly there is no comment of the voyage in the minutes of the first RGS Council meeting to follow the expedition's return, and Markham (still president at that time) makes no mention of it in his personal journal. But Bruce was widely acclaimed both in Scotland and in the British scientific community. He was awarded the Gold Medal[72] of the Royal Scottish Geographical Society; Scotland rejoiced in and celebrated its polar heroes.

Jessie was delighted with her husband's success and pleased to see him after a twenty-month absence. Bruce was happy to be reunited with Eillium, an active two-and-a-half-year-old, and began to get to know his son. He was also eager to supervise the unloading of the *Scotia*'s precious cargo. However, a month after he returned he was incapacitated by a prolonged attack of influenza and was confined to his room, isolated from both his family and his work. The illness prevented him from active involvement in *Scotia* matters for weeks.

8

THE SCOTTISH OCEANOGRAPHICAL LABORATORY

Scotia returned from Antarctica with a collection of barrels and cases containing the biological, zoological and geological specimens collected in Antarctica. Additionally, she carried the meteorological information from the voyage and the weather station on Laurie Island. Bruce needed to house his Antarctic haul with his Arctic collections.

From 1902, and while *Scotia* was in Antarctica, Bruce had been allowed to store the yield from his Arctic expeditions in a building close to the Surgeons' Hall of the Royal College of Surgeons of Edinburgh. It was here that the expedition's secretary, James Ferrier, was based, and it was here that he received the specimens sent by Bruce from various stages of the voyage, looked after the expedition business and dealt with the endless demands of publicity, correspondence and financial worries. The building was not a salubrious venue; its main entrance was via a courtyard that led to a pickle factory which gave off a noticeable stench. When the college decided to use the venue as a laboratory the authorities felt compelled to open another entrance door, but the smell lingered; in addition, heavy drays rumbling across the courtyard shook the whole structure. When *Scotia* returned to Scotland, the scientific collections were transferred there. It was this building that was to become the Scottish Oceanographical Laboratory. Bruce had enormous hopes that it would become an internationally recognised centre of excellence.

The laboratory was not opened officially until 1907, but Bruce started immediately on his crucial priority: the reports on *Scotia*'s oceanographic, meteorological and zoological data. Indeed, it could be said that the real work of the expedition only started when *Scotia* returned to Scotland. The laboratory, which also acted as a museum, was divided into an Arctic section (birds and mammals in lifelike settings) and an Antarctic room (tableaux of Antarctic seals and penguins lighted by electric lamp, plus specimens of fish, invertebrates and deep-sea mud from the trawls). The basement was crammed with the equipment from all of Bruce's various polar explorations, from 'deep-sea trawls to teacups'.[1] Over the years the laboratory was to become a hub of activity, the centre of a spider's web from which the *Scotia* reports were painstakingly produced and a public space which allowed the expedition's specimens to be examined by interested visitors from the UK, Europe, America and the Far East – some knowledgeable, many not, but all welcome. In addition, there were visits from well-known explorers including Ernest Shackleton, Fridtjof Nansen and Roald Amundsen.

The work involved in producing the reports was to be all-consuming; Bruce had understood the enormity of the task from the outset. He refused to write a general book about *Scotia*'s travels – he said that the expedition had been purely scientific and lacked general appeal, even though Shackleton advised him that he ought to do more window dressing; both his and Scott's books describing their expeditions not only raised significant funds but gave them celebrity status as well. Bruce was also reluctant to make time for a lecture tour on the same basis. In short, he avoided time-consuming ploys that would have taken him away from the laboratory but which might have publicised his efforts, increased the appeal of his work and raised his public profile as well as his funding.

On 22 August 1904, at a meeting of the British Association for the Advancement of Science in Cambridge, Bruce presented a paper on his expedition. The lecture was a success, and because of this he agreed to a lecture tour later in the year.[2] However, his serious attack of flu (he was unwell for months) made it impossible for him to leave Edinburgh, so his faithful 'assistants' Rudmose Brown and Dr Harvey Pirie filled in for him. Although the timing was unfortunate – *Discovery*, Scott's ship, reached England on 10 September and Rudmose Brown thought that the *Scotia* story seemed pale by comparison with the attempt on the South Pole[3] – the newspapers did give attention to a 'very interesting story ... enhanced by limelight and cinematograph pictures'.[4]

Because Bruce was so unwell, Rudmose Brown, Harvey Pirie and Ferrier continued temporarily with the work in the Scottish Oceanographical Laboratory. It is difficult to overestimate the amount of work involved. Hundreds of species had to be sorted and sent to experts at home and in Europe for description, analysis and reports. In making use of experts from the Continent as well as the United Kingdom, the laboratory followed the example of the *Challenger* expedition. This work would take Bruce and his assistants years – some 'expert' reports had to be rejected, which only added to the problems; a Miss Thornely's work on 'Bryozoa' (tiny aquatic invertebrates) was refused as a careless piece of work abounding in inaccuracies.[5] Bruce characteristically described it as 'abominably put together, as you see there is no beginning, no middle and no end'![6] Later a report by a colleague named Pearcey was considered inadequate and was rewritten by a Mr Earl; Bruce thought, rightly, that this would be 'a case of the heather raging horribly', meaning Pearcey would be seriously upset and would be 'too angry to write'.[7] Another paper was said to be amateurish and misleading; Bruce could only be relieved that when corrections were made to a paper on plankton the author was acquiescent.

In 1906, Bruce went to the Exposition Coloniale Nationalle in Marseilles. This was an international meeting organised by his patron the Prince of Monaco. The Scottish Oceanographical Laboratory's submission was awarded the exhibition's Grand Prix – this was a significant accolade; it showed the respect with which the international oceanographic community viewed Bruce's expedition.

In October 1906, *The Voyage of the* Scotia, written by 'Three Members of the Staff' (R. N. Rudmose Brown, Dr Harvey Pirie and Robert Mossman), was published. It was dedicated to 'William Speirs Bruce, Our Leader and Comrade and to the memory of Allan George Ramsay, Chief Engineer S.Y. Scotia, died in August 6 1903'.[8] Bruce contributed the introduction. This included a strong message of Scottish nationalism: 'While "Science" was the talisman of the expedition, "Scotland" was emblazoned on its flag.' He wrote that by adding 'another link to the golden chain of science, we have shown that the nationality of Scotland is a power that must be reckoned with'.[9] He also wrote that the book was especially for Scots throughout the world. Some reviewers approved of this bias, one journalist writing in *The Athenaeum* that 'there is something delightful in the irrepressible spirit of nationality which pervaded this book ... when even penguins on the floe are treated to a skirl of the bagpipes'.[10] But these nationalistic statements must have weighed against Bruce when he needed assistance from non-Scottish patrons.

In the years that Bruce spent in the laboratory he had to dovetail oceanographic work with other interests. He had visited Spitsbergen with Prince Albert of Monaco in 1898 and noted shale oil, coal and gypsum. Subsequent visits in 1899 and in 1906 and 1907 convinced him that the archipelago contained valuable resources that could be developed. He promoted a private prospecting company, 'The Scottish Spitsbergen Syndicate', in 1909. For the remainder of his life he worked unstintingly to promote the syndicate and over the years he became increasingly concerned about the geopolitical future of Spitsbergen. A good deal of his time and energy was to be devoted to repeated approaches to the government about its ability to protect British interests. This saga was to deflect his focus from his other commitments, and may have been counter-productive since it was partnered awkwardly with his pressing demands to the same government for grants to help defray the printing costs of the *Scotia* reports.

Bruce seemed unable to prioritise. In a period already crammed with activities such as writing pamphlets, making presentations and dealing with the voluminous correspondence about the *Scotia* results, he still took on other projects. In 1907 he became a founder member of the Scottish Ski Club, which aimed to promote all types of skiing for men and women (ladies skiing in big skirts and big hats). Bruce took the chair at the club's first meeting, was involved in drawing up the constitution and remained on the committee. His expertise in skiing was in marked contrast to that of Shackleton, who even by the time of the *Endurance* expedition was not able to ski properly, as is shown by his comment to Orde-Lees during the traverse across the sea-ice: 'Do you know, I had no idea how quickly it was possible for a man on ski to get about.'[11]

The Scottish Oceanographical Laboratory was opened on 16 January 1907 at 4.00 p.m. by Albert, Prince of Monaco. It was a grand occasion; the Lord Provost opened proceedings and invited Albert to address the assembled dignitaries. The prince praised Bruce's Antarctic work and pointed out that his expedition was probably the most economical of all the explorations in the early 1900s. Bruce made a formal reply, and speeches were contributed by Lord Dunedin,[12] representatives of the Scottish Museum, the Scottish University, the Science Society and other dignitaries. Paul Rothenberg, chair of the Glasgow Branch of the Royal Scottish Geographical Society, spoke and a Mr McVittie offered a vote of thanks. The fact that the laboratory fuses blew in the middle of the formalities did not spoil proceedings in the least; proceedings continued by the candlelight. Bruce hoped that his laboratory would be the first permanent oceanographical laboratory and museum in the United Kingdom.

Newspaper reports agreed on the purpose and excellence of the collection, but were united also in their concern about the fabric of the building.[13] Bruce's model for the future was Prince Albert's Musée Océanographique de Monaco; he dreamed that his laboratory would eventually be housed in a purpose-built building in the University of Edinburgh. He had good reason for his hopes; the laboratory contained a wealth of Arctic and Antarctic specimens and, importantly, a legacy of local (the *Challenger*) and international (Prince Albert and others) scientific mentors. The plan was that a Scottish Oceanographic Trust would own the collection and arrange financial support for the laboratory via a small committee.

A few weeks after the opening, Bruce was elected as an honorary Doctor of Law at the University of Aberdeen. His contributions to science and to the Scottish nation were being honoured. He could now write 'Dr' before his name. Jessie must have been proud; the grand laboratory opening, the praise and the degree were all things to cherish.

Although the Scottish Oceanographic Trust oversaw the finances of the laboratory, inevitably the endless day-to-day duties remained primarily with Bruce and the laboratory's secretary, James Ferrier.[14] The sale of *Scotia* had to be organised, letters had to be written to colleagues about scientific data, further explorations and requesting advice (he consulted Sir Joseph Hooker, the naturalist and doctor on Ross's expedition of the 1840s). There was a seemingly endless list of reports to be prepared: biology (tow-netting records, lists of birds and their details), oceanography (deep-sea deposits and float logs), soundings, geology, meteorology, magnetism and tides. In addition, sketches, paintings and photographs had to be sorted and a financial statement prepared. It was work that would take years to finish. Bruce did not want his results to be published piecemeal in scientific papers only; he wanted them to be collected in an integrated publication series which was to be his magnum opus. He planned for ten volumes (seven were eventually published) entitled *Report on the Scientific Results of The Voyage of S.Y.* Scotia *during the years 1902, 1903 and 1904; under the leadership of William S. Bruce.*

He would not skimp on anything that related to his journals, insisting on the best-quality paper and the best engravers irrespective of cost (the engravers A. J. Searle of the British Museum charged £200 for engravings of fish) and finding the money to cover the cost of the reports became a long-term struggle. Also, in spite of the £5,000 raised by the sale of the *Scotia* to a Dundee whaling syndicate,[15] Bruce still owed money for expedition costs. The Royal Society of Edinburgh printed many of the *Scotia* results in their 'Transactions' and in this way the expedition's data was initially disseminated, but Bruce wanted the papers to be in a 'collated' form; additionally, some papers were not within the scope of the Royal Society.

After the first volume of the report (on physics, price £1 1s) was published in 1908 to an appreciative scientific establishment, a public appeal for finance was necessary. The Carnegie Trust[16] did give help with some of the volumes,[17] but Bruce was destined to continue his increasingly frustrating hand-to-mouth financial struggle. Repeated requests for finance are always irritating, and many of the people Bruce approached must have felt that they had already made their donations to the expedition, but he did not flag in his efforts; he gave talks, sent articles to the press, sold some specimens, accepted help from friends and benefactors and managed to swallow his irritation at unsolicited advice (remarkably staying silent when a secretary of one of the Scottish scientific societies told him, condescendingly, that the South Pole would be a good project for a local Scottish athletic club!).

All his efforts were for the advancement of science. He did not mind poverty for himself and was seemingly oblivious to its effects on his family; his whole energy was directed at keeping his laboratory going, getting his reports published and maintaining his prospecting company. He lived his work, taking it home with him, and had little residual energy to direct towards his family; the strain on his wife must have been considerable. He estimated that £3,000 would be needed to produce the remaining volumes. He submitted a request for a grant to the Grant Committee of the Royal Society, London, in December 1908, but was unsuccessful.

Interspersed with this focus on his laboratory and his syndicate, Bruce managed to divert some energy into developing plans for a completely new concept – a Scottish Trans-Antarctic expedition, which he presented to the RGS in 1909. The fact that he was prepared even to consider another Antarctic adventure whilst deeply embroiled with his laboratory, his reports, his debts and his syndicate perhaps suggests an overly optimistic mindset. But at this stage he was probably just speculating, assuming that nothing would happen for years and hoping that by such a time his affairs would have been settled.

Whether grounded in reality or not, this plan shows that Bruce now appreciated the importance of spectacular adventure to attract interest and sponsors. He wrote that the expedition would follow up on the *Scotia* work but would make its base on the Antarctic continent. He would sail from Buenos Aires to Cape Town, continue his bathymetric survey of the South Atlantic and then land a party on Coats Land, as far south as possible. He planned for the ship to sail on from the Weddell Sea round the Antarctic to the Ross Sea (always continuing the oceanographic work), whilst the party left on Coats Land would attempt a Trans-Antarctic crossing, aiming to meet up with the supporting Ross Sea party at a previously arranged point. Having previously spurned the South Pole as a goal, he now wrote that this Antarctic crossing would be of greater value than a journey to the Pole and back.[18] He asked Dr Mill to 'come and say a few words in support of the project'.[19]

The presentation to the RSGS went well and Bruce thought that he would get support for his plans. He hoped that one man, 'or two, or three would give big financial support'.[20] He wrote of 'stumping the country for money'.[21] But although there was support from Scottish scientific societies and Edinburgh University, and general backing in Scotland, Bruce was unfortunate in his timing when he applied to the government for support. In 1909 the authorities in London were preoccupied both with Scott's *Terra Nova* plans and with a grant to Ernest Shackleton of £20,000 to help cover his debts from the *Nimrod* expedition of 1907–09.

His application was rejected by the government within a fortnight. This was perhaps understandable as Bruce's bid consisted of a one-page letter without supporting detail or any indication of wider support[22] (see appendix 3 for a detailed account of the correspondence relating to the proposal). Bruce wrote, with little insight, that 'London does not care a rap about us in the North'.[23] He clearly did not appreciate that his application had been woefully inadequate. He certainly never understood that the government's priorities were for 'British' or 'Imperial' undertakings. His nationalism seems to have blinded him from seeking opportunities in this wider arena. It is interesting, however, that he discussed the plans fully with Ernest Shackleton, whose ambition was to be the first to reach the South Pole. Both accepted that support for either man's plans depended firstly on the outcome of the *Terra Nova* expedition and secondly on whichever of the two would be the more successful in raising funds. (In the event, Shackleton achieved financial support and, with Bruce's blessing, attempted this Trans-Antarctic crossing in 1914. He failed in his attempt. The Commonwealth Trans-Antarctic Expedition of 1957–58 finally made the crossing under the leadership of Sir Vivian Fuchs.)

In an article in *Nature* in 1910, a columnist approved the concept of a Trans-Antarctic expedition, suggesting that if British expeditions (Scott and Bruce), approached the Pole from different bases (Scott from the Ross Sea) then this would make for national credit and scientific progress – however, the columnist went on to say that claims for support should be scientific: 'It is undesirable to appeal to the Scottish public to stand up for this and other Scottish rights.'[24] Rudmose Brown wrote tartly about the 'Scottish rights' remark: 'When the Editor says that such a question should be a scientific & not a political one, he grants our contribution. That is exactly what we say. Give the grant to the best man and don't necessarily give it to a man because he is English. The Government has shown political bias but that blessed fool of an editor of *Nature* can't see it'.[25]

A column in *The Field* magazine sympathised with Bruce's ambitions, but not with the letter issued to the press by the Scottish Oceanographical Laboratory asking why there was 'a persistent refusal on the part of the government to recognise the Scottish Antarctic enterprise, while it showers money and honours on those doing similar but no better work in England'.[26] The *Field* piece stated that Bruce had attempted, not for the first time, to introduce petty national division into a work that demanded a united British enterprise. Money was scarce, the columnist stated; better to support one venture well than several poorly. He wrote, unfairly, that Bruce had shown no particular genius as an explorer.[27] Rudmose Brown wrote to *The Field* to defend Bruce (to whom he gave his £2 fee).

In his failure to fully understand the government's priorities regarding 'British' or 'Imperial' rather than 'regional' enterprises, Bruce continually banged the Scottish nationalistic drum in a way that must have been counterproductive. A further attempt to rouse public support found him writing to the press to advertise his laboratory's shaky financial base and to highlight the fact that *his* expedition had sailed with no government support – in marked contrast to the £45,000 that had been given to Scott's

Discovery expedition. His letters flagged up his feelings of injustice relating to the government's unequal treatment of Scotland and England. This provocative opinion, heightened by comments in the Scottish press such as 'The Scots are simply not in it', 'the "Predominant Partner" recognises no nationality save that of the "boys of the Bull-dog breed"' and 'the Fiery Cross of Scottish Nationalism is quietly being passed from hand to hand',[28] can only have damaged his reputation with the government in London.

In 1909 Bruce and Jessie were delighted that their daughter Sheila Mackenzie was delivered safe and well, especially as Jessie was thirty-eight years old. But family tensions began to appear. Bruce was stretched financially with the expenses of the Oceanographical Laboratory and his attention was pulled towards increasingly active involvement in his prospecting company, the Scottish Spitsbergen Syndicate, which he anticipated would provide him with financial security. He was 'with' the family but not 'in' it. He had little time to spare for family activities, and the family also struggled with financial anxieties – as mentioned, friends sent cash to help with his family expenses. Gradually Jessie had to shoulder the responsibility for managing the uncertain finances of the home and the children, apparently without much contact with her own family. Their granddaughter Mrs Moira Watson (Eillium's daughter) says that when Bruce was at home he would bury himself in his study; his dinner would be put outside the study door, where it remained untouched.[29]

In November 1909 Bruce made a further grant application to the Treasury towards the printing of his *Report*, this time for £6,800; £5,000 for the publication of the scientific results and £1,800 to cover his personal debts from the expedition.[30] On this occasion the application was put together by James Ferrier on behalf of the committee of the expedition, rather than as a personal letter from Bruce. As such it was a comprehensive package of documents, including testimonials from distinguished figures and a detailed budget, and this time the application broadened its base by claiming that *Scotia*'s achievements could be considered as a celebration of what had been achieved for Britain as a whole. Thus, for the first time, a wider political perspective was introduced alongside the nationalistic view.

Official minuting shows that in the normal course of events there would have been no chance of a grant, but because of sensitivities relating to Shackleton's grant, plus the financial support that had just been offered for Scott's second expedition, officials, though reluctant to agree to any grant, decided to refer the matter upwards to the Chancellor of the Exchequer (David Lloyd George[31]). Sadly for Bruce, the timing was unfortunate; the General Election of January 1910 had led to a hung parliament, and government attention was diverted. By March, when there was still no decision, a strong sense of favouritism bubbled up again among Bruce's supporters; the delay was a slight to Scotland, an insult to all scientific opinion.

The delay opened the way for Charles Price,[32] the Edinburgh Liberal Member of Parliament, Bruce's constituency MP and a strong supporter of Bruce, to raise the matter in the House. A personal letter of support quickly followed this from the Secretary of State for Scotland,[33] Lord Pentland,[34] to the Chancellor. As a result of this political intervention it was agreed that Lloyd George would meet a deputation of senior figures, but on the agreed date Lloyd George was ill, and so the meeting was cancelled.

Predictably, resentment festered. In Scotland indignation was expressed as the response being 'typical of a step-fatherly attitude to Dr Bruce'.[35] The St Andrew Society and other Scottish patriotic societies wrote, with distinctly political overtones, to all the Scottish parliamentary candidates – Unionist, Liberal and Labour – asking them to support 'in every way possible the claims of the National Antarctic Expedition upon the Government for a Treasury grant as already given to two expeditions that sailed from England'.[36] The candidates' replies were encouraging and the application was linked in order to draw public attention, with a suggested reduction of £100 in Shackleton's grant and an abstract of the accounts, details of loans and a prospectus of the volumes already published.

Finally, Lloyd George agreed to a grant of £3,000 to meet the costs of publication; the remaining £3,800, Lloyd George suggested, could be raised in Scotland. Even this small grant came with a caveat: it had to be controlled by the Scottish Office as opposed to being paid directly to Bruce, none of it could be used for Bruce's personal debts, and the Treasury refused to agree that 'publication' included running costs for the laboratory and salaries for Bruce and his staff to prepare the reports. Arguments over these restrictions meant that no money came through until 1911,[37] when the Treasury eventually agreed to be flexible over the meaning of 'publication', allowing Bruce and his staff to be remunerated and the laboratory overheads to be supported. It remained adamant, however, that no money should go towards Bruce's debts.

The *Report on The Scientific Results of the Voyage of S.Y. Scotia* was Bruce's work for posterity. Each one had to be written, edited, illustrated and printed. Rudmose Brown, who fielded the botanical work, sent mosses and grasses to several European experts for comments which had to be collated into what would become Volume III.[38] The invaluable Rudmose Brown also edited Seals and eventually helped with Birds after Bruce got into a 'fix', when his ornithologist colleague, the eminent Eagle Clark of Edinburgh, had 'shied' away from doing the report.[39] Eagle Clarke did in fact write three reports, with pages of illustrations in the *Ibis*. These were reprinted in the Ornithological Report.[40]

The year 1909 was also the beginning of the long-lasting saga concerning the Polar Medal, which in one form or another has continued for more than a century. The medal was created in 1904 when the First Lord of the Admiralty petitioned Edward VII for its creation to mark the successful return of Scott's British National Antarctic Expedition. The medal was only to be awarded to members of expeditions mounted, or officially recognised, by His Majesty's Government. Clearly Bruce's expedition, proudly backed and executed in Scotland with private funds, was not considered (not least by Bruce) to be a candidate for the award. This view changed dramatically when members of Shackleton's 1907–09 expedition, another expedition backed by private rather than government funds, were awarded the medal. The Admiralty had petitioned persistently for an exception to be made in Shackleton's case because of his exceptional achievements; this argument the king accepted, and the medals were bestowed in November 1909. This was the touchstone that provoked Bruce in 1910 to petition via the Scottish Office for a similar honour to be awarded to members of his *Scotia* expedition.

He became convinced that his request for the medal to be awarded to the men of the *Scotia* was turned down due to Sir Clements' malign hand. This entrenched view has been questioned by Dudeney and Sheail,[41] who have reported that the decision came from the monarchy;[42] Sir Clements had no part to play in the choice of recipients for the medal. The Scottish Office and Admiralty made another spirited attempt to get the medal awarded in 1913, only to be immediately rebuffed by the palace (see Appendix 4 for a detailed account based on the correspondence of the time). A further attempt was made by Scottish Parliament in 2002, to mark the centenary of the expedition, but this was also rebuffed.

As the first decade of the 1900s drew to a close Bruce seemed to be immersed in his plans for new ventures and the publication of the *Scotia* results, but in spite of these onerous burdens, remarkably, he somehow found time to write a wide-ranging book, *Polar Exploration*, which was published in 1911.[43] In this he offered his idea of how 'modern' polar scientific exploration should be conducted, and what the main topic areas should be. The book showed not only his broad and deep mastery of research fields as diverse as glaciology, meteorology, magnetism, oceanography, biology, and aurora as they pertained to the polar regions, but also highlighted what was known and where the critical questions remained. He made some prescient connections that have stood the test of time – for instance, he discussed the importance of the cold bottom water originating in the Antarctic (which we now call Antarctic bottom water) and speculated on how much this controlled the wider behaviour of the oceans. *Polar Exploration* is a blueprint on what needed doing and how to do it. One can only speculate just how far the broad range of polar sciences would have been advanced had Bruce ever been able to lead a second expedition to the Antarctic, or had he not died so relatively young.

The book is very easy to read despite its subject matter and it is interesting to note that, given the complex relationship between Bruce and his wife, Jessie seems to have played an important secretarial role in the preparation of the work; among the acknowledgements in the book is the statement 'Mrs Bruce has been my amanuensis throughout'.[44] Since it is likely that Bruce had autistic tendencies, it is possible that Jessie actively edited the book, dedicated to Sir Joseph Hooker, to make it so accessible.

In 1911 the laboratory contributed to an Antarctic exhibition in Glasgow. Bruce was in Paris for the inauguration of Prince Albert's Institut Océanographique, but he came rushing back to immerse himself, typically, so completely in the preparations that Ferrier felt compelled to remind him of the pressing importance of the government grant, 'however interesting and necessary the exhibit may be. As if you did not know that!'[45] The attendance at the six-month exhibition was huge. This shows that Bruce was successful in promoting his laboratory and his expedition's national credentials in the public mind, but not, unfortunately, in ensuring financial support for his work.

By May 1912 volumes IV and VI were 'going steadily ahead'.[46] Volume III was complete. 'Bacteriology' was ready for press. Some headings of plates had to be corrected.[47] Bruce wrote that the classification of the dimensions of the different seals was finished; he sent Rudmose Brown Belgian, Swedish and other reports on seals and asked for help with birds.[48] Clark of Aberdeen had delivered the phytoplankton section; the correspondence about 'foraminifera, salinities and specific gravities was reaching a conclusion. But there was still a 'tremendous pile of work'.[49] Rudmose Brown advised Bruce on the layout of the manuscript and where to site the maps and plates.[50] He had completed proofs of the zoological section by June. But others were predictably slow in sending in their work, two papers on algae needed revision and photos still had to be put in the right place. Throughout, Rudmose Brown was the most remarkable friend and supporter. In spite of being Professor of Geography at Sheffield University, he was 'only too glad to be able to do this work and help in any way I can' – and he did.[51] He also helped by re-reading chapters.

Bruce became increasingly and doggedly diverted into the politics of the scientific world both nationally and internationally. In 1912 a proposal was made that the Royal Scottish Geographical Society should do something towards running the geographical section of the British Association at its Dundee meeting. Bruce wanted to make the geographical section thoroughly Scottish, but his correspondence is mostly interesting for his trenchant views and ill feeling towards the society: 'The council are an obsolete body of old men who have no other idea than to make a lecture agency of the Society and the secretary Bartholomew (the eminent co-founder of the RSGS, to whom he had written very politely on his return from the *Scotia* expedition) is not interested in anything beyond filling his purse.'[52] Rudmose Brown agreed that the association should be sorted out, along with the 'London crowd'. But he was a restraining influence; he cautioned Bruce against involving the St Andrew Society, with its predictable nationalistic sentiment. Any decisions should be a 'matter of national capacity and intellectual standing, which must be voiced by a scientific society such as the Royal Scottish Geographical Society'.[53]

It is difficult, in reading of the number of hurdles that he increasingly created for himself, to avoid the thought that Bruce had some characteristics that today would be classified as part of an autistic spectrum disorder; Rudmose Brown himself wrote that no man, and certainly no woman, ever got close to Bruce,[54] who seems to have had a lack of empathy, poor verbal skills and an inability to pick up those non-verbal signs that are so important for successful communication. He was impatient, quarrelling easily and frequently.[55] He could not be deflected from any task once he had started it. These are traits that must have affected him and those around him significantly both in his personal and professional life.

His isolation would have been exacerbated when Jessie, it seems, developed a drinking habit. According to Moira Watson, Bruce's granddaughter,[56] Jessie would be called an alcoholic today. She became a neglectful mother; the neighbours often had to look after Eillium and Sheila while Jessie sold household items to feed her addiction, so exacerbating the family's parlous financial state. It can be suggested that Bruce's aloofness and absences pushed her to the solace of alcohol, and her drinking caused him to retreat from the family unit to a greater extent. As a result their relationship appears to have spiralled downwards to an inevitable end. Although Bruce did pay attention to his children to the best of his ability, family problems obviously had an ongoing effect on the children: Bruce's granddaughter Moira understands that Eillium grew to dislike his mother; alcoholism and debt must have caused long-lasting scars. With Bruce's consent, Eillium 'escaped' when he was fourteen, joining the Incorporated Thames Nautical Training College, HMS *Worcester*, where he trained for a career at sea.

Although Sheila later described her father as concerned and interested, Bruce's single-minded involvement in his projects and his inability to comprehend the requirements of his family unit meant that he could not give them the attention and time they needed and must have been damaging.

In 1913 the pressures mounted up. In February Bruce had to investigate rival companies in Spitsbergen – a company claimed to have raised capital of £1 million to start quarrying for marble and coal, a claim that Bruce described as 'all rot'.[57] He also had enquiries from the Foreign Office about the syndicate's claims.[58] These matters could be dealt with, but must have deflected his time and energy from the Oceanographical Laboratory. He was also occupied with plans for a zoo in Edinburgh and acted as vice-president of the organising committee.[59] His correspondence is typical of the concentrated focus he gave to any project he took up.

Given all Bruce's other commitments, it is amazing that he also approached the Governor of the Falklands, and through him the Colonial Office, to return to the South Orkneys in the summer of 1913/14. The government was prepared to employ him in the post of 'Government Representative' for the whaling industry based in the South Orkneys, and he seems to have been willing to take this lowly position. The duties were not onerous and would have allowed him time to carry out a personal programme of research. He would have earned £15 per month. However, the government was not prepared to provide him with an assistant and he did not, in the event, take up the post.[60]

Also in February 1913, word reached the waiting world that Robert Falcon Scott's team had reached the South Pole in January 1912, five weeks after the Norwegian team led by Amundsen, and that Scott and his four companions had died on the return journey. Bruce privately thought that the expedition had been badly managed – he wrote that he felt that the 'whole business is a colossal blunder and that Scott, Bowers, Wilson and possibly Oates too should never have been allowed to die with the base camp 155 miles off and full of provisions, transport and healthy men'. He thought that it 'looked as though there was nobody capable at the base station of judging the position'.[61]

In relation to these statements it is interesting to note appears that Robert Scott had actually visited Bruce's family home in Portobello[62] in 1909, before setting out on the *Terra Nova* expedition. Eillium recounted to his daughter Moira that her grandfather advised his children to be 'as quiet as mice' during Scott's coming visit. Eillium told Moira that there was an argument between the two men, with Bruce (unusually) shouting and Scott storming out of the house. Bruce apparently stood shaking his head, muttering that Scott did not understand that his proposed food caches were too far apart.[63] It is fascinating to wonder whether Bruce was reflecting on the problems encountered on Shackleton's *Nimrod* expedition and advising Scott to put his depots on his expedition closer together. But in spite of this private opinion, he and Burn Murdoch organised an Antarctic exhibition in Edinburgh, both to encourage continued Antarctic interest and to underline the fact that the Scots had not been in competition with Scott's men.

Notwithstanding his heroic efforts, Bruce's campaign to keep his treasured laboratory open was doomed to failure. In December 1913, Ferrier began another appeal for £3,800 to finish the *Scotia* results and pay off Bruce's debt of £1,800. He received a very prompt rejection from the Treasury which included the tart response: 'It was clearly stated in the correspondence dealing with the original grant of £3,000 that in assenting to this grant, My Lords relied upon "sufficient funds being forthcoming from other sources to complete the publication of the whole of the material", and that "in no case would any further contribution be made from Public Funds".'[64]

But this did not stop Bruce sending over one hundred letters to Members of Parliament[65] to canvass support again for his Member of Parliament,

Charles Price. On this occasion Price aimed at attracting support from English as well as Scottish Members,[66] and tabling a question in the House of Commons. He submitted an appeal (thirty-two pages long) to the Lords Commissioners of His Majesty's Treasury.[67] His argument was that a refusal would be an insult to all the scientific community of Great Britain. The request carried the signatures of principals and vice-chancellors of the universities of Scotland, presidents of Learned Societies of Scotland and distinguished scientists, both in Scotland and England. But even with the keen support of Ramsay MacDonald[68] (the Scottish Member of Parliament and future Prime Minister),[69] the support of the RGS[70] and the British whaling group Messers Salveson, which offered to pay for the cost of the whaling report (which would help with the publication of Volume IV of Bruce's report), the Treasury again refused the request. The Treasury Chambers' reply stated that 'their Lordships have nothing to add to (the) Treasury letter of the 23 January on this subject'.[71] The *Glasgow Herald* reported this as 'rather absurd' on 17 April 1914 considering that 'money is being spent lavishly in the interests of other expeditions which have not achieved anything, and a meeting of Scottish members of Parliament to-day resolved to take such steps as will compel the Government to reconsider its decision'.[72]

So Bruce, again emphasising the Scottish nature of his appeal, prepared himself for yet another fight. Charles Price and Lord Dalrymple (Unionist MP for Wigtowshire) led the assault, which they said would continue 'until they got money (or some of it)',[73] and Bruce wrote of signs of a strengthening of the national spirit in Scotland. But the big fight he was working up to never took place. The outbreak of war in August 1914 put all his plans on hold.

9

THE IMPACT OF THE FIRST WORLD WAR ON BRUCE

Many of Bruce's problems came from situations well outside his control, and indeed the First World War dealt a serious blow to his hopes and ambitions. Its immediate impact related to the future of the Oceanographical Laboratory. Bruce had planned that the laboratory would transmute into a prestigious Oceanographical Institute of Edinburgh, and at a meeting of the Royal Society of Edinburgh in May 1914 a group of eminent scientists agreed that such a National Oceanographic Institute should be founded as a memorial to Sir John Murray, who had been killed in a car accident in March.

They planned for a lectureship at the University of Edinburgh associated with the institute (for which Bruce would have been a prime candidate, and which would have given him financial security), and Bruce agreed to gift his collection to the new institute. But the war put paid to this cherished plan; even before the appeal for a building fund was launched, the assassination of Archduke Ferdinand in Sarajevo in July led to Great Britain declaring war. As a result, attention and all available money were diverted towards the war effort.

Bruce's attitude to the war reflected his patriotism and his long-term distrust of Germany. The build-up of the German fleet fuelled fears of a foreign takeover of Spitsbergen; a *Scotsman* article of 25 July, in the approach to the declaration of war, stated that the Germans were on manoeuvres close to Norway and that this had been a long-standing practice. Moving from his customary antagonism towards Norway, Bruce wrote that such manoeuvres were 'greatly to the discontent of the Norse population, a violation of Norwegian independence and international law'. He wrote correctly that 'it would not be possible to prevent an attack from a fleet in a neutral harbour though this would be an action against international law and British security'.[1] He was sure that the government was aware of this, and said that the public had a right to know and that diplomatic pressure should be used to stop the practice. Such comments, from a man with a very personal interest in the outcome but no knowledge of international diplomacy, must have strained the patience of government officials wrestling with the awful pressures brought on by the outbreak of war.

Bruce, at forty-seven, was too old for active service in August 1914. In the early part of the war he stayed in Edinburgh, struggling to keep the laboratory going. He wrote to Rudmose Brown that 'the whole burden of this place is on my shoulders and I have many accounts to settle. The best I can hope to do is to keep it alive until happier times.'[2] He worked briefly for the Admiralty, but the Admiralty did not take up a proposal that he should compile Antarctic and Southern Ocean sailing directions and revise all the Admiralty charts, so he decided to accept an offer from Burn Murdoch to manage a whaling station in the Seychelles, leaving his wife and twelve-year-old son and five-year-old daughter in Scotland. The station was in a poor state, and with shipping routes disrupted by the war, he was unable to prevent its closure in August 1915.

When Bruce returned to Scotland it became obvious that he and Jessie could no longer live together as man and wife. They separated in

1915, though they continued to live in the same house. Eillium joined the Merchant Navy in 1916 as a cadet, also automatically becoming a cadet of the Royal Naval Reserve. Moira Watson understands that apart from his dislike for his mother he did not care much for his sister; the sea was a way to escape. Bruce was certainly concerned about his son, writing to Rudmose Brown on several occasions; the Rudmose Browns looked after Eillium and his 'heavy sea chest' as he passed through London on his way to and from the training college.³ Bruce wrote, 'My boy must be planted as firmly as possible for the future and there must be nothing haphazard if it can be avoided, about him joining the *Worcester*.'⁴

Bruce returned to his 'home' in the Scottish Oceanographical Laboratory and to his correspondence. He replied positively to a query about whether the missing Shackleton party could have survived their Trans-Antarctic sortie (although reflecting ruefully that the Treasury had systematically refused money for the scientific results of the only expedition that had actually explored and charted the Weddell Sea). Bruce's opinion was that Shackleton could have survived and that it was possible that no news would appear until May 1916. Opinions predictably differed on this point: a Mr MacKellar wrote that he had been told that 'spiritualists "met Shackleton's spirit" and he [Shackleton] told them that he and his party had died'.⁵ MacKellar also wrote to Bruce relating to the *Aurora* party (*Aurora* was the ship that Shackleton sent to the Ross sea base to provide support and receive him and his party after his proposed Trans-Antarctic crossing) that 'it does not seem to me even possible that the party left on shore could lay depots to the foot of the Beardmore Glacier, 360 miles; and if they did not, and Shackleton really got half way across the continent, then if no depot met him at the foot of the Beardmore – if he could get so far – then his men MUST have perished'.⁶ Bruce disagreed. He thought that the *Aurora* party could have got to the Beardmore. He did 'not see that there was any news at all that indicates that any calamity has befallen him or his party'.[7] He offered support to Lady Shackleton.

In April 1916 Bruce wrote a four-page letter to R. H. Boyle of the *Daily Chronicle*,[8] quoting a piece in *The Scotsman*: 'I do not share the somewhat alarmist views of its London correspondent, who apparently speaks with no special knowledge of the Weddell Sea.'[9] In this letter he suggested plans for a possible rescue for Shackleton if this was needed. He pointed out the particular dangers of the Weddell Sea and offering himself to organise and, if necessary, conduct the relief operations. In fact in London the government were already organising a search-and-rescue expedition and Bruce, along with the Australian explorer Douglas Mawson and Captain Davis, were invited to provide expert advice. Bruce's detailed suggestions (dogs, portable wirelesses, men) were accepted. But as preparations for a rescue proceeded, Shackleton materialised in Port Stanley at the end of May 1916. If the rescue expedition had actually set off to search the Weddell Sea, it is likely that Bruce would have been part of it and probably would have led the proposed wintering group.[10]

Even though Bruce had been invited to the planning for the rescue mission, he could not contain his bitterness. In his letter to Boyle he affirmed that he had 'no intention of urging that any special knowledge I consider I have of the Weddell Sea in particular and of ice navigation in general should be made use of by those who do not want it, but it is there if it is wanted'. Also, in a letter to Rudmose Brown in May 1916, he said that 'there must be something hereditary surely in Presidents of the RGS, the way they systematically ignore the work of the *Scotia* and the existence of many people who took part in the expedition ... Myself, I supposed being north of the Tweed, they think dead. While I do not wish to oust Mawson, Davis or Evans, I do think that we might get some friends of the *Scotia* to point out to these Cockneys that the people who have been to the Weddell Sea should be consulted more particularly than any others.'[11]

Bruce doggedly pursued his efforts with publications and journals, but he wrote to Rudmose Brown that he and the laboratory were on their 'beam end'.[12] By February 1917 it had been known for some months that Shackleton had survived, but Bruce's suggestion that his paper on the Weddell Sea should be published without waiting for Shackleton's return home was refused on the grounds that it would be better to wait for Shackleton arrival. Bruce's complained in his reply that Shackleton might take months to return, and when he did Bruce's paper might be delayed for an inordinate length of time, but he was ignored by the RGS.

Some welcome financial relief came via Rudmose Brown,[13] who invited Bruce to be an external examiner in Geography at the University of Sheffield, with the added inducement of a fee of £15 per year plus payment for papers examined and costs for any overnight stay in Sheffield.[14] And Bruce kept going with his reading and correspondence. He noted with satisfaction that the naval officer and explorer Edward Bransfield (1786–1852), one of the first men to see Antarctica, was, in fact, Irish and born near Cork. It was not England but 'good old Ireland that had discovered the Antarctic continent'[15] – a possibly deliberate provocative statement since the Irish Uprising had occurred in 1916. He also found time to write seeking help for Lady Hooker, the widow of Sir Joseph Hooker, who was in financial difficulties and forced to rent or sell her home. Bruce wanted the house to be taken by someone 'with a sense of reverence for the eminent original owner'.[16]

But by early June 1917, Bruce was writing bitterly that he did not know how much longer he could manage: 'God help me and my family if the Scottish Oceanographical Laboratory goes after my life's best work on it ... One gets no chance with London centralisation at 400 miles distance, especially when the Tweed blocks the road and wets English feet.'[17]

Although he had battled with what he considered English prejudice, Bruce would have been surprised to know that he was actually valued by the Admiralty and the Colonial Office. By 1917, the government was already considering what would be needed for post-war reconstruction. Southern Ocean whaling development was a priority, and a key figure with regard to this was Roland Darnley[18] of the Colonial Office. Darnley had discussions with Bruce in June 1917 and wrote an influential memorandum focusing upon how the Falkland Islands Dependencies remained 'one of the major undeveloped estates of the Empire' and what might be done to realise its potential. Bruce was asked to give evidence to an interdepartmental committee established to develop detailed plans. Here the Admiralty apparently appreciated his 'extraordinary and unique knowledge'.[19] Out of this committee were born the post-war *Discovery* investigations, which aimed to provide a scientific underpinning to the whaling industry. The Colonial Office recorded its thanks to Bruce in a letter in December 1919 and provided him an honorarium of 100 guineas in recognition his service.[20]

The laboratory struggled on until 1919. At this time Bruce was admitted to hospital suffering from mental and physical exhaustion. He developed a psychotic illness in addition to his physical problems. He improved sufficiently, however, to lead a further expedition to Spitsbergen in 1919. But in this year, defeated by the crippling costs of publishing his results, he arranged for the dismantling of his precious laboratory. Originally he planned to donate the collection to the Royal Scottish Museum (now the National Museum of Scotland), but because of the financial problems and his physical and mental deterioration, the contents of the laboratory, which included over 1,000 books, were offered for sale. The advertisement attracted interest from overseas, but Bruce's whole working life had been to promote Scotland, and he wanted his collection to remain there to become the basis of an oceanographical museum in Scotland. Poignantly, he told the director of the Royal Scottish Museum that he wished for the collection to be available to all students of oceanography and to be kept, as much as possible, in Scotland.

The huge collection was eventually dispersed between the Royal Scottish Museum, the St George's Society, the University of Edinburgh, the Royal Scottish Geographical Society and museums throughout Scotland (Aberdeen, Glasgow, Paisley, Perth, Dundee).[21] Duplicate specimens could be sold to England, or other countries!

The First World War had torpedoed the plan for a laboratory based in the university, and this, combined with the perennial financial problems faced by Bruce, dealt a killing blow to the Scottish Oceanographical Laboratory. But Bruce, through unceasing work and grim determination, eventually achieved a triumph with the publication of his *Scotia* volumes, and his laboratory contributed significantly towards the development of the science of oceanography.

Six volumes of the *Report on The Scientific Results of the Voyage of S.Y. Scotia* were eventually published by 1920. Five of the cloth-covered volumes had a Scottish lion in a crest that reads '*Nemo me Impune Lacessit*' ('Let Nobody Harm Me With Impunity') on the frontispiece – a polarising statement.[22] The first volume, Bruce's *Log of the* Scotia, the narrative of the voyage, which would have had the most interest for the general public, was virtually complete by the time that *Scotia* arrived in Scotland, but Bruce gave priority to the scientific volumes. The printers' proof of the log was only ready in 1913,[23] and by this time money for publishing had dried up. The volume was filed with papers kept by Alfred Aitken, Bruce's friend and supporter, the secretary of the Scottish Spitsbergen Syndicate, in his offices in Edinburgh. In 1947 the collection was donated to the Scott Polar Research Institute in Cambridge. Peter Speak, a research associate at the institute, rediscovered the log and published it in 1992, nearly ninety years after it had been started.

Also, during these years of increasing disappointment and resentment, Bruce's achievements were actually recognised more widely. He was awarded the Patron's Medal of the Royal Geographical Society (of London) in 1910, although he would have been awarded it two years earlier had he not irritated the powers that be at the RGS over a claim for expenses (see appendix 5 for the text of the citation). In November 1913 he was approved as a Life Member of the RGS by the council under chapter 111 (para. 6 of the Bye-laws, which meant that his membership was approved free of charge).[24] He wrote that he was delighted at 'the high honour they have done me by electing me to the Life Fellowship of the Society, in recognition of what they are pleased to consider are distinguished services to geographical science'.[25] These and other awards in England and America recognised Bruce's vision and scientific achievements. He achieved remarkable successes.

10

THE ARCTIC: THE SCOTTISH SPITSBERGEN SYNDICATE

This is a story of hope, adventure and enthusiasm, but also ultimately of disappointment. Bruce had high hopes of a successful mining enterprise in Spitsbergen, which he had visited with Prince Albert of Monaco in 1898 and 1899. He wrote that in 1898 he had found oil shale on Barents Island, coal at Advent Bay and gypsum in Sassen Bay. After the *Scotia* expedition his mind turned to the development of a commercial enterprise. This project, which was to involve Bruce heavily in the geopolitics of the area, was to obsess him for the rest of his life.

Any idea of exporting coal and other minerals from this inhospitable and remote environment – especially to Great Britain, which had a sufficiency of coal – may seem implausible, but Bruce planned alternative outlets and he knew that there was already one successful functioning enterprise, run by Americans. His aim was to be a successful entrepreneur; he wanted financial security.

Once involved in the enterprise, Bruce became fiercely determined to protect his company's interests. Throughout the years one of his arguments was that history supported British claims to the archipelago. The Dutch mariner Willem Barentsz had discovered the island (Spitsbergen means 'jagged mountains') in 1596, when he was searching for the Northeast Passage to China. The Muscovy Company of London visited it thereafter in 1604, when coal and walrus ivory were seen. Later the presence of whales, walruses, reindeer and bears as well as coal was recorded. In response to these findings, King James I of England awarded a charter to the company in 1614, granting them the rights for whaling in the seas around Spitsbergen. Robert Fotherby,[1] the master's mate on the whaling ship *Thomasine*, claimed a small bay on the south shore of the island for King James. A wooden cross was erected on the land and the king's arms set up, 'under which I also nayled a piece of sheet Lead, whereon I set the Muscovie Companies Marke, with the day of the moneth and yeere of our Lord'. Fotherby then cut out a piece of turf: 'I take this piece of Earth, as a sign of lawful possession of this countrie of King James his New – land, and of this particular place which I name Trinitie Harbour.'[2]

Rudmose Brown wrote that the claims were never rescinded and should therefore still be considered valid,[3] but this is debatable. Legally, a territorial claim requires three steps: firstly, a flag must be planted and a claim made over the territory on behalf of the country planting the flag; secondly, that country has to accept the claim by enacting some internationally accepted legal instrument; finally, the country making the claim has to administer the territory. The first stage only gives what is known as an 'inchoate claim', which lapses after a period of time if no further action is taken. Fotherby's claim was 'inchoate', but it could be argued that the award of the charter to the Muscovy Company by King James signified the start of stage two. However, even if this is accepted, to make the claim firm (to 'perfect' it), James would have had to not only agree to the claim, but also to enact legal instruments proclaiming his territory and, more importantly, to arrange for its effective administration. None of these steps were taken between 1614 and 1908, so the British claim would have effectively lapsed. This makes Rudmose Brown's conclusion legally shaky.

Spitsbergen makes up the western bulk of the Svalbard Archipelago (74°–81°N. Latitude and 10°–35°E. longitude). It is the largest and the only permanently populated island of the archipelago. It was a whaling base in the eighteenth century and coalmining began at the end of the nineteenth century. The land is rugged and glaciated, with many fjords and inlets. Bruce wrote that its total area was about equal to that of Scotland.

The major advantage relating to commercial development was that from the end of the nineteenth century Spitsbergen was classified as *terra nullius* (belonging to nobody). This meant that the right to hold and mine an area could be obtained simply by staking out a plot and registering the claim with the claimant's country. Bruce hoped, as did others, that the archipelago had an untapped quantity of natural resources. He knew that a commercial shipment of coal had been made by a Norwegian ship in 1899 and that thereafter American, Norwegian, Russian, Dutch and three English companies had staked claims. Bruce's claim was the fifth to be registered in the early 1900s; the Arctic Coal Company of Boston was registered in 1905, as were the Spitsbergen Coal and Trading Company of Sheffield and the Spitsbergen Mining and Exploration Company. The Northern Exploration Company of London was registered in 1906.

Bruce gave an account of his first exploration of Prince Charles Foreland in the *Geographical Journal* in 1908.[4] He wrote that he had seen Spitsbergen in 1899, when he returned to the Arctic Islands with Prince Albert and sailed along almost all of the coastline, as well as 'seeing something of its interior'.[5] In 1906 he revisited the archipelago at Prince Albert's invitation. The prince wanted to make a detailed plan of the Foreland and to investigate its atmosphere with kites and balloons. Bruce wrote to Rudmose Brown in June, suggesting that a few men under his (Bruce's) direction, a subsection of the main party, should explore the

Foreland as well as undertake the topographical survey. He said that little had been done there since the work of Nordenskjöld, the Finnish/Swedish geologist, in 1869.

In relation to coal, Jonas Poole[6] had discovered this in Spitsbergen in the 1600s, but the first shipment was not made for two hundred years and it was this latter shipment that raised the possibility of further commercial developments in the bleak northern islands. But in spite of this hopeful example, Bruce would have been well aware that good-quality coal, in thick, easily accessible, seams, and low-cost shipping, were prerequisites for any coal deposits to be commercially viable. He thought that this was achievable.

The original exploration and fieldwork of the Foreland took place in the summers of 1906 and 1907. On these visits Bruce found that the Admiralty had given 'more or less a definite map of the island but, on inspection I found this to be, as I expected, little more than a conglomeration of a series of indefinite sketches, all inaccurate but each one less inaccurate than the resulting conglomerate'.[7] Published comments like this can hardly have endeared him to the authorities in London.

In 1906, Bruce and two companions were on the Foreland for three months. They made a topographical survey of much of the island. The Prince of Monaco picked them up in the *Princesse Alice* in August as she sailed south to Norway. Bruce took a sample of coal with him.

On his second visit in the summer of 1907, Bruce hired a steamer, the *Fonix*, to take him and a larger team to the Foreland. The team was Stewart Ross MA, Victor Burn Murdoch (a geologist and the cousin of Bruce's friend William) and the piper Gilbert Kerr. Hjalmar Johansen, Nansen's companion in Franz Josef Land and later a member of Amundsen's expedition to the South Pole, joined the party later.[8] On this visit Bruce hoped to complete the survey of the Foreland. The party was split into groups, and with two companions Bruce surveyed Cape Cold (the conditions were awful; they were away for so long that, at base, Johansen and Burn Murdoch thought that there had been 'some disaster').[9] The team returned to base camp on 12 September after a trek of thirteen hours, much to the relief of Burn Murdoch and Johansen – Bruce was physically very strong at this time.

These surveys were important. The coastline was dangerous; there were stormy seas and frequent fog. Bruce wrote that 'he saw seven steamers going up and down the coast and that shipwrecks around the island gave a vivid indication of potential difficulties'.[10]

The team surveyed the Foreland save for two sections of the coastline and produced a 1:100,000 topographical map, which was to be completed in 1909 and placed in the public domain. The survey also included the geology, zoology, botany and meteorology of the island.

The direction of Bruce's life was changed by an analysis of the coal samples that he brought back to Edinburgh. This confirmed in his mind the possibility of commercial development of Spitsbergen's natural resources. The report, dated 30 March 1909, stated that the coal was long-flamed steam coal. It had a high calorific value and could be used in steam locomotives. The samples were said to resemble Yorkshire coal, which was used as good household fuel.[11] Experts in Glasgow also examined the coal and said that it was clean, free from sulphur and ash, and could be used for steam engines in general. The coal was in tertiary measures (from the Tertiary Era of 65 million years ago – what geologists now refer to as the Palaeocene) and was of a comparable quality to coal from Glamorgan, South Wales. Although tertiary coal is often not as commercially viable as other forms of coal, this is not the case in Spitsbergen. The coals, though 'young', have been buried deeply and been subject to high temperatures, so for their age they are of good quality. Temperature and time expels water and other volatile substances, and as this process proceeds the coal becomes richer in carbon and of higher calorific value.[12]

Bruce did receive a warning from the geologist H. M. Cadell, who wrote that in view of freight costs and iceberg worries, commercially successful mining in Spitsbergen was doubtful.[13] Bruce chose to ignore this; he was genuinely encouraged by the reports on the quality of the coal, and with Victor Burn Murdoch he established the Scottish Spitsbergen Syndicate with the aim of exploring the mineral resources of Spitsbergen. His Scottish venture would follow other companies already registered. The main British rival to the syndicate was to be Northern Exploration of London.

A prospectus for the syndicate was issued in September 1908 'for private circulation only' under the names of William S. Bruce and J. Victor Burn Murdoch. The prospectus, from the Scottish Oceanographical Laboratory, went to prominent businessmen in Edinburgh and Glasgow. It described the plan to equip an expedition to Spitsbergen early in 1909 to secure at least two considerable areas known to Bruce and Burn Murdoch (which in 1908 had not been claimed), plus any other available areas and stated that coal had been known to be present on the archipelago for years and was still there in commercially exploitable quantities. The prospectus emphasised that effective occupation was required to establish the claim and it was envisaged that exports could be made to Archangel (and thence Moscow), to Norway and to countries in the Baltic.[14] It reassured prospective investors that the Gulf Stream made the west coast of the archipelago more free of ice than other Arctic islands so that navigation and shipping into natural harbours and fjords on the coast should be possible from June to September. Good coal seams were close by. The prospectus stated that mining, as opposed to shipping, could continue throughout the year, and alluring prospects of oil, marble, iron ore and gypsum as well as coal were referred to, as was the possibility of dealing in game skins and hides and even building houses. Subscribers were invited to 'subscribe immediately'.[15]

Bruce's company would be a prospecting company concerned primarily with coal – it was envisaged that the rights would be sold on. The original plan was for a detailed survey, with the aim of exploiting primarily coal resources, but also to look for oil and marble. The private company, of no more than fifty members, aimed to raise £6,000 in £10 shares of which £3,000 would be used for the 1909 expedition (ship hire, staff, purchasing of scientific equipment and insurance). It was intended that the two expedition leaders would receive salaries and a number of fully paid-up shares in lieu of their past expenses.

As Frigga Kruse points out in *Frozen Assets*, Bruce mainly recruited from his earlier Antarctic connections, his scientific network and the Scottish elite.[16] There was a variable response: among others Dr Paul Rottenburg, a Glasgow merchant who later became the President of the Glasgow RSGS, gave £300 (conditional on £2,000 being raised),[17] and Prince Albert of Monaco gave £300. T. Leslie Usher, an Edinburgh businessman, gave £50, Sir John Murray £200, Robert Morton Paterson £50, and Robert Rudmose Brown and John Mathieson (who were to go with Bruce on the 1909 and subsequent expeditions) £50 each. In total, only thirty subscribers contributed a total of £4,000, taking up 400 shares of £10.

The Foreign Office was informed in February 1909 and the Scottish Spitsbergen Syndicate was incorporated on 15 July 1909.[18] Five directors were appointed[19] and Bruce and Burn Murdoch transferred their claims, rights and interests in Spitsbergen to the syndicate on the 16 July.[20] They each received 100 shares (valued at £10 each) and Bruce was made chairman of the board of directors, a role to which his expertise and personality were perhaps not best suited. It also appears that several people who had been of assistance during previous expeditions plus family (including Jessie) and friends were rewarded with a number of shares. It is not clear whether these were part of Bruce's allotment.[21] Bruce telegraphed Rudmose Brown, who was in Aberdeen, that the expedition was ready to leave. He told Rudmose Brown to keep the syndicate's plans private; it was obviously important that other interested parties did not know of the Scottish plans.

During these challenging months Bruce continued with numerous other commitments. He gave lectures, for example on Prince Charles Foreland (on one occasion in tandem with the Antarctic explorer Louis Bernacchi).[22] He wrote numerous articles on polar history and on his personal experiences. He was involved with the Scottish Skiing Club and the Scottish Oceanographical Laboratory, and he worked on *Scotia* reports. He had family problems (his son had measles, his wife neuralgia); there was a possibility of a lectureship in Glasgow; he made submissions to the government for grants (for his planned Trans-Antarctic expedition and for the costs associated with publication of the *Scotia* results). Throughout, he remained heavily involved in his Scottish syndicate.

Apart from Spitsbergen, he still dreamed of southern ventures and actually applied to the government for a lease of the South Sandwich Islands for sealing and whaling. This surprising side venture seems to have been treated positively: an assistant undersecretary in the Colonial Office wrote that Bruce might be given 'a right of priority, but there could be no question of a permanent monopoly'. A deputy undersecretary agreed, though he warned that a one-year lease should 'suffice to disgust him of this scheme'.[23] It seems that Bruce did not follow this project through, probably because he heard about the explorer Carl Larsen's visit to the islands. Larsen's health had been so severely affected by fumes from active fumaroles (openings near volcanoes sending out sulphurous gasses) that he had formed a completely negative impression of the island group.[24]

Bruce 'juggled many balls' – too many to carry through. This incessant energy and anxiety to be completely involved in many options must have related to his chronic financial insecurity, but it would be interesting to know what his Spitsbergen backers would have thought if they had realised that he was making plans to travel south while simultaneously planning the Spitsbergen Syndicate.

On 19 July 1909, the SY *Conqueror* sailed north from Leith harbour. The scientific staff was Bruce, Rudmose Brown, the surveyor John Mathieson,[25] two geologists Major Harry Hannay RE and Angus Peach, Alastair Geddes (son of Patrick Geddes, Bruce's early mentor), Victor Burn Murdoch and Gilbert Kerr. Bruce was in charge with a salary of £200.

Conqueror sailed to Spitsbergen reaching Recherche Bay (Bell Sound), some distance south of Ice Fjord, on 31 July; where a search for coal was made. She then sailed north to Prince Charles Foreland where John Mathieson led a surveying party that completed Bruce's 1906/07 survey of the island. The Foreland was claimed on behalf of the syndicate. *Conqueror* sailed next to Kings Bay in Spitsbergen to make further claims and she subsequently sailed to Advent Bay in Ice Fjord, the home of the American mine run by Arctic Coal Co. of Boston. From here Bruce and Hannay trekked across West Spitsbergen to its eastern coast adjoining Stor Fjord. Along the way they pegged and boarded new claims. The two men trekked back to Temple Fjord (at the eastern end of the Ice Fjord), regularly staking further claims. The area of these new claims represented 2,430 square kilometres bordering the eastern coast of West Spitsbergen. Each claim was confirmed by boards stating the boundaries of their claims in longitude and latitude and was dated 1909. The expedition returned to Norway in September 1909.

The syndicate claims therefore covered much of West Spitsbergen and Prince Charles Foreland. Later Barents Island was added. The claims were registered with the British Foreign Office in January 1910, with an appendix added in 1913 which laid claim to the whole of Barents Land.[26] A note to this effect was delivered to the British Legation at Kristiania (Oslo). The British Foreign Secretary, Sir Edward Grey,[27] subsequently notified his Norwegian counterpart.[28]

Harry Hannay's geological report was not as encouraging as the reports of 1908 and was a disappointment to Bruce.[29] Hannay stated that much of the coal from Bell Sound was below sea level, in seams that were too thin for profitable mining. Also, the coal-bearing areas that had been investigated in Kings Bay and Advent Bay were reported as commercially unviable.[30] Hannay stated that the gypsum (used for plaster of Paris and cements) on Temple Mountain was of good quality and suitable for mining if there was a sufficient margin for profit, but the phosphates examined were of little commercial value. However, Rudmose Brown wrote that 'the expedition had been successful and opened the way for further work'[31] (a new claim map was sent to the Foreign Office in 1910, to include the gypsum, coal and oil shale that had been identified within the claim areas of 1909).[32] Bruce reassured himself that the report was that of a cautious scientist.

Finance remained an ongoing problem. The 1909 expedition had run through the syndicate's reserves, the little that remained of the £2,000 allotted to the actual expedition having been swallowed up by general expenses. Also, after initial hopeful enthusiasm, excitement among the shareholders died down at the precise time when Bruce needed to promote his claims. Bruce was not a good self-promoter; neither urbane nor charming, he was intense and focused while also lacking real commercial expertise – or indeed interest. Promotion of the syndicate's potential would have benefited from a publicity agent both to generate newspaper coverage and wider public support, plus a professional managing director committed to making his syndicate a commercial success.

Instead, Bruce focused his efforts on the archipelago's strategic importance in his correspondence with Whitehall. He wrote that if Norway was to gain control of the archipelago, her government would lay claim to Spitsbergen's valuable resources, and that the syndicate's existing claims would either become invalid or hidebound by red tape. He claimed 'that a British subject knows as much about Spitsbergen as anybody'[33] and aimed for British and American companies to work together to maintain their mutual interests.[34] He became increasingly vociferous in demands for British annexation of the island group, basing his claim on Sir Martin Conway's *No Man's Land*.[35] By this time Germany had made claims to Magdalena Bay and Hamburg Bay, thus underlining the syndicate's fears. Rudmose Brown wrote that if only they could make a German scare over this they might get British annexation.[36] The whole basis of the syndicate's modus operandi in Spitsbergen was Bruce's fervent wish to protect its claims.

The attempt to whip up support did attract many Scottish Members of Parliament, especially Bruce's particular supporter Charles Price. A deputation to David Lloyd George aimed to convince him of the value and importance of Spitsbergen and to heighten patriotic indignation by demonstrating other countries (particularly Norway's), increasing involvement in the area. Appeals on these lines were doomed to failure. Great Britain was involved in an international poker game, not only with Norway but also with other European countries; Spitsbergen was only one small piece in the complex jigsaw puzzle of geopolitics. The government was never going to force an issue over coal, which was easily available in Britain. It was this consciousness that commerce was never going to be the decisive factor which drove Bruce towards emphasising the strategic benefits of annexation.

In 1911 Bruce was distracted by an offer of a well-paid post in Burma to work with the Pearl Fisheries Company of the Mergui Archipelago, a company that Rudmose Brown had previously dealt with. Could he fit this in with Spitsbergen? Eventually he decided against the offer.[37]

In an attempt to keep the syndicate's interests in the public domain, he and Rudmose Brown continued their valiant attempts to canvass support and overcome public apathy by giving lectures. But canvassing was based only in Scotland, and little interest was expressed until the erstwhile explorer Joseph Foster Stackhouse[38] approached Bruce with the proposition of opening up Spitsbergen to the tourist market. Stackhouse confidently proposed hotels and tourist parties[39] and said that the first tourists would be able to visit by July 1912. Little capital would be needed – the travellers could pay their fares in advance. 'Arctic Explorations Ltd' was planned with an initial capital of £2,000. But Bruce learnt not to trust Stackhouse.[40] Meetings were remarkably difficult to arrange. A *Times* report suggested that the French government had commissioned Stackhouse to make relief maps. The report was not true, and this led Bruce to doubt Stackhouse's credibility. No money appeared after Stackhouse had agreed to purchase shares in Arctic Exploration Ltd, though he said that he had £2,900 and been promised £5,000 more. Bruce wrote that Stackhouse had got them (the syndicate) into a mess. He considered suing. In the end he was pleased to get out of the arrangement with his business honour intact.[41]

In relation to the practical plans for Arctic Exploration Ltd, or indeed any expedition in the North Atlantic, new problems arose in 1912. On 14 April, the *Titanic* sank on her maiden voyage after collision with an iceberg. This disaster caused serious problems with both charting and getting insurance for shipping in the North Atlantic. Cover for above 72°N on the west and north-west of Spitsbergen (80°N) became excessively high.

Bruce's life, already a tapestry of interwoven complexities, became even more complex. In March 1912 he took up his appointment as an examiner in Geography to the University of Sheffield for a three-year period.[42] In June, the *Geographical Magazine* published a paper by that 'old fool and humbug'[43] Sir Clements Markham. The paper traced Sir Clements' Antarctic work in the RGS since his appointment as president in 1893, but to Scottish fury it also belittled the achievements of the *Scotia* and other expeditions in favour of Markham's protégé Scott.[44] Bruce, understandably angry, became involved in a time-consuming counterattack to defend his expedition's reputation. He wrote to Lord Curzon (1859–1926), the president of the RGS, with bluntness and a lack of tact to ask if the magazine 'should have printed these defamatory statements', or whether this had been 'an error of judgment on the part of the editor'. He said that Markham should be checked and asked whether 'members of the Council of the Geographic Society agreed with the statements'.[45] Curzon replied, reasonably, that authors alone were responsible for statements they made, and however much one might disagree from the view expressed by Sir Clements Markham it was impossible for the *Geographical* to decline to publish a paper by a man in his position on such a subject. Dr Keltie, the society's secretary, added that the society had shown its appreciation of Bruce's work by awarding him a medal (the Patron's Medal).

Bruce was not pacified; he decided to send copies (anonymously) from London to leading polar figures in Belgium, Germany, Sweden, France and other Antarctic leaders and organisers.[46] The society had published statements that, he said, 'reflected discredit on the society of which such a journal was the official organ'.[47] He asked Rudmose Brown to write a general defence of the *Scotia* expedition, suggesting that Rudmose Brown should send the letter to the *Daily Mail* if other papers refused. The *Daily Mail*, Bruce said, would definitely publish because Markham had attacked the paper when it raised money for Mawson (the Australian explorer) through its columns. He thought of returning his RGS Patron's Medal,[48] but was advised by Rudmose Brown that doing so would be 'too great a compliment for old Clem' and would be 'cutting off your nose to spite your face'.[49] Bruce heeded his friend's advice.

He was to meet Sir Clements face to face in September, nine months after this correspondence, at the British Association meeting in Dundee when both men presented papers on Antarctica. It must have been a frosty encounter but seems to have been one where Bruce won the 'sympathetic vote' of the audience. *The Scottish Geographical Magazine* (SGM) reported on the presentations. Markham spoke first and the SGM reported that 'it was felt that in his desire to do honour to Captain Scott, he dealt scant justice to other explorers'. Markham had concentrated on glorifying Scott almost to the exclusion of all else. He did not mention the *Scotia*, or other recent expeditions by name, arguing that 'they were not directed to the object he advocated i.e. continental exploration and that some were mainly confined to the Southern Temperate Zone and hardly reached even the Antarctic Circle'.[50] This comment can only have been aimed at disparaging the French, Swedish and Scottish expeditions.

Bruce, according to the SGM, followed Markham with a scholarly and comprehensive review of all Antarctic work since Cook, giving proper consideration to the various expeditions (including Scott's), and summarising the achievements of the *Scotia* expedition. The SGM article concluded that an animated discussion followed. Bruce must have felt vindicated when, though all the speakers generously acknowledged the value of Scott's work, they strongly deprecated the exalting of one living explorer at the expense of others. It seems that the eighty-two-year-old Markham received a serious rebuke from Bruce's supporters. Markham, however, was characteristically unperturbed, writing in his journal: 'I read my paper on Antarctic discovery to a very crowded audience. Then a long paper by Bruce trying to belittle Scott and magnify the gadfly (here he was probably referring to Amundsen) and Shackles. It was by then too late to answer them and perhaps it was better not.'[51] This is one of the very few entries in his journal when Sir Clements actually mentions Bruce. It reveals much about Markham the man, his dismissal of Bruce and his very particular view of his own role in promoting Antarctic exploration.

Bruce made visits to Spitsbergen on behalf of the syndicate in 1912, 1914 and 1919. The purpose of the visits was to review the syndicate's claims, to ward off rivals and to extend surveys. Up to 1919 the syndicate only engaged in prospecting, and none of the claims had been sold to developers.

In 1912, to support the proposed expedition, a fundraising circular was sent to all syndicate subscribers. This focused on the dangers lurking over their claims and warned of possible Norwegian threats. It stated that the expedition would fail without further support. The shareholders rallied, though sluggishly. Bruce wrote to Rudmose Brown that unless he could raise cash quickly 'the Expedition falls through, and, as I have explained, it is most important that this Expedition should start'.[52] Bruce and J. V. Burn Murdoch, the largest shareholders, had to offer £500 worth of their shares as an incentive to anyone interested in subscribing the remaining £150 that was apparently needed to secure the departure of the expedition.[53] The solicitor Alfred Philp took over secretarial duties. The expedition members were reduced from four to two.

Bruce and Rudmose Brown sailed from Edinburgh in July. They made a six-week visit, inspected their claim boundaries, reinforced them, and looked at the houses belonging to the Spitsbergen Coal and Trading Company of Sheffield with a view to taking them over. From Tromsø they sailed to Green Harbour on the south side of the Ice Fjord entrance. Here, Bruce noted suspiciously, Green Harbour had a post office and a telegraph station, which boasted poles of 60 metres and a permanent staff of six men. This, he thought, was well out of proportion to the size of Green Harbour. Almost certainly, he must have recalled the situation that had arisen on Laurie Island and feared that the Norwegian government was using this post office to justify de facto administration of the archipelago. He was already fearful that this administration might be accepted internationally.

The men visited the American Arctic Coal development at Longyear City. This was followed by a detailed topographic survey of Bjona Haven in Sassen Bay, where the anchorage possibilities were noted with a view to developing a hotel company. All claims from Gips Valley to the Post Glacier at the end of Sassen Bay were walked to check whether they had been respected. Any rival claim boards infringing on the syndicate's land were removed and new claim boards, dated 1912, erected.

When the two arrived in Edinburgh in September 1912, they emphasised again the need for British sovereignty in Spitsbergen. The American mine at Longyear City was said to have exported 40,000 tons of steam coal in two or three months.[54] Also, Russia's interest continued: 'If Britain does not look out Russia will grab the place, have an excellent supply of Welsh coal and be within two days steaming of a modern steamer of British coasts … we intend to do all we can to induce the Government to wake up out of its usual lethargic state.'[55] They noted Norway's significant presence (whaling companies, the wireless station and her involvement in the animal life of Spitsbergen). Germany also had made claims to bases, of importance in relation to her naval build-up.

Bruce wrote to the Earl of Morton, quoting from the *Daily Telegraph*, which stated that Swedish, Norwegian and Russian representatives were meeting to discuss Spitsbergen in Kristiania.[56] He was angry and frustrated that neither Great Britain nor Scotland was represented in this international gathering. He stated, again, that Spitsbergen should be annexed by Great Britain, pointing out that the 'Foreign Office has certain written data regarding British interests in Spitsbergen'[57] and saying that it was important to get answers as to how far these interests had been safeguarded – 'we should perhaps, in the first place, ask certain Members of Parliament to raise the question in the House of Commons'.[58] He opined that the Americans at Advent Bay would prefer a British to a Norwegian administration, because British mining laws were more helpful for the development of American concerns than Norwegian. He wanted representations to be made to the Foreign Office as well as to Parliament. He needed the syndicate to have indisputable rights in Spitsbergen so as to encourage continued investment.

Correspondence with Keltie of the RGS alerted Bruce to official British reluctance to interfere with Spitsbergen. Such an involvement would result in trouble with 'all the three Powers: but she might do something to prevent Russia getting possession'.[59] Keltie suggested that Bruce approach Winston Churchill, then First Lord of the Admiralty. Churchill's reply was unhelpful. He wrote that there was no sound reason to consider annexation. (Churchill was to stick with this opinion, writing in 1917 that there was no naval reason to annex Spitsbergen; a formal annexation would require an armed force to safeguard the claim and to 'perfect' it, which would not, in itself, affect whatever possibility existed of the island being used by enemies.)

As Bruce had anticipated and feared, Norwegian claims in Spitsbergen increased after the Kristiania meeting. June 1914 saw a further conference on Spitsbergen's future. This time Great Britain was represented. No changes were made in the status quo because of the outbreak of war, but the underlying *terra nullius* remained a Scottish concern. Norway, Sweden, Russia or the USA might use the hiatus to develop their claims and so override the claims of the Scottish Spitsbergen Syndicate, which were, after all, only protected by claim boards and flags. Even if the war diverted the British authorities' attention, other countries might not be equally diverted.

Bruce's anxiety was underlined by claims on some of 'his' territory, particularly on Prince Charles Foreland. He noted that the Norwegians had named Mount Jessie as one of their boundaries and Nathorst Bay as another boundary. He said their claims were wrong He needed to get back. A small expedition was arranged for 1914. To fund the expense of this, the syndicate's capital was increased to £1,000[60]. The issue of preference shares – 100 shares issued at £10 each – raised this.

Three men – Bruce, J. V. Burn Murdoch and R. M. Craig, a geologist from the University of St Andrews – set out from Scotland. John H. Koeppern, a Scottish zoologist of German descent who paid for Bruce's travel expenses, met them at Bergen. The plan was for the geologists to make a survey of Stor Fjord from Ginevra Bay as far south as 76° 30'N, to look for any oil shale deposits, make soundings in the fjord and map uncharted islands. They did not achieve this plan. When they finally reached Green Harbour on 12 August 1914, the men heard (via the Norwegian wireless station) of Great Britain's declaration of war against Germany. Bruce met an old friend, Captain Staxrud of the Norwegian Army, in Green Harbour. Bruce wrote that Staxrud 'summed up the position with Norway in relation to the war, showing us that if Germany prospered in the campaign, in spite of Norway being most unwilling to take any part in the war, yet she might be compelled to side with Germany against Russia'.[61]

Bruce was desperate to return to Scotland, but he was in a difficult position. He was obliged, so as to defray expenses (and 'because I wanted to be in absolute command of the ship and give my skipper orders'),[62] to keep to a contract to deliver a cargo of fish and paraffin to the Russians at Green Harbour, and – probably to his dismay – coal to the German meteorological station at Cross Bay. This was problematic as the whereabouts of the German fleet in the North Sea was unknown, but he succeeded. The team managed to visit Prince Charles Foreland, where deposits on the rocks suggested iron ore (though it was unlikely to be of economic value), but no coal. The men noted also that Norway had made inroads into some of the Scottish syndicate's claims. They felt that there was absolutely no evidence that the Foreign Office had real concerns for British interests in the archipelago.

On his return Bruce immersed himself in the work of both the syndicate and the Oceanographical Laboratory. New maps of Spitsbergen were noted to contain inaccuracies and sometimes suspicious name changes[63] (Wyches Island to King Karl Island, Nordenskiöld Land to Nathorst Land, changes to the Greenland Sea, etc.).[64] He was particularly annoyed to find that some names on Prince Charles Foreland had been changed. This problem was finally sorted out with meetings with the Prince of Monaco and the surveyor John Mathieson. The names on the Foreland were left to Bruce.[65] After a careful study of reference books and consideration of those names that had been changed, Bruce reverted to the original names!

Scottish apprehensions were increased when a Swedish expedition of 1916 recorded that coal of good burning quality was present in deep deposits over an area of about 100 kilometres. Two areas in Spitsbergen were calculated to yield 3 million tons of coal.[66] By contrast, the Scottish Spitsbergen Syndicate still had had no return for its investment.

Bruce and J. V. Burn Murdoch visited Arthur Robert Hicks[67] of the RGS on 16 November 1916 and made a comprehensive presentation in relation to annexation of Spitsbergen. It was mentioned that British companies claimed about 4,000 square miles in Spitsbergen, which could be amalgamated with the American Coal Company at Advent Bay to make a block of territory that could be administered as a single unit; that the syndicate's claims, which had coal, oil shale, iron, gypsum and possibly gold, were vulnerable and needed protection; and that the previously abundant wildlife had been almost exterminated by hunters (mostly Norwegian). Russia was said to have attempted to purchase the American claims. Germany had made claims in Spitsbergen and had a high-altitude station and a wireless station there; finally, there was the suggestion that Britain had already claimed Spitsbergen in 1615. During the meeting, the presence of the Norwegian post office and wireless station was flagged up as well.

Hicks was impressed. He brought the matter before the council of the RGS, which offered support, and Foreign Secretary Sir Edward Grey (soon to be succeeded by Arthur Balfour)[68] was approached. But again there was little immediate government support, though the Foreign Office gave 'sympathetic' consideration to the request for British protection both from an economical and commercial point of view. It was said that British claims and protests would only be lodged *after* the war since Britain had entered the war as a protector of smaller nations. The annexation of Spitsbergen (except if Norway or Sweden actually sided with Germany) would be misrepresented and Spitsbergen's future could not be decided without consultation with several governments. For this, the timing (1916) was such that the matter could not be considered.

In fact, a decision not to annex the archipelago had probably already been made, based on discussions at the 1914 Spitsbergen conference.[69] The archipelago's future was to be decided eventually as an addendum to the Treaty of Versailles in 1918, when the major powers met at the end of the First World War to decide on the future of Germany, her allies and her dependents. The Spitsbergen Treaty was signed on 9 February 1920. Spitsbergen became part of the kingdom of Norway, but with special provision for the mining rights of foreigners.[70]

The syndicate lodged a formal protest with the Foreign Office immediately after the decision was announced and before the actual signing of the treaty. Reference was made again to previous assurances and frustration and indignation expressed that the syndicate had only read the outcome in the press. This was the result that Bruce had anticipated and feared. In late 1918 a Foreign Office official gave an interview to Bruce and Maples (Secretary of the Northern Exploration Company) and explained the dawning international consensus. Denmark would 'get' Schleswig (southern Jutland), Sweden would receive the Baltic Islands and Spitsbergen would become part of the Kingdom of Norway, given away without any consideration of its mineral wealth or strategic value, although under the treaty British 'rights' were reserved. In world politics British interests were focused on the east, in Mesopotamia and elsewhere. The British government had never had any intention in getting into a diplomatic row defending small companies in Spitsbergen whose output was virtually non-existent, especially not over an archipelago that it dismissed as being of no strategic importance.

As the war drew to a close, the prospects for financial gain from claims in Spitsbergen seemed to wax brighter, as shown by the increased price of rival companies' shares quoted on the stock exchange and a report in the *Times* of piles of iron.[71] In the autumn of 1918, J. V. Burn Murdoch, who was more business-minded than Bruce, began to agitate for fundamental change. He contrasted the performance of the Scottish syndicate with that of the Northern Exploration Company, which was listed on the stock exchange and whose share price was benefitting greatly. He wrote on 21 September to Alfred Aitkin, the company secretary, saying that neither Bruce nor Rudmose Brown were businessmen. 'Their legal and general knowledge is not exactly what is needed to cope with the present golden opportunity. With a fairly large number of shareholders and a quotation on the stock market we would be in a much better position than the little provincial syndicate that we are at the present.'[72] It clearly was a golden opportunity, and Bruce agreed, writing on 26 September that 'Northern Exploration Company shares (face value 10s) are now 47/6s and it is now time for the Scottish Spitsbergen Syndicate to be in the field'.[73] Bruce also recognised his limitations, writing to Rudmose Brown on 15 October that 'it will probably be wise of me to resign as chairman of the board if we can get a man like Leslie Usher to replace me or a prominent Glasgow businessman. I am not a businessman myself.'[74]

So on 8 January 1919 the syndicate met to consider a scheme of reconstruction. The (present) company was wound up and its assets transferred to a new company,[75] to be formed with the same name but now changed from a prospecting company to a prospecting *and mining* company with a nominal capital of £100,000 made up of 10,000 shares of face value £10 each. The reconstruction documents stipulated that £30,000 should be raised to meet the costs of an expedition that would take place in the spring of 1919. But although a float on the stock exchange was planned, the company initially remained private, and limited to a maximum of fifty shareholders who were approached for funds.

Bruce wrote to friends asking them to subscribe to the expanded syndicate, which aimed to carry out a detailed survey of the commercial value of the claims with a view to further development.[76] The response was slow: £26,390 had been raised by June 1919, requiring that the expedition costs be reduced.

It may seem remarkable that any backers could be found for another expedition to Spitsbergen, over which so much political uncertainty hung, but the Scots had invested money, enthusiasm and support in the syndicate over the years and hoped that this time they might secure their investments – they did not want to 'spoil the ship for a ha'penny worth of tar'. However it was clear that no further calls could be made in the foreseeable future from the small group of current shareholders. Thus, in August 1919, in order to raise more funds, the company became public and offered 85,000 shares at £1 each on the London Stock Exchange.[77] Bruce stood down as director; the new directors were businessmen, with the exception of William Gordon Burn Murdoch. The syndicate of 1919 now seemed healthy and its future relatively bright.

The new company's expedition was one of the largest to visit Spitsbergen. The prospectus was an ambitious catch-all proposal. It included rights to develop the syndicate's land; to prospect for gold, silver, platinum, copper, iron, coal, gypsum[78] and (particularly) oil shale and free oil; to carry on whaling and fishing; to provide shipowners, hotel keepers, etc. with fish and game; and also to provide ships, boats and equipment.

The Treasury agreed to charter a sloop (a single-masted sailing boat) and provide coal,[79] but refused to fit out, insure or recondition the craft. No wonder the syndicate's secretary, Alfred Aitken, wrote that he could not understand the malign influence that seemed to dog Bruce in his dealings with the Foreign Office.

Bruce was in charge of the expedition, which set out in the summer of 1919 (Rudmose Brown was his deputy) with a large scientific and mining staff.[80] Bruce and Rudmose Brown received £600 and £500 respectively for their services. John Mathieson accepted the post of chief surveyor at £60 per month; other staff received smaller amounts. J. V. Burn Murdoch was senior geologist, and A. Flemming Campbell and George M. Cowen were the mining engineers. The accompanying party, too numerous to list in detail, included a surveyor, three other geologists and two naturalists.

Bruce led the Main Party. John Mathieson led the Advance Party, which landed on the eastern shore of Klaas Billen Bay and made surveys for coal in the Ebba Valley, Gips Bay, Gips Valley and an area south of the Nordenskiöld Glacier. A large-scale map of the Ebba Valley was made together with another of the region south of the Nordenskiöld Glacier. In two months, 80 miles of coastline had been surveyed and some valleys investigated as far as 10 miles inland. Claim boards were put up regularly whenever they were necessary. A number of 'illegal' claims were removed.

The main expedition departed from Tromsø on 22 July 1919. Sailing on *Petunia*, the party reached Prince Charles Foreland where a small prospecting party was landed to examine the land, rock formation (tertiary formation) and iron outcrops. *Petunia* then sailed through Ice Fjord in Spitsbergen to Klaas Billen Bay, anchoring on 29 July 1919. Here they met with Mathieson's advance party and the syndicate estates were revisited. A serious attempt at mining was made on syndicate property. Three boreholes were sunk under the supervision of Flemming Campbell, the mining engineer. The first borehole was near a group of houses ambitiously named 'Bruce City' (built to underline the syndicate's property rights and sited across of the Ice Fjord from Pyramiden). No coal was found. The second (discontinued) was south of the River Gerrit. The third was further inland; no coal was found at 50 metres when drilling was stopped, but when the riverbed was investigated a 9-inch seam was found at a depth of less than 2 metres. Campbell recommended further investigation and two bores were drilled in the riverbed near to bore number 3. Here coal was finally found. Drilling went on for over two months and samples were taken before boring was stopped at 117 metres.

'Bruce City' consisted of two prefabricated houses near to bore number one. Each carried the uncompromising text 'This house and contents are the property of the Scottish Spitsbergen Syndicate Ltd, 37 Queen St, Edinburgh. Please close the door.' Interestingly, to underline the point, Union Jacks (rather than the Saltire) were painted on the walls. Bruce City gave rise to the name of the Bruce City Coalfield. Two more houses were subsequently erected.

In all, the 1919 expedition made an extensive review of the syndicate's holdings, including Barents Island. Mathieson, the surveyor, had thought that large areas could be opened up and coal seams of 3 to 4 inches could produce a significant tonnage, but in reality the coal seams that were investigated were found to be thin. An analysis by a Mr Ernest Bury concluded that after washing and briquetting, their by-product yield was too low for them to be useful as coke or lighting gas, and that by comparison with the average British coal they were of poor quality[81]– the samples appeared to be commercially unviable.

Bruce also had had high hopes of finding shale oil. He knew there was a profitable market for oil in Russia, in spite of high import taxes.[82] But when geologists James Wordie and George Tyrrell and mining engineer George Cowen examined the spot at the foot of the Usher Glacier (on the east coast opening into Stor Bay), where Bruce and Hannay had been impressed by the reek of gas in 1909, they decided that the smell was due to the release of gas from bituminous rocks. No shale oil was found. Bruce's hopes died. On 1 September the ships returned to Advent Bay to coal. Campbell remained at Klaas Billen Bay and sunk bore number 6, again close to bore 3. No commercially useful coal seams were found.

In this expedition Bruce increased the company's holdings by 3,345 square kilometres, placed claim boards and laid claim to Bruce City Coalfield (backed up by the erection of the two houses), but the expedition was a commercial failure. Although there was coal in Spitsbergen, the areas claimed by the Scottish company did not include fields of sufficient yield for economic success. Further exploration would be prohibitively expensive. Funds were too low for a systematic examination of the hopeful coalfields to be undertaken, though Campbell continued to investigate bore 3. He concluded that there were two distinct coal horizons in the Klaas Billen area, and surveyor John Mathieson continued with his observations. Bruce City remained as it had been left in 1919.

Bruce's health deteriorated. He was admitted to hospital for an operation in December 1919, but there were also hints that he was suffering from mental as well as physical problems. The operation was for a hammertoe, a painful condition treated by a painful operation, but this does not explain his mental deterioration. However, Bruce admitted other problems when he wrote to Prince Albert to congratulate him on his granddaughter's wedding. Bruce said he had had an operation but that he had also suffered from more serious mental problems from which he was recovering. He does seem to have recovered temporarily, and actually visited Spitsbergen again in 1920, but the recovery was followed by a serious relapse.

Bruce's condition was finally stated unambiguously in a letter from Bruce's friend Alfred Aitken when he wrote to Arthur Hinks, secretary of the RGS, stating that 'Dr Bruce has had a nervous breakdown.'[83] Aitken was answering an enquiry from the RGS as to whether Bruce could be in London to receive the David Livingstone Centenary Medal.[84] This was to be a grand occasion, with the medal presented by the American Ambassador, but Aitken wrote that Bruce was in a nursing home under the care of a Professor Meakins. His mobility was not improving; any attempt to do a little more than on the previous day set him back. Aitken wrote that Bruce had 'quite broken down' when he learnt of the subject of the evening's lecture was 'The Future of Polar Research' and that he wanted his father (now aged eighty-six) and his sister to attend. Frank Debenham,[85] who would become the first director of the Scott Polar Research Institute, read the paper. Bruce's father and sister did attend and were interested, and surprised, spectators. Rudmose Brown accepted the medal on Bruce's behalf.

By late 1920, Bruce was bedridden. By 1921 he was too unwell to go on a smaller expedition to Spitsbergen. He would live just long enough to see the publication of the final volume of the scientific reports. He had always been a poor promoter of his cause, considering that scientific publications should stand on their own merits. He never understood the importance of popular interest, a point that Shackleton made to him and which Scott understood completely.

The syndicate continued until 1952, but without Bruce the driving force and leading enthusiast for Spitsbergen development was gone. The Norwegian government took over the company eventually in 1952. The British liquidator issued a statement to this effect, stating that a final distribution of assets at the rate of 0.8784p per share had been declared.

11

BRUCE'S FINAL ILLNESS AND DEATH: REFLECTIONS ON HIS LIFE

Bruce's health deteriorated sharply. He died in Liberton Cottage Hospital, Edinburgh, on 28 October 1921.

The death certificate (number 58), records William Spiers (*sic*) Bruce as aged fifty-four, a scientist, married to Jessie Mackenzie. The cause of death was listed as 'Arteriosclerosis, Softening of the brain'. The informant was Jessie Bruce of 'Antarctica', 17 Joppa Road, Portobello.[1]

On 2 November 1921, after a simple service, on the nineteenth anniversary of *Scotia* sailing from Scotland, Bruce's coffin, covered with a Scottish lion and St Andrew's cross and with a bunch of highland heather beside it, was conveyed to Glasgow for cremation.

His spirit and determination never left him. He requested that he be cremated and his ashes scattered in the South Atlantic at a high southern latitude, so as to draw attention to the need for further research in the area. On 2 April 1923, the magistrate of South Georgia, some of his officers and the manager of Messrs Salvesen's whaling station formally cast the ashes over the sea at latitude 54°S, longitude 36°W. The explorer had returned to the seas that he loved.

His loyal friend Rudmose Brown wrote Bruce's obituary in the *Geographical Journal*. Rudmose Brown praised Bruce's scientific work highly. He said that Bruce had suffered a long illness due to strain and overwork. In a letter to Dr Samuel Bruce he said that Bruce was a true friend; a man who never spared himself to help his colleagues and a man who never expected as much of them as of himself. He felt that Bruce had been a martyr to unselfish scientific devotion.[2]

An inventory of Bruce's assets was filed in Edinburgh Sheriff Court (Ref. SC70/1/675) on 15 February 1922. Pathetically, he had 3 shillings in cash in his possession. Assets in household furniture, medals and scientific instruments amounted to a little over £74, credit at the Commercial Bank of Scotland was £9 11s, and the balance at his accountants was just over £183. But he had a number of life insurances, war bonds and shares whose combined value totalled over £6,663.[3] The grand total of his estate was £6,714 8s 1d.

His will was registered on 8 November 1921, eleven days after his death. He made provision for his children but he did not entirely abandon Jessie, who was left the 'liferent' on Joppa Road (in Scottish law this is the right to receive the benefits of a property or other asset, owned by somebody else, for life, but without the right to dispose of that property or asset) and various assets therein. These assets included all the household furniture with the exception of 'my upright grand piano, which I direct my Trustees to store and hand over to my daughter, the said Sheila Mackenzie Bruce on her attaining majority'.[4] Jessie apparently did not abide by this and sold the piano promptly.[5]

His friends William Gordon Burn Murdoch and Thomas Leslie Usher of Edinburgh, along with his sister Helen Violet Bruce of London, the chartered accountant Thomas Whitson and the solicitor Alfred Aitken of Edinburgh, were appointed as trustees. Their duties were to continue until the children were twenty-one. In this way Bruce kept much of his financial assets away from his wife, and secured his daughter's education and his son's future in the merchant marine.

After her husband's death, Jessie emigrated to Australia. It is relevant that from then on her dependency on alcohol appears to have diminished. She remarried and worked again as a nurse. She died in 1942.

Eillium was left £1,500 ('payable on his attaining the age of twenty-one years complete, or in the discretion of my Trustees the age of twenty-five years complete').[6] He was nineteen when his father died and had joined the Merchant Navy aged fourteen. Many of the cadets in HMS *Worcester* rose to a high rank. Ultimately Eillium became a captain on a fisheries research vessel. He was made an officer in the Order of the British Empire (OBE) for his services during the Second World War. He died in 1969.

Sheila Mackenzie was twelve when her father passed away. She was left £1,500 pounds also, with the same conditions attached to her legacy as to Eillium's. She was sent to a boarding school in Hertfordshire, presumably chosen by her aunt. Moira Watson, Bruce's granddaughter, understands that Sheila ran away from school and was then sent to a finishing school in Switzerland. She trained as a secretary, married and moved to South Africa. After the Second World War she returned to England. When her husband died she moved to Merseyside. She died in the mid-1990s.[7]

Bruce left bequests also for his wife's sister Bella Mackenzie Tain, his sister Violet, Thomas Whitson and to the Royal Infirmary Edinburgh in recognition of the services he had received.[8] The capital on any residue of his estate was to be given to his children after his wife had died (again at the age of twenty-one, or, at the discretion of the trustees, twenty-five).[9]

Bruce's most enduring legacy lies with his work in the south. Because of his work on Laurie Island we now have well over a century of continuous meteorological, geomagnetic and sea-ice information, by far the longest run of data from anywhere within the Antarctic. This is a crucial resource for climate change studies.

His comprehensive meteorological recordings led to an understanding that conditions in one area, in this case the Weddell Sea, can affect far-off meteorological conditions, namely the rainfall in South America. The meteorologist of the *Scotia* expedition, Robert Mossman, concluded in 1909 that when there was a low pressure in the Weddell Sea and the South Orkneys, the winter rainfall over the lower part of Chile and the greater part of the Argentine Republic would be below average; when there was high pressure in the Weddell Sea and South Orkneys, the rainfall in South America would be above average. This was illustrated by the height of the River Parana in central South America, which rose and fell in sympathy with the barometric pressure in the Orkneys in the previous months.[10]

Bruce wanted his *Scotia* expedition to coordinate results with other expeditions that were heading south in the early 1900 – ships from Germany and Sweden as well as the UK. This ambition was undoubtedly an inheritance from his teachers in Edinburgh, particularly Patrick Geddes, a man committed to a holistic approach to the environment, which concludes that every part of a problem interconnects and is explicable only by reference to the whole problem, a suggestion remarkably supported by weather patterns over the South Atlantic. International coordination was Bruce's early dream as a scientist. He aimed at cooperation between observatories in South America, the Falklands and the South Orkneys and it was this ambition to achieve a coordinated network that was his main drive to offer the Laurie Island Observatory to Argentina. He believed that Argentina would be a major beneficiary of the regional network of observatories, as Robert Mossman (who subsequently joined the Argentine Meteorological Service) amply confirmed. This dream was fulfilled and the development of a network of stations in the south has made Bruce, it can be said, the father of the modern coordinated observatories in Antarctica.

As regards the broader geopolitical importance of Laurie Island, in 1904 Bruce had not actually reached a definite conclusion – in January

Haggard wrote, 'In conversation with Mr Bruce, he seemed to me not to have made up his mind whether they were likely to be of any use whatever to Great Britain or no'.[11] Whatever his musings on the island's long-term general usefulness, Bruce would never have anticipated that the Argentine government would designate one of their personnel as postmaster on the island, that a stamp would be issued stating that the South Orkneys base was an integral part of Argentina, or that the Argentine flag would be raised when *Scotia* left the islands. So it is a matter of speculation whether Bruce gave consideration to the possible long-term geopolitical implications of his decision. It would not have been his intention to bequeath the diplomatic impasse that festers today. He simply aimed at continuing valuable scientific work. It was the government that made an error of judgement in not collectively recognising the potential value of Laurie Island to the British Empire early enough and in not defending its position with sufficient vigour. The decision showed a lack of foresight for which the government blamed itself later (as illustrated by the government official's comments some years later that 'Mr Round's chickens are now coming home').[12] The outcome has influenced policy in the South Atlantic throughout the twentieth century; the continued operation of the British Antarctic Survey base on Signy Island (an island near Laurie Island in the South Orkneys archipelago) is a direct consequence of this decision.

In relation to his achievements, Bruce was a poor self-publicist. He never understood the need to stimulate wide, popular interest. He would have done much better with fundraising if he had started his reports by publishing the *Log of the* Scotia (recording the highs and lows, the problems and successes of the expedition), but he insisted on publishing the section on physics first, a subject unlikely to engender a popular following. So the *Scotia* expedition never gripped the popular imagination as Scott's and Shackleton's did. The voyage tended to be overlooked by contemporary observers, and when *Scotia* returned in

1904 the expedition got neither praise nor publicity from the RGS. When Sir Clements wrote later that the main object of the expedition seemed to have been deep-sea sounding, his comments diminished the value of the expedition's work and lessened its lasting impression.

A further problem in garnering support from scientific colleagues may have related to the fact that after he gave up his medical training, Bruce did not achieve any further scientific qualification. In late Victorian/early Edwardian days it was still possible to be a 'gentleman' scientist (as was shown by Patrick Geddes and John Murray), but this deficiency may have been reflected in how he was viewed by the broader scientific establishment when he sought academic positions. It may also have dented his own self-esteem and fuelled the somewhat abrasive approach he employed with the 'great and good' in learned societies such as the Royal Society.

As an idealistic youth Bruce's interest in a Scottish national identity developed slowly but forcibly. During his years in Scotland he became increasingly pro-Scottish, and resentful of the London authorities. Much of his resentment was fuelled by his lack of insight into the workings of the British government and this in turn funnelled itself into fiery Scottish allegiance. However, his intentions were always peaceable. He wanted Scotland to be a nation proud of her Celtic tradition, an equal rather than a subservient partner to England. But though he used Scottish politicians to make his case he does not appear to have embraced Freemasonry, unlike Scott and Shackleton, who were both members of the Navy lodge. Again, unlike his polar contemporaries, he never attempted to go over the heads of senior officials at the Treasury by cultivating senior ministers in the government. Nor did he engage in lobbying the London establishment, on the contrary blaming the establishment for his lack of success. All of this will have shaped the response to his demands for support. When he really needed help with the *Scotia* results, his relatively modest demands were turned down at a time when the government provocatively (as far as he was concerned) awarded large sums to his fellow explorers, Shackleton with his debts from the *Nimrod* and Scott with funds for his second expedition. But it must be emphasised again that Bruce's ambitions were scientific. He retained a sense of loyalty to the British monarchy, empire and constitution.

He was a man who focused on his work. He was persistent, intense, determined; his main concentration was clearly on his scientific aims, though he did plunge into some community appointments such as the zoo and the Scottish Ski Club with total involvement. But he was often tactless, and unable to compromise or back down. He was reserved, had poor communication skills and, seemingly, a lack of awareness of non-verbal signs. He was unbending; once he felt he had been slighted he would never forget the slight. In this context he firmly believed that Sir Clements Markham had maliciously blighted his career, though in fact there is no evidence that this was the case. Markham was undoubtedly difficult and quite uninhibited in recording in his journal his opinions (good or bad) of people he had met. It is telling, therefore, that Markham only mentions Bruce three times from the mid-1890s until his death in 1916 and these comments are short and neutral. It is likely that Markham did not see Bruce as a serious competitor to his protégé Scott and disregarded him. Bruce's permanent antagonism should be seen a manifestation of his persona.

Making a retrospective diagnosis is always difficult, but it seems that Bruce exhibited characteristics in his behaviour which would now be considered as being part of an autistic spectrum disorder. This suggestion is based on Bruce's difficulties in social communication, social interaction and social imagination. He had a highly focused range of interests, was obsessive about his work, had a low tolerance for mistakes, excellent visual skills, a dogged persistence in following a single project. He had a collecting mania, keeping every scrap of paper he received. [13]

Professor Rudmose Brown published his book on Bruce, *A Naturalist at the Poles*, in 1923. The work is a celebration of Bruce's life by a loyal companion, but even Rudmose Brown acknowledged Bruce's stubbornness, irrepressible critical facility, spiky sensitivity and poor lecturing skills[14] – Rudmose Brown was also concerned (rightly) that Bruce was liable to be misjudged in relation to his continued and increasing emphasis on Scottish patriotism, the Scottish Oceanographical Laboratory and the Scottish Spitsbergen Syndicate.[15] Rudmose Brown said that writing the book 'was no easy task; neither Jessie Bruce nor Bruce's father and sisters could help',[16] but he felt he was the right person to do it.

However, even Rudmose Brown, with all his loyalty and sympathy, admitted that he had not truly penetrated Bruce's reticence and reserve. He wrote that Bruce never fully confided in him. He commented that 'there seemed to be a barrier that no man and certainly no woman ever crossed' and that 'he seldom if ever spoke of his family and childhood, rarely of his private concerns, and never of his philosophy of life'.[17] This suggests that Bruce was encased in his own determined, introspective persona. Although he engendered loyalty in a small number of colleagues, for example Rudmose Brown, Pirie and Mossman, none of them became intimate friends. It could be said that he had no such friends, though when he hand-wrote letters to Ferrier he would begin, 'My dear James'. Ferrier was the only person he seems to have addressed regularly by his Christian name. It appears rather that his close colleagues respected him for his work and felt protective towards him, particularly Rudmose Brown.

He was argumentative – after the *Scotia* expedition Mossman wrote to Mill at the RGS saying, 'I hear Bruce has had a row with Keltie. I do not know what about but I think it is a great pity that he should "fall out" with so many people. Even when one is slighted it is just as well to keep quiet. If a man is doing good work and he is respected he is bound to come out on top sooner than later.'[18] This was a prescient comment. It seems that Bruce was 'argumentative' quite frequently (see appendix 6 for a typical example of this single-minded and argumentative attitude), and certainly he must have offended many people in his lifetime – he offered no words of regret over the deaths of Scott's party and was objective over Ramsay's death. These aspects of his personality, along with his strong nationalistic sympathies, certainly contributed to his not getting as much support as he might have done, and contributed to him being misjudged and his significant scientific achievements being somewhat overlooked.

Bruce's extreme reticence must have made his married life with Jessie very difficult. It might be said that a man with Bruce's personality should never marry, and Bruce's inherent focused and isolationist traits must have created great strain within his family. The effort of keeping up appearances must also have been great. His ultimate deterioration and 'softening of the brain' may have been exacerbated by concomitant depression.

Bruce's death certificate stated that he had suffered from arteriosclerosis. This is a build-up of fatty plaques in the walls of arteries which reduces the blood flow to organs, in this case the brain, which may result in dementia, personality changes, mobility problems, depression and an inability to live independently. Vascular dementia can develop quickly, and Bruce's deterioration seems to have been rapid. He was incapable of independent living, could not walk, his personality changed and he broke down on occasions. As no post-mortem appears to have taken place, the death certificate diagnosis remains speculative. Bruce could have suffered from a number of problems (such as a brain tumour, dementia with Lewy Bodies,[19] or infection); the important point is that he rapidly and unexpectedly deteriorated at a relatively early age.

His legacy should be considered not only for his remarkable scientific achievements in the Antarctic and the Arctic, but also for his impact on Anglo-Argentine relations.

His observatory on Laurie Island has been in continuous operation for 114 years (in 2017). This is the longest-running observatory in the entire Antarctic by well over forty years,. His ambitions that the observations would continue forever have been amply fulfilled, though the act of inviting the Argentine Meteorological Service to take on the Laurie Island Observatory set in train a complex diplomatic two-step between Argentina and Britain that continued unabated until the signing of the Antarctic Treaty in 1959. The fallout still continues, rendered yet more complex by their perception in the official mind as being closely entwined with counter-claims to the Falkland Islands. Bruce's actions inadvertently resulted in his most significant and long-lasting impact, leading as they did to the permanent occupation of Antarctica by the British government in 1944[20] and contributing to governments being forced, in the late 1950s, to make serious efforts to secure an effective international arrangement to govern the continent. Out of this came the outstandingly successful Antarctic Treaty, whose focus on science can surely be seen as part of Bruce's legacy and something he would have whole-heartedly applauded.

His Arctic and Antarctic collection in the Scottish Oceanographical Laboratory should have been the basis for an internationally recognised laboratory. Here he was ultimately defeated by world events. His hopes, when agreement had been reached for such a laboratory in Edinburgh University, were demolished by the outbreak of the First World War.

In Spitsbergen, one of his hopes has been comprehensively vindicated: oil has been discovered below the seas around the archipelago and an oil rush looms. Importantly in relation to this, the Spitsbergen Treaty of 1920 runs out in 2020. This will undoubtedly add to the existing diplomatic complexity in the Arctic. But he would have rejoiced over the Svalbard Global Seed Vault near Longyearbyen. The vault preserves a huge number of plant seeds, duplicates of seeds held in gene banks worldwide, with the idea of insuring against loss of seeds in existing gene banks due to regional or global crises.

Bruce was a complex man, sometimes hard to warm to, and hobbled in his achievements by his withdrawn personality, possibly autistic tendencies and emphasis on Scottish nationalism, which must have been counter-productive. His grievances about what he perceived as unfair prejudice on the part of the British government made him unable to see the bigger picture. Had he been able to sell his ideas, book rights, films and photographs of the *Scotia* expedition to the waiting world (as did Shackleton and Scott) he would have received far greater recognition, but he did not and so he was to a great extent ignored by the general public. Perhaps his greatest achievement is what he did accomplish in spite of (or because of)[21] these handicaps.

During his lifetime Bruce received many awards from scientific societies: the Gold Medal of the Royal Scottish Geographical Society, the Patron's Medal of the Royal Geographical Society,[22] the Neill Prize and Medal of the Royal Society of Edinburgh[23], the David Livingstone Centenary Medal, plus an Honorary LLD degree from Aberdeen University. In 1926, a memorial prize, the Bruce Memorial Prize, was created in his honour and awarded to the first recipient, Mr James Wordie (see appendix 7 for an account of how it came about and a list of recipients). In this century he has been further recognised for his scientific advances. An exhibition in Edinburgh, organised by Professor David Munro[24] in 2002, demonstrated and lauded Bruce's achievements. Further recognition came with the naming of a sea in the South Atlantic, the Scotia Sea, and from the polar research community, who named a laboratory in the British Antarctic Survey Research Station on Signy Island for Bruce in 2016, an event celebrated by his descendants.

In our judgement, Bruce was equal to, if not greater than, any of the other more famous names from the Heroic Era, if judged on his contribution to our understanding of the polar regions.

Appendix 1

CAPTAIN THOMAS ROBERTSON,
1855–1918

Captain Robertson was a man with whom Bruce never fell out. Bruce admired the captain's superb ice-navigation skills and his 'miraculous' ability to anticipate and avoid the numerous potential emergencies that *Scotia* encountered on her exploration to the south in 1903.

Thomas Robertson was born in Peterhead in 1855. His father and both his grandfathers were whaling captains, and from childhood he had a close association with the sea. His apprenticeship was served on a Peterhead merchant vessel trading with Australia and China, but on his return to England he decided to join the whaling and sealing industry. In this work he went to the Arctic, first as mate on the *Jan Mayen* of Dundee and then, at the age of twenty-four, as master of the *Polar Star*, in which role he made voyages to the seal and fishery grounds off East Greenland and the Davis Straits. These voyages gave valuable experience; the ships were sail driven – this was before steam was in general use on whaling ships – and the knowledge he gained in handling these sailing vessels through the iceberg-laden north was an invaluable asset when later he commanded ships with steam auxiliary power.

Bruce first encountered Robertson on the Dundee Whaling Expedition to the Antarctic of 1892–93. Bruce sailed as surgeon/naturalist on

Balaena, one of five whalers going south in search of right whales. Robertson was captain of one of the smaller ships, the *Active*. Bruce was accompanied on the expedition by his friend and fellow student Burn Murdoch. When Burn Murdoch wrote a book, *From Edinburgh to the Antarctic*, criticising the captain for the few opportunities allowed for scientific work on the expedition, Robertson wrote a defence. He said that it was difficult for the 'passengers' to be aware of the petty tyrannies imposed on a whaling captain.

The two men met again in the summer of 1897. Bruce was a scientist on the Franz Josef expedition when Captain Robertson, now captain of *Balaena* and on a whaling sortie, visited the archipelago. The meeting led to Robertson being later appointed as captain of the *Scotia* in 1902 when his skill in avoiding getting trapped in the polar ice was pivotal. His plan to avoid the ice that swept up from the south-west of the Weddell Sea by sailing eastwards to the north of the ice edge became a benchmark for later expeditions. His contribution to the success of the *Scotia* expedition was readily acknowledged by Bruce.

He was naturally ambitious to further his career. At this time Shackleton was secretary of the Royal Scottish Geographical Society. Robertson wrote to him in October 1904:

Lieutenant Shackleton RNR

Edinburgh

Dear Sir

As I was in command of the ship of the Scottish Antarctic expedition I would esteem it as a great honour if your society would make one a fellow. I did some work in the Antarctic some years ago and I think that an FRGS would help one in getting charge of some expedition where I would have a chance of doing some geographical work in the future.

Trusting you will lay my request before your council I am yours faithfully, Thomas Robertson.[1]

At their meeting on Thursday 20 October 1904, the RSGS council awarded the society's silver medal to Captain Robertson upon the return of the *Scotia*. Bruce was awarded the Gold Medal. The council also approved Robertson's Fellowship of the Royal Scottish Geographical Society.

Following the Antarctic expedition it was planned that *Scotia* would see further use by the universities of Scotland as a research vessel; however, it became necessary to sell her to recoup some of the expedition costs, and she and Robertson were reunited as Robertson sailed her as a sealer and whaler off the Greenland coast. On 15 February 1913 she was requisitioned (still under Robertson's command) by the Board of Trade for use as a weather ship on the Grand Banks of Newfoundland in order to give iceberg warnings to shipping; for this a Marconi wireless was fitted, allowing communications with stations on the coast of Labrador and Newfoundland.

When members of Shackleton's *Nimrod* expedition were awarded the Polar Medal, Bruce submitted a request for the crew of *Scotia* to be similarly honoured. The request was refused by Edward VII. Another attempt was made in 1913 but the request was refused again by Edward's son, George V (see appendix 4 for more details). Bruce wrote[2] to Charles Price, Edinburgh MP and Bruce supporter, in August 1917, that 'Robertson was dying without his well won white ribbon! The Mate is dead! The Second Mate is dead!! the Chief Engineer is dead!!! everyone as good men as have ever served on any Polar Expedition yet they did not receive the white ribbon. Surely it can merely be treated as an omission by the King, the public need never know that King Edward ever considered the matter.'

The medal was not awarded.

But Robertson's reputation as an outstanding seaman is assured. He had a remarkable record; in nearly forty years of Polar work he neither lost a ship, nor a man. He was 'a man to ride the waters with'. In numerous emergencies, when a moment's hesitation could have resulted in disaster, his natural gifts as an ice pilot were complimented by an intuition that on occasions seemed miraculous.

Appendix 2

EXCERPTS FROM THE LOG OF THE SCOTIA BY WILLIAM SPEIRS BRUCE[1]

Sailing South

February 2 1903. – Lat. 60°28' S.; long. 43°40' W

A course in west-north-west direction was steered for about thirty miles in fog until 11.40 A.M. when we pushed into the pack and proceeded in a more or less southern direction. For the officers and nearly all of the crew of the Scotia as well as for myself, this was no new experience, but except for Wilton, none of the scientific staff had seen ice before. The whole working of the ship through the ice, and the wonders of this new world, were therefore to them of intense interest. As the wind was blowing, and the swell was running into the ice from the open sea, a tight sea-bar had been formed over which the seas were breaking and the effect of the swell was felt well into the ice. Great blocks many weighing several hundred tons, rolled, tossed, and crashed into each other.

March 26 – Scotia Bay Lat. 60°44' S.: long. 44°39' W

What a peaceful night and how restful this morning, lying comfortably at anchor in the head of the new-found harbour, which I have named Scotia Bay! This probably is the first time any ship had dropped anchor in the South Orkneys. As I have already said, we were disappointed in not finding anchorage either in Spence or Elleson Harbour and indeed Captain Robertson didn't expect to find any harbour here or elsewhere. He called the Orkneys an ugly-looking group as we were approaching them from the south-east. He was by no means so sanguine as I was that in this fine bay a suitable place might be found. But we tried, and here we are in a magnificent anchorage and in as good a situation as could be for a magnetical and meteorological station.

May 1903
Constructing the Meteorological Hut

Bruce had originally intended to spend the winter months north of the ice, but conditions in the Weddell Sea made this plan impossible and he and Captain Robertson returned to the South Orkneys, which they made their base from March to November 1903.

May 4 1903

The house building continues. The wall, up to the level of the new door, is finished: we are rebuilding the inner portion of the east wall, south of the window. The stones we used were mostly the debris of the hard grey-wacke cliffs of Church Hill, that overhang The Beach to the westward, between Jessie and Scotia Bays. These stones varied in size from 2 or 3 cwt. to 20 or 30 lb., and were bound together by an obstinate tough, hard, and almost unfracturable interstitial matrix of ice. Pick after pick was destroyed in this heavy work, and the solid Omond House and monumental central cairn will be long standing memorials of the energy and perseverance of the crew of the Scotia. I never heard a murmur, and the crew were encouraged the more when they found that their officers and the scientific staff, who had been mostly unaccustomed to this hard manual work, were ready on every special occasion to work side by side with them, and vie with them in doing the work as willingly and well as they did.

Bruce realized that the South Orkneys were in a good position between South American and South African Observatories. The winter was spent in disciplined scientific observations.

August 25

The dredge contained a nudibranch, many entomostraca and small mollusca chaetopods zephyreans and two worms, sea –spiders, bryozoa, and two yellow star-fish. The trap (13) contained only a few cushion-stars. I finished the Giesbrecht net, and flensed the Lobodon for its skin (No.16) The old anchor was taken up to replace the patent new one, and was fixed up. We put over five floats in Jessie Bay, which is all open water with only very thin pancake ice. The mean temperature was 44°F to-day, with squally southerly and south-westerly winds, and overcast or foggy weather. Only one snowy petrel and one black-backed gull were seen to-day, all birds having vanished with the frost.

Bruce was determined that his scientific work should continue after his expedition had returned to Scotland. He decided to offer the observatories on Laurie Island to the Argentine authorities when he went to Buenos Aires for refuelling.

December 25, 1903 to January 21, 1904

My trials had only begun, and we were not to sail from Buenos Aires for another month. The funds of the expedition were exhausted, and I was only able to keep things going by a few subscriptions sent out by friends. The first to arrive was a welcome £100 from my old college friend the Balaena *Antarctic artist W. G. Burn Murdoch. Except Mr Ferrier and*

Excerpts from The Log of the Scotia by William Speirs Bruce [1]

Mr Whitson at home, and myself in Buenos Aires, no one knew what an anxious time I was having and even these two could not realize what a wretched time it was, fighting our way through a prolonged dock strike, during which the authorities had to keep a guard of marines to protect the ship from molestation. One thing was certain, that at all costs I must get back again to the South Orkneys, even if I dismissed half the crew and mortgaged the ship. Mossman and four other Scotia men were there, and must be relieved and provided with more stores if they were to winter. So I wired urgent appeals home for more money, while Ferrier, Whitson and others backed up those appeals The result was successful ... This not only secured the relief of Mossman's party but another season's work in still higher latitudes, during which we were rewarded by adding greatly to our previous year's exploration of the sea and also by the discovery of the coastline of the Antarctic continent, 500 miles further north than it had been previously been believed to exist. The land I have called Coats Land, in grateful appreciation of not only the munificent support of Mr James Coats, Junior, and his brother, Major Andrew Coats, but also for their continued interest in the expedition from beginning to end.

In the meantime in Buenos Aires I had got in touch with Dr Francisco Moreno, donor and Director of the La Plata Museum and with Mr W. G. Davies, Director of the Argentine Meteorological Office, as well as Señor (Escalante), Minister of Agriculture and they accepted my proposal, with the sanction of President Roca, that the Argentine Republic should take over the Meteorological and Magnetic Station I had set up in Scotia Bay, and which I had left in charge of Mossman. My offer included passing over free of cost the houses and stores I had already landed at Scotia Bay, and taking down with me, passage free, four Argentines and additional coal and stores for the station. If Mossman was willing, I was given leave to appoint him head of the observations under the Meteorological Office of the Argentine Republic ... Thus I was able to secure the continuance of the Meteorological and Magnetic Observatories started by the Scotia *and it is pleasing to relate that up to the present time (1912) the Argentine Republic are still continuing, uninterruptedly, for the tenth year, these observations, which have already proved not only of scientific but also of great economic value.*

January 21, 1904

Eventually on January 21, 1904, we set sail. The great heat we experienced in Buenos Aires so soon after our wintering in the Antarctic greatly told on our health: and the plague of flies, especially on board the Scotia, *which lay not far off the cattle-boats and sheds, made us ill, and the crew, I regret to say, especially suffered. I often wished that I had money enough to put most of them ashore at the sailor's home. All of us were almost continually victims to diarrhoea, which greatly weakened us, and we were heartily glad to get away to sea again to recuperate.*

New Land, Which Bruce Named Coats Land

March 6 – Coats Land. Lat. 73°30' S,: long. 21°28'W.

After lying all night, we started steaming slow at 5 A.M. endeavouring to go on a south-south-west course, and making about a south-west course. A stream of ice diverted us at one time to a north-westerly course, but we got more southerly on rounding the point of it ... At 8 A.M. we were nearer the ice face, having crossed a bight to the east-north-east. The ice-face then bore east-south-east and east-north-east, with the ship's head south ... There were many flat-topped bergs here at 9 A.M.; at that time at the masthead I counted sixty-six of large size. Two were about a mile long, and more than half a dozen were over a quarter of a mile long. None of them were, I think, over 100 feet high, and most of them probably rather less, but it is very difficult to judge ... We now steered across this bay in a south-south-east direction, and prepared to take a sounding. When we neared the ice-face we steered a south-westerly course keeping about three miles off it, and here I took photographic and cinematographic records; Willie also made drawings. The light was very bad, however, though bright, there being a vague glare without shadows. At 1.30 P.M. I sounded, and struck a rocky bottom with 159 fathoms, securing a sample and temperature of water at that depth, I did not expect less than 300 fathoms. We were at that time 4800 yards off the ice-face – a distance that we could not have accurately determined without a range finder, since dense and heavy pack-ice barred us from getting nearer, and the lines of the ice-face and glacier are so ill-defined. At this time (1.40 P.M.) I saw what appeared to be irregular hills at the back of the rising glacier, between east-north-east and north-east, which merged into the clouds. Captain Robertson, Mr Davidson and Dr Pirie also believed these to be hills.

James Ross had recorded a sounding of 4,000 fathoms in the Weddell Sea – the mystical deep – Bruce had never believed this reading, and disproved it on his own expedition.

March 23 – Lat. 68°32'S. long.12°49'W

... At 8 A.M. MacDougall reported an appearance of land, which I also saw. It looked remarkably like land, with the loom of land over it; it bore north by east to north-north-east. The appearance lasted a considerable time, and then the clouds thickening and becoming lower, it vanished. The sounding we got was against it, viz. 2660-deeper than yesterday. By chronometer and dead reckoning but without a meridian altitude, we were within two miles of Ross's sounding of 4,000 fathoms no bottom – which is thus disproved.

Near the End of the *Scotia* Voyage
April 19 – Lat.48°57'S.; long. 8°13'W

... The tempestuousness of the weather and the sea during this time may be better realized by my quoting from the log of Mr John Fitchie, mate of the Scotia.

We carried this type of weather with us almost without a break from 65°S to 40°S, that is through 25 degrees of latitude, or fully 1,500 miles during twenty-three days, viz. from March 28 to April 20. Sounding during intervals when it was less violent, and on these occasions trawling successfully in water respectively of 2103, 1332, and 1742 fathoms south of 48°S. These operations were conducted with the greatest possible difficulty, and not without accidents and loss of much gear, and would have been impossible had we not learnt from hard experience during the last two seasons. I do not believe that any ship had previously attempted to undertake such operations under such difficult and even dangerous conditions of weather and sea. Except Ross's one sounding, no one had attempted to even take a sounding, much less trawling in deep water south of 40°S. between the longitudes of South America and South Africa before the departure of the Scotia. *I therefore risked loss of valuable gear, especially as we were homeward bound, and the results of our efforts has been to show that the game was worth the candle, for these operations revolutionized all previous ideas of the South Atlantic Ocean.*

Appendix 3

PLANS FOR A TRANS-ANTARCTIC JOURNEY

It was not Ernest Shackleton who first conceived the idea of a Trans-Antarctic expedition; it was William Speirs Bruce who started planning such a journey in 1908 to confirm that there was a continent to be crossed. This was well before Shackleton got home from his *Nimrod* expedition. Bruce made his plans public in April 1908, and they were covered by *The Times*.[1]

A New Scottish Antarctic Expedition

Reuter's Agency is informed that Dr William S. Bruce of the Scottish Oceanographic Laboratory, who returned from a journey to the Arctic last autumn, is now planning a new Scottish expedition to the Antarctic. Dr Bruce suggests following and extending the deep sea investigations made by the Scotia in the South Atlantic, Weddell and Biscoe Seas. The work, mainly oceanographic, is divided into three parts; first a thorough investigation of the South Atlantic Ocean and islands south of 40deg. South; secondly, similar investigations in the Weddell and Biscoe Seas, including the mapping out of the limitations of those seas by the coastline of Antarctica; and thirdly, to investigate the lands adjacent to the Weddell and Biscoe Seas and to make an attempt to cross the Antarctic Continent. Dr Bruce estimates that an expedition fitted out with one ship of about 250 tons register and 36 men, including six men of science, would cost some £40,000. Additional funds, including the cost of a second ship, would be required to carry out efficiently the project for the exploration of the land. It is estimated that the expedition would last more than two years.

Bruce received enthusiastic backing but no promise of funds from the RSGS at its meeting on 16 November 1909.[2] In October of that year he sought support from the government for his plan, before he had secured any significant funding from private sources.

Below is a letter from Bruce to Prime Minister Asquith dated 22 October 1909:

Herewith I have the honour to enclose a pamphlet reprinted from the Official Publication of the Royal Scottish Geographical Society, viz 'the Scottish Geographical Magazine' for April 1908, which outlines a plan for a British Antarctic Expedition to be organised in Scotland.

The special objects of this expedition are briefly:

i) Extensive Oceanographical research in the Weddell and Biscoe Seas, and general circumpolar Oceanographical research.

ii) The crossing of the Antarctic Continent from the Atlantic Ocean to the Pacific Ocean across the South Pole.

A map is herewith enclosed shewing (sic) the intended route across the Continent by way of the South Pole.

The President and Council of the Royal Scottish Geographical Society have expressed their hearty approval of the project, and have instructed a committee to consider and recommend how the Society can best help to carry the project through.

I am already known as a Polar Explorer having taken part in seven Arctic and two Antarctic Expeditions since 1892. In five of these I was leader, notably in the Scottish National Antarctic Expedition of 1902–1904, in recognition of which I received the Gold Medal of the Royal Scottish Geographical Society and other honours.

Fully Fifty Thousand Pounds (£50,000) is required to fit out this important Expedition and I beg to ask His Majesty's Government to consider the claims of this British Expedition by giving a grant towards its outfit. [3]

Although this letter was accompanied by a more detailed description of the proposed expedition, it is startling in its brevity, lack of detail or list of notable figures offering their support. There is no breakdown of how the figure of £50,000 it arrived at, how much of it is being asked of the government, and what any grant would actually be spent on. It is also at best economical with the truth in claiming leadership of five expeditions! Unsurprisingly, the government's response was quick (dated 5 November) and to the point:

The First Lord of the Treasury has laid before the Board your letter of 22nd ultimo requesting His Majesty's Government to consider the claims to a grant from public funds of an expedition to be organised in Scotland for the purposes of Antarctic exploration.

In reply I am directed to inform you that they regret to be unable to submit to Parliament a Vote for assistance to this enterprise. [4]

Bruce's approach to the government must be seen in context: Scott was in the process of raising money for his second expedition and received a grant of £20,000 from the government in early January 1910. This incensed Bruce, as can be seen from the following letter, which appeared in *The Scotsman* on 10 January (page 10) and *The Times*, published on

11 January. Although it is not actually signed by Bruce, but by his close colleague Ferrier, it obviously has Bruce's fingerprints all over it:

SCOTTISH ANTARCTIC ENTERPRISE
TO THE EDITOR OF THE TIMES
Sir, – I should be much obliged if you would publish the enclosed letter, which is an answer to a letter from Dr. William, S. Bruce to the Prime Minister, asking if a Government grant might be expected towards the equipment of an Antarctic expedition then being organised in Scotland, and thus enable me to ask publically why Dr. Bruce should be refused a grant in November which Captain Scott is given in January. No one appreciates the work of Captain Scott more than Dr. Bruce and myself, and no one is more pleased that his enterprise should be supported by the British Government; but why should the same support be refused to Dr. Bruce, and why has there been throughout persistent refusal on the part of the Government to recognise Scottish Antarctic enterprise, while it showers money and honours on those doing similar, but in no way better, work in England?

I may mention that the Royal Scottish Geographical Society have recently promised to give Dr. Bruce their official support. In doing so the president, Professor James Gelkie, F.R.S., said that 'no one was better fitted to carry such an enterprise to a successful conclusion, and he ventured to say that the scientific results he had obtained had not been surpassed in interest or importance by the work of any living explorer in high latitudes'. In the face of this opinion, which is the opinion of men of the highest scientific standing, not only in Scotland but also abroad, the refusal of a grant to the Scottish enterprise is an insult to Scottish geographical research and Scotland generally, and is quite on a par with the niggardly treatment successive Governments have shown towards Scotland.

The facts are these: Dr. Bruce publishes his plans in the Scottish Geographical Magazine in April 1908, and in the Standard, London, on

April 13, 1909. Dr. Bruce asks for Government support on October 22 1909, and is refused on November 5 1909. Captain Scott publishes his plans in the summer of 1909, and is promised a grant on January 6, 1910.

It has become a matter for the Scottish public to consider seriously, and in the forthcoming election to support only those candidates, irrespective of party – Unionist, Liberal, or Labour – who will faithfully promise to stand up for this and other Scottish rights.

Yours Faithfully,

JAMES G. FERRIER, Secretary,

Scottish Oceanographical Laboratory,

Surgeons Hall, Edinburgh, Jan. 8.[5]

The letter produced an editorial commentary in the same issue of *The Scotsman* praising the support given to Scott and Shackleton but going on to bemoan:

But what of the Scottish Antarctic, to which Mr J.G. Ferrier calls attention in a letter published elsewhere? The generosity with which the appeal of Captain Scott has been met serves to throw into stronger relief the shabby and neglectful manner in which Scotland's national enterprises, of this and of other kinds, are treated. Financial aid has been refused to Dr Bruce's expedition, notwithstanding that his scheme was laid under the eyes of the public more than a year earlier than that of Captain Scott, and that the gallant projector is able to support his application with a record of work done, both in the Arctic and Antarctic areas, which, in the words of Professor Geilkie, has not been surpassed in the interest and importance of the scientific results achieved by the labours of any living explorer in high latitudes. These labours have been hitherto directed to reaping solid scientific fruits rather than to achievements that strike the popular sense. But Dr Bruce's new scheme includes, in addition to a bathymetrical survey of the Antarctic area south of the Atlantic Ocean, an attempt to penetrate Poleward from Coats Land directly south of British South Africa. So that it could claim support not merely on account of the promise of valuable practical investigations in regions whose physical conditions have special bearing on climate and navigation under our flag, but as an auxiliary to other Antarctic enterprises to which help is being accorded out of the public purse. But this is an appeal on behalf of a Scottish enterprise, and it meets the usual, and in present circumstances the inevitable, fate of being pigeon-holes or dropped into the wastepaper basket.[6]

Letters in a similar vein appeared in *The Scotsman* on 11 January from A. G. Smith FRGS and on 13 January from Rudmose Brown. Smith opined:

Why Dr Bruce's petition was shelved in spite of priority and Captain Scott's was granted, we shall doubtless have explained one day. It might almost be prophesied that the explanation will lie in the distinction between 'British' and 'Scottish'. That explanation would serve as well as any other, however unsatisfactory it may be.[7]

Rudmose Brown emphasised:

Because he prefers to place the sensational attainment of a high latitude in a position secondary to scientific research, he has never met with that measure of recognition and honour in the public estimation which he has richly deserved.

In consequence, his treatment by Government denotes a policy which is as short-sighted in the interests of geographical science as it is unjust to Scotland.[8]

It appears that the editor of *The Times* contacted Keltie at the RGS for a view, producing the following response from Keltie on 13 January 1910:

With reference to the enclosed, there is no doubt that Dr Bruce is a very good man and has done very good work in scientific exploration in the past, but it is absurd of him and his friends to base his claims for a Grant from the Government on the plea that his proposed expedition is a Scotch one. So far as exploration goes, the only consideration of the Government ought to be the promotion of National scientific work, irrespective of whether the leader of the enterprise is English, Scotch or Irish.

Capt. Scott has already showed (*sic*) himself a thoroughly capable man, and his propose expedition is on broader and more National lines, it appears to me, than that proposed by Dr Bruce, and if it was a choice between the two, I do not see how the Government could avoid giving the preference to Scott. Moreover, Scott has had substantial support before he applied to the Government, and the Grant of £20,000 is after all, only a supplement to the subscriptions obtained from private sources. I should think, if Dr Bruce were able to come forward and show that he had equally substantial support for his proposed expedition, and if his plan had the approval of competent scientific men, then it might be fair for the Government to seriously consider his request for a Grant.

I hardly think it is necessary to publish the enclosed letter.[9]

But Bruce could not let the matter rest there, because on 25 January Keltie again replied to a letter from the editor of *The Times*, which presumably referred to a letter seemingly written by Bruce himself:

I doubt very much whether it would do Dr Bruce any good to publish the enclosed letter. I think he certainly deserves some consideration at the hands of the Government on account of the value of his scientific work which he did in the Antarctic, and the results of which it would be to the benefit of science to publish. But letters like that already published from Dr Bruce and the enclosed seem to me calculated to irritate any Government and defeat the purpose for which they are intended.

Dr Bruce is a very excitable man and has a great want of tact, otherwise I believe, he would have got what he wanted long ago. On the whole, it would no (*sic*) do him any good to publish the enclosed letter. Moreover it would fall quite dead at the present moment.[10]

There is no evidence from the *Times* archive that any further correspondence appeared on this subject in spring 1910 from Ferrier, Keltie or Bruce. But even then the matter did not rest as Bruce had made representations to Col H. W. Feilden, a noted soldier, Arctic explorer and Fellow of the RGS. The latter must have contacted Keltie, eliciting the following response on 28 January 1910:

Bruce has evidently been at you as he has been at a great many other people and trying all the papers in order to attract attention to his troubles. If he had been a man of more tact than he seems to possess he would have fared better probably. I may tell you confidentially, as a member of the Council that he would have been proposed for a medal last year – in fact, he was proposed for a medal last year, but he so irritated everybody by the way he behaved with reference to his expenses for a paper which he gave to us, that his name was withdrawn.

However, if you thought he really deserves a Medal, why not propose him for one of this year's medals? That incident I refer to, is over and forgotten, and his claim might very well be brought up. I send you the statement which was drawn up by Mill; that you might make some use of with any additional point that you think might be brought forward on his behalf.[11]

On 7 February 1910, Bruce wrote again to Keltie on this matter of competition, showing both the best and worst sides of his character:

I enclose a copy of a letter I am sending to Captain Peary which you may like to publish in the 'Journal'.

It is most important that Peary, Scott, & I should work hand in hand. Cooperation is essential for success, & by cooperation the work of one expedition will enhance that of the others besides its own.

I was very glad indeed to see that the Government had helped Scott, but I cannot understand their stupid boycott of Scottish Antarctic efforts. One would imagine that a Scottish expedition was not a British one, & that it was a crime to dare to organise an Antarctic expedition in Scotland.[12]

Keltie replied on 9 February:

Thanks very much for sending me a copy of your letter to Peary. I think you are right in what you say in the letter from you which I received this morning. Probably there is no harm in you writing to Peary as you have done, but I think it would be unwise to publish anything on the subject in the papers at present; it might lead to any angry correspondence which would do more harm than good.

It is a difficult matter, but Peary should not forget his own relations with Cook, and his objections to his interference in what he conceives to be his own peculiar sphere. However, this project evidently did not originate with Peary and he does not intend to go himself that is quite evident, but if asked for his advice by the Peary Arctic Club and the National Geographical Society, I do not see how he could very well object to give it. But the fact of the matter is, I doubt very much whether they will get the money in time to start this year, or perhaps even next year. Perhaps not at all. Moreover, as you know very well, it is a very different thing starting in from the Weddel (*sic*) Sea from starting from McMurdo Bay. So far as I can make out you get into Mountainous land at once, with no idea what is before you, and with a distance I suppose of 200 or 300 miles further to go than from the other side if you want to reach the Pole.

I hope you will be able to get the money for your own expedition. Personally I doubt whether it is advisable to write too many strong letters to the papers on the subject. If you want money from the Government there are other ways of going about it I think, that would be more effective than going at the matter through the press. Please consider all this confidential.[13]

Bruce continued to lobby and in March secured a special meeting of the RSGS to discuss his proposal. On 3 March 1910, he wrote to Hugh Robert Mill asking for his support at the meeting:

I am desired by the Council of the Royal Scottish Geographical Society to ask you if you could attend a meeting of the Society on the evening of March 17 which has for its object the promotion of the new Scottish Antarctic Expedition, and to ask if you would say a few words in support of the project on that occasion, The arrangement is that I give them an outline of the plans with lantern illustrations and that about half a dozen speakers who are authorities on the subject speak in support. Your special association with the history of Antarctic Exploration and the fact that you were the first one to support me in Antarctic research is the special reason of asking you to do this. I enclose an outline of the plans, which include reaching the South Pole, because they include crossing Antarctica from Atlantic to Pacific. Anything, however, in the nature of a Marathon race is not included in the programme.[14]

The special meeting of the RSGS was held on 17 March 1910, where Bruce presented his plans in detail and launched a national appeal for funds. The meeting received extensive coverage in the following morning's edition of *The Scotsman*.[15] Bruce was looking for significant contributions from Scottish individuals and enterprises, but still held on to the belief that if a significant sum was raised this way a government grant to cover the balance would be forthcoming. However, he not only had a serious

British competitor in Scott, whose expedition was funded, but he also had a German competitor in Wilhelm Filchner, whose aim was to do just what Bruce planned: a trans-Antarctic crossing from the Weddell Sea to the Ross Sea via the South Pole. The latter expedition set off in early May 1911 and spent the winter of 1912 trapped in the Weddell Sea before finally escaping in September of that year. Captain Peary was also rumoured to be planning an Antarctic expedition. In May 1910 the Scottish Patriotic Association passed a resolution condemning the government which it sent by letter to Asquith on 4 May 1910. The resolution read as follows:

In view of the fact that Treasury Grants amounting to £139,000 have been made or promised to recent and projected Antarctic Expeditions sailing from England, the Scottish Patriotic Association regards as entirely inadequate the reported grant of £3000 in aid of publication of the scientific records of the Antarctic Expedition which sailed from Scotland under the Leadership of Dr William S. Bruce F.R.S.E. The weightiest testimony has been given to the practical value of the work of the Scottish Expedition, and the Association feels the proposed grant to be as open to exception upon scientific as upon national grounds. Further, it would point out that this unequal treatment of Scottish Antarctic enterprise by the Treasury is the more likely to excite feelings of resentment in the fact that His Majesty's Government has but recently refused any financial assistance whatever to Dr Bruce's projected expedition next year. It would therefore respectfully but strongly urge the desirability of a reconsideration by His Majesty's Government of the claims of Dr Bruce as regards both his past and his projected expeditions.[16]

There is no evidence in the relevant Treasury file that His Majesty's Government deigned to reply. In the event, Bruce was not able to find any private donor to underpin his plan and did not succeed in prising any more money from the government, so his plan never saw the light of day.

Appendix 4

BRUCE AND THE POLAR MEDAL

As has been pointed out, uniquely among the British Heroic Age Antarctic expeditions, the Polar Medal was not awarded to Bruce and the staff of the Scottish National Antarctic Expedition. A myth has been built up that this was as a result of the malign influence of the president of the Royal Geographical Society, Sir Clements Markham. Dudeney & Sheail (2014) have shown that Markham played no part in the matter, and we have further developed that argument. In this appendix we provide transcripts of the key source material on which the argument is based, calling on primary material held at the National Archives and the National Records Office of Scotland.

The Polar Medal as redefined in 1904 was to be available as an award for meritorious performance to the members of expeditions funded or sponsored by the government. Privately funded expeditions were excluded. Bruce would have been aware of this. His attempts to get his expedition recognised for the award only started in 1910, as the result of the award being made to Shackleton's expedition of 1907–09.

The key document concerning the latter award is a letter from the Admiralty dated 9 August 1909, addressed to the secretary of HM Treasury:

Sir,

I am commanded by my Lords Commissioners of the Admiralty to acquaint you, for the information of the Lords Commissioners of the Treasury that it is proposed to issue the Polar Medal to the Officers and men who took part in the recent expedition to the Antarctic regions.

My Lords fully recognise that it has not been usual to grant this and similar medals to members of expeditions which have not been sent out under the direct auspices of His Majesty's Government; but they consider that on this occasion the exceptional achievements of Mr Shackleton's undertaking justify an exception being made, and that, although the work performed has no immediate connection with the Royal Navy, it will probably be convenient that the small expenditure involved should be borne by the Navy Votes.

I am to request you will invite the sanction of their Lordships of the Treasury to the foregoing proposal.[1]

The reader may wonder why the Admiralty did not just proceed without bothering the Treasury, but in those days the Treasury had the power to sanction or block expenditure even of the most trivial kind. Their reply was short and to the point:

In reply to your letter of 9th ult, I am to request you inform the Lords Commissioners of the Admiralty that, in the special circumstance, the Lords Commissioners of the Treasury sanction the issue of the Polar Medal and that they agree that the small expenditure involved should be borne by Navy Votes.[2]

The award was gazetted in November 1909, and it seems that it gave Bruce the idea to petition for the same for his expedition. While visiting

London in pursuit of the grant to assist in publication of the *Scotia* results, he wrote to Ferrier on 23 November:

> Many thanks yours for the Polar Medal papers. I have an appointment with Lord Pentland today and saw Dodds and Lamb yesterday. I will make my chief theme with Pentland the medal but this will give me an opportunity of discussing the whole business with him[3]

He wrote again to Ferrier the next day:

> I was received by Lord Pentland yesterday who was most cordial he said he could sum up the position he and the whole office took by saying he had & intended to back up our claims in every possible way.[4]

Lord Pentland was at that time the Secretary of State for Scotland and he did indeed take up the matter, writing directly to the king's private secretary, Col Sir A. J. Bigge, on 26 November 1910:

> My Dear Bigge,
>
>   I have been approached by Dr W. S. Bruce, the leader of the Scottish Expedition to the Antarctic in the years 1902–04, asking for consideration of the case from the award to the members of his Expedition of the Polar Medal which was instituted by the late King. I understand that the Polar Medal was awarded to the members of the 'Discovery' Expedition, which returned in 1904, and also to the members of the Shackleton Antarctic Expedition of 1907–09. Dr Bruce's Expedition was one of great importance, and it achieved valuable results in the direction of exploration and scientific observation. There is indeed such good ground for according to Dr. Bruce and his colleagues a similar decoration to that granted to the members of other expeditions, that it seems quite possible that some

accident prevented the making of such a request, or interfered with its consideration. But this must have happened, if at all, in 1904, and I have no means of ascertaining the facts: possibly the Medal was not then instituted. I venture to submit the case for consideration. It is strongly urged upon me on the grounds that its work is coupled in the public estimation with that of the other Expeditions which I have named, and stands on the same footing, but I shall be happy to endeavour to obtain any further information that you may think necessary.[5]

The reply from the palace on 6 December 1910, written by Sir Frederick Ponsonby, could not have been more negative, and firmly shut the door on any further consideration by the palace:

Your letter to Bigge of the 26th November has been standing over until I returned, as the King wished to know what King Edward's views had been on the subject. I told His Majesty that the Polar Medal was originally instituted for Arctic and Antarctic Expeditions equipped and sent out by the Government, but that certain exceptions had been made, notably in the case of Shackleton, who had been first told that he was not entitled to receive the Medal, but who had subsequently been given it owing to the success of his Expedition.

I explained to the King that if the Medal was extended to private enterprises generally without any definite limit, it might be eventually impossible to refuse anyone who had made a voyage in Arctic or Antarctic waters, and I pointed out the difficulty in selecting a judge who would be capable of deciding whether an Expedition had earned the medal or not.

The King desired me to explain this to you and express regret that he found it impossible to make an exception in the case of Dr. Bruce, whose Expedition had been sent out some years ago. His Majesty said that whilst he reserved to himself the right of making a special exception in any case that might occur during his reign, he thought that to go back to former Expeditions would only lead to discontent and confusion. Dr. Bruce should, therefore, be told that as his Expedition was not sent out by the Government he is not entitled to the Medal, and that the King fears it would not be possible to make an exception in his favour.[6]

There the matter rested until 1913 as far as Bruce was concerned. However, in the meantime the medal was awarded to the members of Scott's second expedition and to the members of Shackleton's attempted trans-Antarctic expedition. This spurred Rudmose Brown to raise the issue with the president of the Royal Scottish Geographical Society, Lord Stair:

Soon after the return of the British Antarctic Expedition in Discovery in 1904 the Polar Medal was initiated and awarded to all members of the expedition. It was also given to those who served on the two relief ships of the expedition, the *Morning* and the *Terra Nova*. The Scottish National Antarctic Expedition of Dr W. S. Bruce which returned in 1904 received no award of the medal although it was subsequently bestowed on the members of Sir E. H. Shackleton's expedition in the *Nimrod*. This neglect of the Scottish Expedition is a slight to Scotland and to Scottish endeavour and it is as a medallist of the R.S.G.S. and a member of Dr Bruce's *Scotia* expedition that I write to ask whether in your Lordship's opinion it is not a matter that the R.S.G.S. might not take up.

The *Discovery* was not a naval ship but sailed under the blue ensign. The *Nimrod* the same. The Scotia also flew the blue ensign. These expeditions were thus all on the same footing. That the medal was not struck exclusively for the *Discovery* is proved by its award to the officers and men of the Nimrod.

The neglect of Government to grant the award to the officers and men of the *Scotia* signifies but scant appreciation of the work of the expedition and is unfair to those who have earned it.

If the R.S.G.S. were able to cause the oversight to be rectified they would show again the interest in Scottish exploration that they have already done so much to foster.[7]

Lord Stair took up the case with the Scottish Office, prompting the assistant undersecretary John Lamb to write to the Admiralty on 24 September 1913, raising the case again:

Sir,

I am directed by the Secretary for Scotland to state for the information of the Lords Commissioners of the Admiralty that he has received a representation from the Council of the Royal Scottish Geographical Society pointing to the fact that the Scottish National Antarctic Expedition of 1902–04 is the only British Antarctic Expedition to the members of which the Polar Medal instituted after the voyage of the Discovery under Captain Scott in 1904 has not been awarded, and urging that the medal should be bestowed on the members of the Expedition. The Secretary for Scotland is in strong sympathy with this representation, and trusts that Their Lordships will be pleased to give it their favourable consideration. The Expedition was not sent out under Government auspices, but the work which it achieved was of national importance, a fact which received recognition when in 1910 a Government Grant of £3000 was authorised towards the cost of the publication of the scientific records of the expedition. A copy is enclosed for Their Lordships's information of the representation which accompanied the application for the grant in 1910, which gives an account of the work of the expedition and of the valuable scientific information which it amassed.[8]

The Admiralty, accepting the case, wrote to the Treasury on 21 October 1913:

> I am commanded by my Lords Commissioners of the Admiralty to acquaint you, for the information of the Lords Commissioners of His Majesty's Treasury, that it is proposed to award the Polar Medal to the Officers and men who took part in the Scottish Antarctic Expedition of 1902–4 under the leadership of Dr W. S. Bruce.
>
> The Secretary for Scotland has represented that he is in strong sympathy with the proposed award, and has pointed out that this is the only British Antarctic Expedition to the members of which the Medal has not been awarded. The work achieved by the Expedition was of national importance, a fact which received recognition when in 1910 a Government grant of £3000 was authorised towards the cost of the publication of the scientific records of the Expedition. The Scottish Expedition, like Sir E. Shackleton's, was not sent out under Government auspices, but in the case of the latter Expedition approval was given for the award of the Polar Medal in the exceptional circumstances represented to their Lordships of the Treasury to their Lordships of the Treasury in Admiralty letter of 9th August 1909 (Treasury reply of 3rd September 1909).
>
> My Lords regard the achievements of the Scottish Antarctic Expedition as sufficiently meritorious to justify the award of the Polar Medal, and I am to invite the sanction of the Lordships of the Treasury to its presentation of this case. The expenditure involved will be small and can be met from the provision under Vote 11.N in the estimates for the current year.[9]

The Treasury replied on 28 October 1913:

> I have laid before the Lords Commissioners of His Majesty's Treasury you letter of the 21st instant, relative to the proposed award of the Polar Medal

The London family home where Bruce grew up in genteel comfort – 18 Royal Crescent, Holland Park. The family moved here in 1871 when Bruce was four years old. (J. R. Dudeney, 2017)

William Speirs Bruce pictured in *The Siege of the South Pole* by Alston Rivers (1905).

The 'Ark' laboratory and marine station in the Firth of Forth, where Bruce first got to grips with marine science. (Etching by Cunningham, 1884)

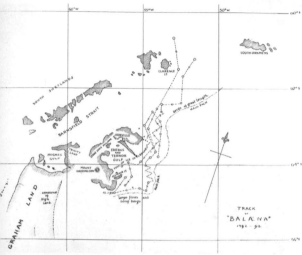

Detailed map of the track of the *Balaena* in the north-western Weddell Sea showing the extent of geographical knowledge at the time. (Glasgow Digital Library - GDL)

Painting by William G. Burn Murdoch, artist/assistant surgeon on the *Balaena* whaling expedition showing three of the ships amongst icebergs in the north-western Weddell Sea. (McManus Galleries, Dundee City Council Leisure and Arts)

The meteorological observatory at the top of Ben Nevis in wintertime. (Photograph from Rudmose Brown's biography of William Speirs Bruce)

A. Rankin, R. T. Omond and R. C. Mossman. Colleagues of Bruce at the Ben Nevis Observatory. (p. 40 of *The Weathermen of Ben Nevis*, Roy M. (2004)

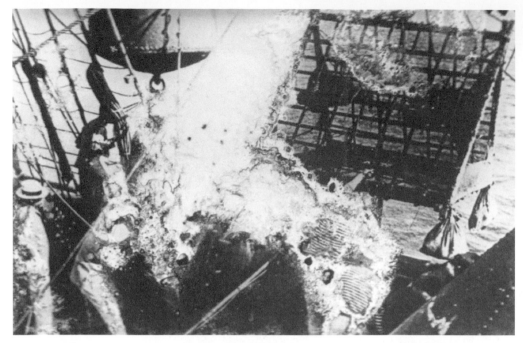

Above: A deep-sea trawl being recovered aboard the *Princesse Alice* in 1898. (RSGS)

Below: View across Klaas Billen Bay (now known as Adventfjorden), from the Port of Longyearbyen on Spitsbergen, Svalbard. (Courtesy of Bernt Rostad under Creative Commons 2.0)

Right: Jessie and Eillium Bruce – Eillium was born April 1902. (Modified from an image from RSGS)

Below: One of the family homes in Edinburgh, 17 Joppa Road, Portobello, Edinburgh. It was given the name 'Antartica' by Bruce, the second house where he lived in Edinburgh to have this name. (J. Sheail, 2017)

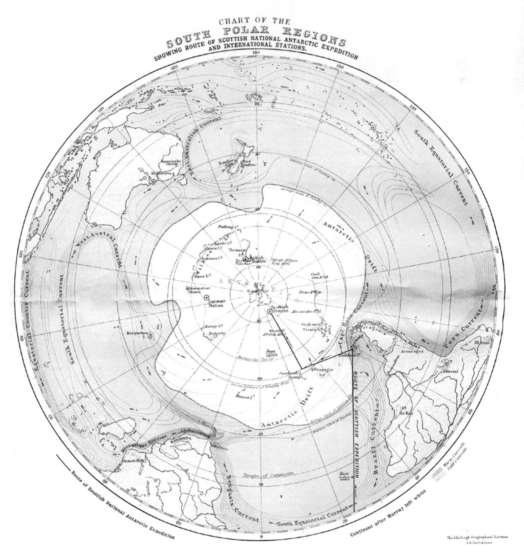

The map showing the original plan and route of the *Scotia* expedition in relation to other international plans (British and German). It would have involved two winters and a station at high Southern latitude (here shown rather fancifully at around 82°S). Bruce was forced to scale back through insufficient funds. (GDL)

Above left: The *Hekla* in dry dock before her transformation from a whaling ship to a state-of-the-art oceanographic ship after which she was renamed the *Scotia*. (GDL)

Above right: Captain Robertson on the bridge of the *Scotia*. (GDL)

The meteorological station (Omond House) under construction on Laurie Island by members of the expedition, pictured in *Report on the scientific results of the voyage of S.Y.* Scotia *during the years 1902, 1903 and 1904, under the leadership of William S. Bruce* (1908). (Public domain)

The telegram that Bruce sent to Jessie on the departure of *Scotia* from Buenos Aires in January 1904. Note that he styles himself as 'Willie'. (GDL)

Piper Gilbert Kerr with an emperor penguin on sea ice. Coats Land is in the background. This photograph was taken at or about the most southerly latitude reached by the expedition, and although it is not obvious, the penguin is tethered to Kerr. (Adapted from the photograph in Rudmose Brown's biography of William Speirs Bruce)

Above: The remains of Omond House, now part of what the Antarctic Treaty designated the Laurie Island Historical Site and Monument No. 42 (J. R. Dudeney, 2013)

Right: The grave of Allen G. Ramsay, engineering officer of the *Scotia*, who died on 6 August 1903 at Laurie Island. Now part of what the Antarctic Treaty designated the Laurie Island Historical Site and Monument No. 42 (J. R. Dudeney, 2013)

Flag of the Scottish National Antarctic Expedition. (RSGS)

The triumphant return of the *Scotia* to the Clyde on 21 July 1904. (RSGS)

Scottish Oceanographical Laboratory Inauguration,

16th January 1907. 4 o'clock p.m.

LIST OF SPEAKERS.

1. The Right Honourable the LORD PROVOST asks His Serene Highness the PRINCE OF MONACO to preside.

2. HIS SERENE HIGHNESS asks the Honorary Secretary to read apologies for absence.

3. HIS SERENE HIGHNESS calls upon the Director, Mr WM. S. BRUCE, to make a statement.

4. HIS SERENE HIGHNESS addresses the Meeting.

5. Principal Sir WM. TURNER, K.C.B., F.R.S., speaks, representing the University of Edinburgh.

Above left: The programme for the formal opening of the Scottish Oceanographical Laboratory in 1907. (EUL)

Above right: The Scottish Oceanographical Laboratory adjacent to the Surgeons Hall in Edinburgh. (EUL)

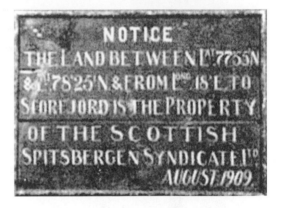

Ten-legged 'Sea Spider' (*Pentanymphon antarcticum*), a type of primitive marine arthropod which was a new deep-sea species in 1904. (RSGS)

One of the 'Claim' boards erected on the boundaries of the Scottish Spitsbergen Syndicate mineral claims to maintain their rights. (RSGS)

W. S. Bruce and J. Matheson surveying Prince Charles Foreland, 1909. (RSGS)

Above: Fridtjof Nansen with his son and William Speirs Bruce at Klaas Billen Bay (now known as Adventfjorden or Advent Bay), Spitsbergen, in 1912 (Adapted from the photograph in Rudmose Brown's biography of William Speirs Bruce)

Left: Railway to 'Bruce City', one of the Scottish Spitsbergen Syndicate sites. (EUL)

Above: Collecting geological samples from the slopes of Mount Pyramiden, Spitsbergen. The mountain overlooks the now abandoned Russian coalmining settlement which operated from 1936 to 1998. (EUL)

Below: The Russian coalmining settlement lies abandoned today; pictured is its coal-fired power plant. (Courtesy of Hylgeriak under Creative Commons 2.0)

Left: William Speirs Bruce in later life. (Lafayete)

Below: A modern photograph of the South Georgia coast, the object of so much of Bruce's single-minded focus. (Courtesy of Liam Quinn under Creative Commons 2.0)

to the Officers and men who took part in the Scottish Antarctic Expedition of 1902–4 under the leadership of Dr W. S. Bruce.

In reply I am to request you to inform the Lords Commissioners of the Admiralty that My Lords feel some hesitation as to the propriety of awarding a medal at the public expense to members of a private expedition not despatched or controlled by His Majesty's Government. They would have thought that in such a case the scientific services of the expedition would be most suitably recognised by the grant of medals by the various scientific societies interested. My Lords are aware that Polar Medals were granted in the cases of the Discovery expedition and of Sir E. Shackleton's expedition, but in the former case a considerable public grant had been made towards the funds of the expedition and many of those serving on it were members of the Royal Navy and in receipt of pay as such, whilst in the latter case the Board of the Admiralty, whilst agreeing that it had not been usual to grant Polar Medals to members of expeditions not sent out under the direct auspices of His Majesty's Government, urged that 'on this occasion the exceptional achievements of Mr Shackleton's undertaking justify and exception' (Admiralty letter of 9th August 1909). Their Lordships would be glad to be informed whether there are any grounds for such exceptional treatment in the present instance. They observe that, though the expedition was concluded nearly ten years ago, no proposal for the grant of a Polar Medal has yet been put forward till the present time.[10]

Meanwhile the Secretary of State for Scotland has become frustrated not to receive a reply from the Admiralty so launches a letter on 9 December 1913 to Winston Churchill, then the First Lord of the Admiralty:

May I bespeak your favourable consideration of a letter which was sent from here to the Admiralty a little time ago in support of the award of the

Polar Medal to members of the Scottish National Antarctic Expedition of 1902–4 which was led by Dr W. S Bruce?

The expedition was planned by Dr. Bruce as the result of a voyage in 1893 with the Dundee whaling fleet which had been sent to try the resources of the Antarctic seas, and by 1902 he had collected his men and material, meeting the cost out of a sum of over £30,000 contributed by public spirited people in Scotland. The First Lord of that day helped with the loan of some valuable scientific instruments.

Picking out what was then the least known of all Antarctic areas the 'Scotia' expedition was engaged for two years in exploring the land, surveying the ocean down to 74°S. and in conducting magnetic, biological and meteorological investigations. In the way of exploration its most noteworthy achievement was the discovery of the Antarctic continent at a point 500 miles north of its supposed limit, and the mapping of this portion (Coats Land) for 150 miles. The survey results have been made over to the Admiralty and I believe the Hydrographer attaches considerable value to them. On its scientific side the importance of the work is recognised by all the world of learning and the Government has contributed £3,000 towards the cost of publication.

Though the exploits of the 'Scotia' expedition were not calculated to make the same vivid appeal to the public as those of some of the other British Antarctic Expeditions, there can be no question that they represent a great triumph over hardships and difficulties and have added lustre to our nation, the more so as other countries, Germany, France and Sweden, were simultaneously at work in the same field.

I gather that the Polar Medal has been awarded not only to the members of the Scott and Shackleton expeditions but also to the relief ships of those expeditions, and I sincerely trust that the same privilege may be extended to Dr. Bruce and his companions.[11]

This appeal to Churchill focussed minds at the Admiralty, with Sir William Greene renewing the submission to the Treasury on 31 December:

With reference to your letter of the 28th October in which you inquire whether there are grounds for exceptional treatment of the Scottish Expedition in the matter of the award of the Polar Medal, I am so commanded by My Lords Commissioners of the Admiralty to represent that apart from purely scientific work very valuable geographical results were achieved by the Expedition in the exploration of Antarctic Lands, viz:-

a) The highly detailed survey of Laurie Island, South Orkneys (probably the most detailed map of any definite area in the Antarctic Regions).

b) The mapping of 150 miles of the coastline of the Antarctic Continent, now know as Coats Land, and previously entirely unknown.

The survey results of the Expedition have been incorporated in the Admiralty works and form a valuable contribution. The Meteorological Office have been supplied with a large number of data which they desired and the British Museum and the Royal Scottish Museum with a large number of specimens.

No comparison can be made between the oceanographical and scientific work of the Scottish Expedition and the purely continental exploration undertaken by Sir E, Shackleton. The objects of the Expeditions were different and, judged merely by results, those of the Scottish Expedition were the more valuable. In their Lordships' opinion the importance of the work done by this Expedition justifies it being regarded as a national achievement, which may be rewarded appropriately by the grant of the Polar Medal.[12]

The Treasury reply dated 22 January 1914:

I have laid before the Lords Commissioners of His Majesty's Treasury your letter of the 31st ultimo, further respecting the proposed award of the Polar

Medal to the Officers and men who took part in the Scottish Antarctic Expedition of 1902/04.

The Lord Commissioners of the Admiralty now state that apart from purely scientific work the Expedition achieved very important geographical results which have been incorporated in the Admiralty records and form a valuable contribution. In these circumstances My Lords will no longer withhold Their assent – They give it, though, with some reluctance in view of the considerations set forth in Treasury Letter of the 28th October last – to the award of the Polar Medal to the officers and men of the Expedition.

They note that the expenditure involved will be small and that it can be met from the provision under Vote 11.N in the Navy Estimates for the current financial year.[13]

Unaware of Lord Pentland's exchange with the palace in 1910 the Admiralty contacted them again, resulting in the following response from Bigge, now elevated to the Peerage as Lord Stamfordham, to Winston Churchill's Private Office:

I now send you the correspondence which I mentioned to you on the telephone.

As the Scottish Office were informed more than three years ago that the King could not confer the Polar Medal upon the men of the Scottish Antarctic Expedition 1902, I almost wonder that that Department has again raised the question.

His Majesty says that he is very sorry that he cannot reverse the decision then come to.[14]

And there the matter rested in the Official mind – if not that of Bruce – for almost ninety years, at which time the Scottish Parliament again opened the question, unaware of the firm decision made by King George V.

Appendix 5

ATTEMPT BY BRUCE TO LEASE THE SOUTH SANDWICH ISLANDS

The South Sandwich Group of Islands is situated to the south-east of South Georgia. They are an island arc of active but snow-covered volcanoes. With the knowledge and blessing of the British government, the Norwegian Carl Larsen had made an exploratory voyage to the group to assess their commercial value at the end of 1908 and had written a detailed report on them for the Colonial Office. The report, which runs to twelve typed pages and includes sketch maps and photographs, was very negative about the commercial prospects, and Larsen found the whole group thoroughly unpleasant.[1] A short extract from the report, which describes landing on Zavadovskii Island, gives the flavour of the island group:

> Then we rowed along the coast to the middle of the island, just to where the fuming exhalations are to be found. A long way off the odour of garlic and sulphur was very strong before landing, and of course it became stronger as we came nearer. Here I went on board the pram again, as the swell was running too high to land with one of the other boats, but it was a risky affair. The pram shipped water before we could put on shore

and all three were thrown into the icy water again. It was with great difficulty that we could save pram, oars, guns, etc. The pram capsized in the breakers, but we succeeded in getting it on shore without other damages than broken tholepins and a hole in the bottom. All the collection of stone samples from the first landing were lost.

Here at the latter place it was almost intolerable on account of the very hot sulphur and other poisonous fumes, which were blown out now and then with such force, that small stone (*sic*) were thrown a long way out of innumerable small holes and cracks in the ground. The fumes were so hot that one could not hold the hand over the holes without burning it. The air was quite poisoned so I turned dizzy, and I am of that opinion that nobody could stay there very long without being poisoned. Pure sulphur was flowing out of some cracks and the whole shore was filled up by layers of it and soft masses from the inner of the island. Some samples of stones and minerals were taken and the island sketched and photographed. As the breakers were still growing worse, we must try to put out with the pram without being thrown into the icy water again, and we succeeded in coming on board without further accidents.

Larsen returned to South Georgia in early December 1908 seriously unwell. He became bedridden due to complications following the poisonous gas inhalation and the serious soakings he had suffered making landings on the islands. This information was relayed by the president of the whaling company to the Colonial Secretary in the Falklands on 4 January, along with a copy of very short report on the voyage prepared by Larsen's brother. However, Larsen's detailed report was not received by Governor Allardyce in the Falklands until April 1909. This he forwarded to the Colonial Office on 19 April 1909 with a covering letter containing the following summary:

The expedition appears to have found neither harbours nor fur seals at the South Sandwich group, though a large number of whales were seen off Bristol Island. In view of the additional information now available it seems that these southern and forbidding Islands still maintain their inhospitable notoriety, and are not likely to be visited any more frequently.[2]

We know that Bruce and Larsen were acquainted with each other, but do not have any documentary evidence that they communicated with each other concerning the economic possibilities of the islands. On 28 May 1909 Bruce wrote to the Colonial Office enquiring about acquiring a lease to them; in doing this it is highly unlikely that he knew of the contents of Larsen's report.

Sir,

I should be obliged if you would let me know under what conditions His Majesty's Government would lease me the South Sandwich Group of Islands, SOUTH ATLANTIC OCEAN[3]

The Colonial Office replied on 4 June saying that 'before considering the matter further, His Lordship would be glad to learn for what purposes a lease to the group is required'.[4]

Bruce responded to the Colonial Office on 20 June 1909:[5]

In answer to yours of the 4th instant, I beg to state that the purposes to which it is desired to lease the South Sandwich group is to establish whaling, sealing, & and other stations there & to thoroughly investigate the commercial resources of those Islands. To ascertain whether there are any mineral deposits, or other substances that may be of commercial value & to establish suitable commercial centres for the working of the same.

As a result of British enterprise with which I was specially associated in the years 1892, 1893, 1903, & 1904, much information has been gleaned regarding the whole region situated in the vicinity of the South Shetlands, South Orkneys South Georgia & South Sandwich Group. This enterprise has largely been taken advantage of by foreigners because in 1894 and 1904 support asked for by myself & others was not given by British Government Departments.

In the present case it is intended to establish a British Syndicate or British Syndicates that will take in hand the commercial development of the South Shetland (*sic*) Group & seas adjacent & thus retain in British hands the commercial wealth thereof.

It is hoped therefore that every possible encouragement will be given by the Colonial Office to foster & encourage this new enterprise by giving a lease on the most favourable terms possible, especially during the first few years of tenure when considerable capital will necessarily have to be expended.

There is a note on the relevant Colonial Office file dated 23 June to the effect:

Captain Larsen's report on his visit to the Sandwich Is., forwarded by the governor in 16550, is now unfortunately with the Admiralty for perusal, but it is clear from the covering despatch that, though whales are to be found in those seas, there is little prospect of there being any great demand for whaling stations, since no harbours have been found. Capt. Larsen found no fur-seals, and the commercial resources of the islands would not appear to be promising. However, if Mr Bruce thinks it worth his while to organise an expedition to the Sandwich Is. (I presume that in the penultimate para, he writes 'S. Shetlands' by inadvertence) no obstacles need be put in his way.[6]

Colonial Office consequently wrote to Bruce on 1 July:

> I am to acknowledge the receipt of your letter of 20th June, on the subject of your application for a lease of the S. Sandwich Is. And to inform you that his Lordship will obtain the views of the Governor of the Falkland Is., under whose administration the islands have been placed.
>
> Subject to the Governor's observations Lord Crewe will be prepared to consider the grant to you of specified rights in the S. Sandwich Is. for a term of years on favourable terms.
>
> I am to add that the Colonial Government will not be willing to grant you a monopoly of the whaling rights in the waters of the S. Sandwich Is., and will probably wish to retain the right to lease whaling stations to other applicants, though it may be possible to give you for a short period the right of priority to the selection of a site.[7]

From the file note and this letter it is clear that the Colonial Office knew just how unpleasant and commercially unattractive the South Sandwich Islands were, but chose not to inform Bruce of the contents of Larsen's report, whilst offering him the opportunity of a lease!

The matter rested there until September, by which time the governor had responded to Lord Crewe. There is a further file note dated 7 September:

> As our present information is to the effect that whaling operations cannot be carried on in the Sandwich Group we shall not be debarring others from access to anything they want by giving Dr Bruce a lease for a year – one year will suffice to disgust him of his scheme. Offer him a lease for a year as proposed by the Council and write as they suggest with regard to the South Shetlands?[8]

This produced the following letter from the Colonial Office to Bruce dated 25 September:

In further reference to the letter from this Department if 1ˢᵗ July, I am to inform you that a dispatch has now been received from the Governor of the Falkland Islands with regard to your application for a lease of the South Sandwich Islands.

The Governor has consulted the Executive Council and recommends that you should be offered a lease of the Dependency for a period of twelve months at a nominal rent of £100 per annum and that a further £100 should be charged in the event in the event of you wishing to obtain also a licence to catch whales. This is the usual fee for such a licence. If after thoroughly investigating the commercial resources of the Islands and ascertaining the prospects of establishing a whaling industry you were desirous of applying for the lease of a site in a selected locality for a period of twenty-one years, this would be placed on a similar basis to the whaling companies operating at South Georgia and has a rental of £250 per annum for a site for a station with the right to employ two steam whalers in catching whales without further payment. The question of sealing would be regulated by the law on the subject which is at present under discussion so far as the dependencies are concerned In the case of possible mineral deposits a small royalty would be imposed on the output.

An annual whaling licence for the South Shetland Islands can be obtained at a cost of £100 on application to the Colonial Secretary, Port Stanley in the same way as is done by the companies now operating there. Particulars of any proposed commercial development on the South Shetland group other than whaling or sealing should be submitted for the further consideration of the Colonial Government, but it is not likely that the Government would consider an application for a lease of lands on the shore of either of the only safe harbours known to exist in the (group).

I am further to add that the Governor and Council have asked that you be informed, that so far as the information at their disposal goes, the prospects with regard to the South Sandwich Group are not encouraging, the leader of the previous expedition having stated that it is impossible to carry on whaling operations there.[9]

We have found no indication in Bruce's correspondence, or in the government record, of Bruce taking the matter any further. We do not have any evidence that he was in contact with Larsen, but equally there is no indication that Larsen's report was in any way confidential, so it is reasonable to suppose that he would have heard of its contents 'on the grapevine' at the very least. Also, the letter offering the one-year lease does reveal Larsen's opinion as to the nonviability of shore-based whaling there, though not of its general unpleasantness. The offer of a whaling licence for the South Shetlands was in principle very positive, but it came with the sting in the tail of having to explore for and establish a new site for a shore-based whaling station. Overall, it is likely that Bruce would have judged the risks to be too great to proceed even if he could have found backers to fund the expedition.

The island group remains a very hostile environment which has never been a focus of any commercial activity. A secret Argentine military outpost was established there in the 1970s but removed at the end of the Falklands conflict. To this day, the group is almost never visited.

Appendix 6

BRUCE AND THE PATRON'S MEDAL

Bruce was awarded one of the major medals of the Royal Geographical Society in March 1910 – this was the Patron's Medal, the patron at that time being King Edward VII. The citation, taken from the minutes of the council of the RGS for 14 March 1910, reads as follows:

Dr William Speirs Bruce raised in the years 1900 – 1902, a sum exceeding £35,000 for an Antarctic Expedition. With Dr Bruce as leader, this expedition sailed in the S.Y. 'Scotia' and mapped 150 miles of the coast line of the Antarctic Continent, naming it 'Coats Land'. Dr Bruce took 75 deep soundings south of lat. 40°S., and nearly 500 soundings of less than 100 fathoms in the vicinity of the South Orkneys. The meteorological observations taken on board the 'Scotia' in this vicinity, and the more extended series taken at the South Orkneys also go to prove that continental land exists in this region. The 'Scotia' trawled in deep water 20 times in depths down to to (*sic*) 2645 fathoms, mostly south of 60°S., and within the pack ice. 150 trawlings were made in water of less than 100 fathoms. The collections of seal skins, skeletons, and embryos are the most complete ever taken from the Antarctic, as are also the collections of bird skins, skeletons, embryos and eggs. The same may be said of the invertebrate collections. About 140 serial temperatures and salinities, down to depths of 266 fathoms, and about 400 surface temperatures and salinities were taken. In addition to the 'Scotia' expedition, Dr Bruce was a naturalist to the Scottish Antarctic Expedition in 1892 – 93; in the Arctic regions he was zoologist to the Jackson-Harmsworth in 1896–97, also naturalist to Major Andrew Coats' expedition to Novaya Zemlya and the Barents Sea in 1892, naturalist to H.S.H. Prince of Monaco's expedition to Spitsbergen and the North Polar regions in 1898 – 99, and again in 1906. During this latter expedition, he assisted in making a detailed survey of the Prince Charles Foreland, Spitsbergen, which is nearly ready for publication.[1]

It is interesting to note how impersonal this citation is. It makes no reference to the personal qualities of leadership, courage and perseverance that must underlie such achievements.

Appendix 7

AN INSIGHT INTO BRUCE'S CHARACTER

Bruce had recurrent cash-flow problems; his friends knew of this and frequently sent monetary gifts to help the family situation. In 1908 the first volume of his *Report on The Scientific Results of the Voyage of S.Y.* Scotia was prepared for publication and the publication significantly amplified his financial concerns.

In the autumn of 1907 Bruce was invited by the president of the Royal Geographical Society, Sir George Goldie, to present a paper to the RGS on his work in Spitsbergen. His reply to Goldie was dated 7 October 1907, and shows again that he cannot let go of his antagonism towards Markham.

It is with great gratification that I have received your kind letter and warm congratulations on my work in Prince Charles Foreland, and I thank you sincerely for it. I cannot but compare your attitude with that of your predecessor; for while you speak of my 'excellent work for the last 20 years', he referred to my efforts as 'mischievous rivalry'. With your assurance and with the assurance of my old friend, Dr Keltie, as Secretary of the Society, that the Royal Geographical Society 'has always followed my work with interest' and that the members of the Council of the Society urge me with the same feeling as yourself to give them a communication during the coming season, I am very pleased to accede to your request.[1]

The talk he gave was entitled 'Exploration on and around Prince Charles Foreland, Spitsbergen' and was delivered on 13 April 1908[2] in London. The expenses incurred exacerbated his anxieties as is shown by this exchange of correspondence over his claim for reimbursement. He was always a difficult man to interact with and this correspondence starkly highlights his prickly behaviour. They are also rather sad demonstrations of his situation, his obsessive personality, his lack of insight and his lack of tact.

From Bruce to Keltie, the secretary of the RGS, dated 19 November 1908:

In reference to yours of September 7th when you returned the account of expenses I sent you, there is no mistake as is perfectly obvious. It is addressed to The Secretary, Royal Geographical Society, 1 Savile Row, London, W. & I am surprised that it should have been returned.

I am not a man of means, I regret to say, & as my outlays for cabs, trains, Hotel, lantern slides, etc, etc. in connection with the lecture to your society exceeded twenty pounds, I naturally sent in my bill in the ordinary course, charging nothing however in name of fee for myself, although I had doubts whether I was expected to do so or not seeing I had received no letter of thanks or the like for my lecture & I did not understand I was to give my services 'gratis' – a thing which I, for financial reasons, am not in the habit of doing.

I did not when sending in my bill for expenses charge a fee, as I thought the bill would raise the question with you & if I was to receive a fee that you would ask me for a note of it on receipt.

In reference to your statement that 'no payments are made to Authors of papers read before the Society', I may say that on previous occasions I myself have received payment for contributions to the 'Journal'.

P.S. I return the account & shall be obliged if you can make early payment.[3]

Keltie replied the following day:

I was surprised to get your letter of the 19th. You must be aware that neither we nor any other scientific Society pay for papers which are read at their meetings. We have never done so in the history of the Society, and never been asked to do so before. If you intended when you agreed to give us a paper, to charge either a fee or your expenses, you ought to have let us know, and I should have submitted the matter to the Council for their decision.

You say you received no letter of thanks or the like. The thanks of the Society were awarded to you immediately after your lecture was delivered, by the President, and it is not the custom of our Society, any more than it is the custom of any other Society to write letters of thanks to readers of papers. However, I am sending your letter to the President who may decide to bring it before the Council.[4]

Keltie followed this letter up with another on 23 November:

I have shown your letter of the 19th, to the president with your demand for Twenty Guineas for your expenses in connection with the paper which you read at our Society last session. He is surprised that you should make such a demand: you must be aware that Societies do not pay for papers contributed to their meetings. We certainly pay for contributions to the

Journal which are asked, but that is a totally different thing. We have never before had such a demand made, any more than any other scientific Society has had.

However, if you wish I shall place your letter before the Council. With regard to lantern slides, we are willing to pay for them, but then the slides would be our property. I must say that you are very ill-advised in making such a demand.[5]

Bruce would not let the matter rest, replying on 25 November:

I have your letter of 23rd

I am sure your advice to forego my claim for personal expenses in connection with my visit to London is given in all sincerity, & if I could afford to accept it I should gladly do so. As it is I can only accept the alternative you offer of submitting my claim to your Council.

With regard to what you say about the remuneration of Lecturers addressing scientific bodies, I cannot altogether agree, on more than one occasion I have been offered remuneration for lecturing to Geographical Societies. I am aware that many lecturers for reasons of their own volunteer to lecture to Scientific Societies without any expectation of remuneration or reimbursement of their outlay. I also know that many Lecturers rightly consider it their duty & their privilege to lecture to such Societies as yours in recognition of assistance (pecuniary or otherwise) afforded to them by such Societies. As you know however, I cannot class myself with either of these.

I need not go into all the circumstances, but I would ask you to bear in mind one or two matters which may have escaped you & of which Major Darwin was doubtless unaware when he expressed surprise at my making a claim. While I did not stipulate for any fee

(& do not ask any) I would remind you that I did not volunteer to read a paper; on the contrary I reluctantly agreed to do so on the invitation of your late President & yourself. After I agreed to do so, you will recollect the nature of my paper was quite changed in order to meet the requirements of your Society. Instead of the scientific paper I prepared, I was requested for the lecture to introduce 'other things, incidents & episodes which would interest an audience which are not of sufficient permanent importance to publish in the monthly Journal'. I was also asked to show 'curios'. These alterations on my original plans involved me in considerable time & expense, which I had not contemplated at the outset.

In naming twenty guineas as my personal expenses I am much within the mark, & I trust on reconsideration you may find it unnecessary to refer to your Council for special instructions. If, however, you still think it is necessary to submit my claim I must ask you to submit this letter & the whole correspondence which took place between your late President, Mr Reeves, & yourself and me, & to afford me an opportunity of making such further representations as I may think desirable in the circumstances

I may mention that I am at present engaged in bringing before another scientific Society the following which practically covers the vey questions at issue between us, that it be a general instruction to the Secretary in connection with any lectures given or papers read to the Society that

(First) For the Secretary to write a cordial letter of thanks on behalf of the Council.

(Second) To offer a first class return railway fare & and the cost of Hotel accommodation for two or three days.

(Third) To offer to defray a small part of actual expenses incurred in writing the communication & in delivering the lecture.[6]

Keltie consulted his opposite number, Major Lachlan Forbes, at the Royal Scottish Geographical Society in a letter of 27 November:

> Strictly 'entre nous' what a difficult man Bruce is! He gave us a paper at our last session, and now sends in a bill of £20 for expenses. We never under any circumstances pay for papers which are read at our meetings, and he knows that; but I think he has some sort of grudge against the Society. He writes rather unpleasantly on the subject. I shall have to bring the matter before the Council, and I do not know that they will agree to pay his demand. I have told him he is very ill advised to write as he has done. He certainly is, for reasons which I cannot enter into. He tells me that he has got certain instructions given to a Secretary of another Society with regard to readers of papers: that he must write a formal letter of cordial thanks, and must offer to pay their fares and any reasonable expenses. Well we have never written letters of thanks; the thanks are given on the spot by the president. Moreover, as a rule, readers of papers are only too glad of have the opportunity of reading them before the Society. However this is all between ourselves.[7]

It seems the 'Society' to which Bruce referred in his letter was the RSGS since Forbes replied to Keltie on 30 November:

> I find Bruce quite impossible, among other things he appears to think that everybody wishes to insult him. I backed up his application for a grant from the British Assoctn. last year and he got £50, this year he made such a mess of the whole thing that he got nothing! he came to me when it was too late and I was unable to get the matter reconsidered although Major Hill did all in his power to help us.
>
> Get him the money if you can, I am afraid that he is very hard up, and in fact I do not understand how he manages to get along at all. I do not think

he is at all strong, and perhaps this accounts for his bad manner and the tone in which he writes, and by which he seems to put everybody's back up that he has anything to do with.

I always write and thank the reader of a paper, and as we do not pay a fee I offer to pay his fare and any necessary expenses. This only in some measure makes up for the long railway journeys in the middle of winter![8]

On Bruce's letter dated 25 November there is a handwritten comment, presumably in Keltie's handwriting: 'Dec 2 08 £20 Cheque signed by President & self sent.' But there is no indication from the minutes of the council meeting held on 30 November 1908 (or subsequent ones on 14 December and 11 January) that the matter was actually brought before the full council either for a decision or for retrospective endorsement. So Bruce won this battle, but at a significant cost to his reputation. The enigmatic comment in Keltie's letter to Forbes – 'He certainly is, for reasons which I cannot enter into' – refers to the fact that Bruce had been proposed for the award of the Patron's Medal of the RGS that year, and this spat scuppered that. He had to wait until March until 1910 before he was so honoured.

Appendix 8

THE BRUCE MEMORIAL MEDAL

This medal, honouring the life and work of Bruce, was awarded for some notable contribution to zoology, botany, geology, meteorology, oceanography or geography, where new knowledge has been gained through a personal visit the polar regions. The first award was given in 1926 to James Mann Wordie.

MEETINGS OF THE SOCIETY

PROCEEDINGS OF THE STATUTORY GENERAL MEETING.

Beginning the 144th Session, 1926–1927.

At the Statutory General Meeting of the Royal Society of Edinburgh, held in the Society's Lecture Room, 24 George Street, on Monday, October 25, 1926, at 4.30 P.M.,

Professor J, H. Ashworth, F.R.S., Vice-President, in the Chair, the Minutes of the Statutory Meeting on October 26, 1925, were read, approved, and signed.

The CHAIRMAN in presenting the BRUCE PRIZE; (first award) to JAMES MANN WORDIE, made the following statement:—

The BRUCE MEMORIAL PRIZE was founded in memory of Dr WILLIAM SPIERS BRUCE, whose enthusiasm and single-minded devotion to science conjoined with great modesty and unselfishness endeared him to a wide circle of friends. Following upon his death in 1921, it was decided at a meeting of his friends, called for the purpose, to inaugurate a fund to commemorate his scientific work in the lands and seas of the Arctic and Antarctic regions. In so doing, the founders perfectly realised that the real enduring monument to Dr BRUCE lay in the work which he had himself accomplished. Since his student days at the University of Edinburgh, which he interrupted to sail for the Antarctic in 1892, he paid many visits to the Arctic and Antarctic regions, and these resulted in a rich collection of knowledge and material in many branches of science.

Of these journeys the greatest was undoubtedly his Scottish National Antarctic Expedition of 1902–1904, during which he discovered and traced for 150 miles a new portion of the Antarctic continent which he named Coats's Land. Of this expedition it has been said in Mr J. K. Maclean's Heroes of the Polar Seas: 'The discoveries made were of great value, and museums were enriched by the unique collections which Dr BRUCE brought back with him. He added to our knowledge in so many departments of science that it would require an expert in each department to describe his achievements. It may be said that no wore enduring work than his has been accomplished in the Antarctic seas.'

Botany, Geology, and Zoology, as well as the sciences of Meteorology and Oceanography, have all been enriched through his energies. A single illustration will indicate the magnitude and value of his work. Of invertebrate marine animals alone, 1100 distinct species have been recorded from his collections, and of these more than 200 were made known to science for the first time. In the last year of his life, Dr BRUCE generously presented these vast zoological collections to the Royal Scottish Museum in Edinburgh.

Such work needs no memorial; and the foundation of a BRUCE PRIZE was due to a desire to signalise important additions to our knowledge of regions in which Dr BRUCE'S distinguished work was done.

In order that the award should meet as closely as possible the strong views which Dr BRUCE was known to have held, the subscribers decided that it should be given 'for some notable contribution to natural science, such as to Zoology, Botany, Geology, Meteorology, Oceanography, and Geography—the contribution to be in the nature of new knowledge, the outcome of a personal visit to Polar regions on the part of the recipient.' Again following Dr BRUCE'S predilections, it was decided that in the making of the award preference should be given, other things being equal, to an explorer of Scottish birth or origin, and to one at the outset of his career as an investigator.

The Medal which forms part of the award itself has a close connection with Polar exploration, for, with an adaptation of lettering, it is the medal, designed by BRUCE himself, which was struck to commemorate the safe return in 1904 of the Scotia from its great Antarctic voyage.

A Committee of the Royal Society of Edinburgh, the Royal Physical Society, and the Royal Scottish Geographical Society, has decided that the first award of the BRUCE MEDAL should be made to JAMES MANN WORDIE, M.A., of St John's College, Cambridge, who more than fulfills the conditions laid down for its bestowal. In the first place, he is a Scot, and a former student of the University of Glasgow. In the second place he has made contributions of value to our knowledge of both Polar regions through his own personal effort; and if it can hardly be said that Mr WORDIE is at the outset of his career as an investigator, it may be said that he has behind him a record of Polar achievement of which any man might be proud.

His first Polar voyage, undertaken with Sir Ernest Shackleton in the ill-fated Endurance in 1914–1916, brought him into close touch with Bruce's earlier discoveries; for it was after drifting along the line of Coats's Land, that the Endurance, hemmed in with ice, was crushed and sank, leaving Shackleton and his men adrift in three small boats to make the hazardous voyage to the inhospitable Elephant Island. Everyone remembers the heroic and arduous attempts which Shackleton made for the release of the stranded crew and how his devotion and courage were after many months rewarded by the safe return in 1916 of every soul which had sailed on the Endurance.

Later Mr WORDIE voyaged to Spitsbergen in the company of Dr BRUCE in 1919 and 1920. Having served so gallant an apprenticeship in the service of masters of polar exploration, Mr WORDIE himself next led an expedition to the distant Arctic isle of Jan Mayen, and in 1923 a strenuous attempt made by him to reach the east coast of Greenland was frustrated, when he was within sight of his goal, by the presence of pack ice unusually heavy for the season of the year. During the summer of this year Mr WORDIE again sailed for Greenland and landed there with success, and we await with interest the scientific results of this most recent of his adventures.

In consequence of these stirring journeys, Mr WORDIE has made valuable contributions to our knowledge of polar problems such as the formation of ice at sea, of the nature of the bottom deposits at great depths in the Antarctic Ocean, and of the Geology of the islands of the Arctic seas, and many of his results have made their first appearance in the Transactions of this Society.

This prize is awarded to him for his geological and oceanographical work in Arctic and Antarctic regions.

THE BRUCE MEMORIAL PRIZE 1926–2016

Award	Year	To	Reason given
1	1926	J. M. Wordie, Esq	His oceanographical and geographical work in both Polar regions
2	1928	H. U. Sverdrup, Esq	His contributions to the knowledge of the meteorology, magnetism and tides of the Arctic, as an outcome of his travels with the expedition in the *Maud*, 1918–25

3	1930	N. A. MacKintosh, Esq	His researches into the biology of whales in the waters of the Falkland Islands dependencies
4	1932	H. G. Watkins, Esq	His important contributions to the topography of the Spitsbergen, Labrador and east Greenland, and the investigation of the ice cap of Greenland
5	1936	J. W. S. Marr, Esq	His work in the southern ocean and more particularly for his monograph of the South Orkney Islands
6	1938	A. R. Glen, Esq	His work in Spitsbergen, including survey in New Friesland and the completion of the map of north east land
7	1940	B. Roberts, Esq	His work in survey, ornithology and general biology in the Polar regions--north and south
8	1942	Dr G. C. L. Bertram	Valuable biological work in the Arctic and Arctic from 1932–1937
9	1944	Lieut T. H. Manning	His valuable survey and biological work, 1931–1939 in Iceland, Lapland, Southampton Island, Hudson Bay and in Foxe Basin (1936–39)

10	1946	Lt-Col P. D. Baird	His valuable survey and geological work with Mr J. M. Wordie on NW Greenland and Baffin Island in 1943 with Mr T. H. Manning's British Canadian Arctic expedition (1936–1937), and later work, during the war, in charge of the Musk-Ox operation in Arctic Canada
11	1948	Dr W. A. Deer	His work in East Greenland, 1935–36, especially in regard to the Petrology of the Skaergaard Gabbro Intrusion
12	1950	Dr M. J. Dunbar	His biological researches in the Canadian Arctic
13	1952	G. de Q. Robin, Esq	His initiative and resource in carrying out glacial and meteorological researches in the Antarctic
14	1954	Dr R. M. Laws	His investigations in the South Orkney Islands and South Georgia, particularly on the biology and life history of elephant seals
15	1956	J. W. Cowie, Esq	His investigations into the stratigraphy and palaeontology of Greenland
16	1958	Dr H. Lister	His glaciological work with the 1957–58 Transantarctic expeditions

17	1960	Mr J. MacDowell	His work in the fields of Antarctic meteorology and geo magnetism and as leader of the Royal Society (London) expedition to Halley Bay 1958
18	1962	Mr K. V. Blaiklock	His contributions by way of navigation to the exploration of the Antarctic continent and for his mapping of lands bordering the Weddell Sea
19	1964	Dr M. W. Holdgate	His work on the zoology of the islands of the Antarctic seas
20	1966	Dr S. Evans	His many applications of physics to scientific exploration in the Antarctic and particularly for his development of radio echo-sounding of ice
21	1968	Dr W. S. B. Paterson	His pioneer work both theoretical and practical on the physics of glaciers
22	1972	Dr P. Friend	His leadership on three visits to East Greenland, and for his valuable investigations into the Devonian sedimentation of the region
23	1977	Dr P. Wadhams	His oceanographic investigations, especially in studying the behaviour of pack ice near Spitsbergen, the North Pole, and off east Greenland

24	1980	Dr A. Clarke	His studies relating to the biochemistry and ecology of Antarctic zooplankton and in particular the Antarctic krill, a shrimp-like organism that serves as a major dietary source for many species of whale, seals and sea birds
25	1987	Dr J. E. Gordon	His geomorphological research in Antarctica, Greenland and other high-latitude regions
26	1994	Dr I. L. Boyd	His contribution to polar studies particularly through his work on Antarctic seal
27	1999	Professor D. Marchan	His contribution to the field of earth science, especially in relation to his work on the East Antarctic Ice Sheet
28	2004	Dr M. J. Bentley	His outstanding work on Antarctic glaciers and ice sheets in relation to global climate change
29	2010	Alison Cook	Her work surveying and mapping the Antarctic Peninsula
30	2016	Dr Andy Hein	His work is recognised as bringing new insights into the history and stability of the Antarctic Ice Sheet

ACKNOWLEDGEMENTS

We have been greatly assisted by the staff at the archives at the Scott Polar Research Institute, also the staff of the Royal Geographical Society (with IBG), the Royal Scottish Geographical Society, the National Museum of Scotland and the University of Edinburgh Library. We also acknowledge the valuable support received from The National Archives at Kew and the National Records Office of Scotland.

Grateful thanks also to Dr John Sheail and Stephen Haddelsey for their helpful comments on the manuscript, to Mrs Moira Watson, Bruce's granddaughter, for her insightful comments on her grandfather, also to Robert Burton, Professor David Munro, Duncan Mackay, Dr John Millard, David Williams, Glyn Matthews, Christine Simm and James Goodlad, for their invaluable insights and factual information.

ACRONYMS

BA   British Association for the Advancement of Science

EUL   Edinburgh University Library

FZS   Fellow of the Zoological Society

GDL   Glasgow Digital Library

NMS   National Museum of Scotland

RGS   Royal Geographical Society

RS   Royal Society

RSGS   Royal Scottish Geographical Society

SPRI   Scott Polar Research Institute

SNAE   Scottish National Antarctic Expedition

TNA   The National Archives

ULE   University Library of Edinburgh

NOTES

Prologue

1 Bruce, W. S. (1908), *Scotland and the Antarctic*, 'Scotia', 2, p. 19

2 Speak, P. (2003), *William Speirs Bruce, Polar Explorer and Scottish Nationalist*, Edinburgh, National Museums of Scotland, p. 15

3 Rudmose Brown, R. N. (1923), *A Naturalist At The Poles*, Seeley, Service and Co, London, p. 297

1 *The Early Life of a Naturalist*

1 The Swedenborgian Church or 'New Church' based its theology on the work of Emanuel Swedenborg (1688–1772), a Swedish scientist and theologian. Swedenborg claimed to have had continuous heavenly visions over a period of a quarter of a century, receiving new revelations from Jesus. Swedenborgians believe that they should worship God in Jesus Christ, rather than the Trinity.

2 Samuel Noble Bruce (1834–1926), a Fellow of the Royal College of Surgeons. He worked as a general practicioner.

3 The daughters were named: Mary Charity, Eveline Rose, Helen Violet, Edith Isabel, Mabel Beatrice and Monica Jane

4 Speak, P. (2003), *William Speirs Bruce, Polar Explorer and Scottish Nationalist*, Edinburgh, National Museums of Scotland, p. 22

5 *ibid*

6 Here he was probably actually referring to the South Kensington Museum on Exhibition Road, as, at this time, the Natural History Museum was located in Bloomsbury, too far for the children to visit.

7 Norfolk County School, was a public school founded by Joseph Brereton to educate the sons of artisans and farmers. It opened in 1873 but was closed in 1895. The building was then bought by Edmund Watts for Dr Barnardo and converted to accommodate boys from Barnardo homes, where from 1903 to 1949, under its new name of Watts Naval Training School, it provided education for the boys before they joined the Navy. It continued as a Bernardo's home until 1953 when it was demolished. (sources: wikipedia.org/wiki/ Watts Naval_School and www.heritage.norfolk.gov.uk NHER 2934).

8 Rudmose Brown, R. N. (1923), *A Naturalist at The Poles*, Seeley, Service and Co, London p. 20

9 Students could only be registered if they had passed the examination recognised by the General Medical Council. The University of London held examinations to allow candidates to be admitted for degree courses from 1838

10 Entry requirements for the University of London 1887–8, *The Calendar*

11 Sir Patrick Geddes (1854 –1932), biologist, sociologist, planner, founder of the first Scottish university student residence. He was born in Ballater, Aberdeenshire and studied at Perth Academy and the Royal College of Mines in London. He did not complete his degree, but was employed firstly as a demonstrator in the

Department of Physiology at University College London and then, from 1880 to 1888, as a lecturer in Zoology at the University of Edinburgh. With a career spanning the fields of biology, sociology and geography, he became known for his innovative thinking in the pioneering field of urban planning. Geddes went on to become the Chair of Botany at University College, Dundee (1888–1919), and the Chair of Sociology at the University of Bombay (1919–1924). He was knighted in 1932, but died later that year in Montpellier, France. Source: http://www.ed.ac.uk/about/people/plaques/geddes

12 Hugh Robert Mill (1861–1950) was born in Thurso, Caithness. He was a geographer and meteorologist who exercised a great influence in the reform of geography teaching and on the development of meteorology. He was educated at Edinburgh University, graduating in chemistry (1883) and specializing in the chemistry of seawater for his doctorate (1886). Love of the sea and of boats led to his famous pioneer survey, *The English Lakes* (1895). Indifferent health and physique—he became totally blind in later life—prevented him becoming an explorer, but from 1892 (when he was appointed librarian of the Royal Geographical Society and settled in London), he became an acknowledged world expert in oceanography and Antarctic exploration. It was through *The Realm of Nature* (1891) that he influenced the reform of geography teaching. As director of the British Rainfall Organization (1901–19), editor of British Rainfall and Symons' Meteorological Magazine, and honorary secretary of the Royal Meteorological Society from 1902 until 1907 (when he became president), he had a profound influence on the development of meteorology. He served as vice president of the Royal Geographical Society from 1927 to 1931 but was compelled by ill-health to refuse the presidency in 1933. His autobiography was in proof when he died. Source: https://www.britannica.com/

biography/Hugh-Robert-Mill. He was influential in securing
scientific positions for Bruce on Arctic and Antarctic expeditions.

13 Bruce, W. S. *The Antarctic*, National Museum of Scotland, Box1,
File1. The *Challenger* expedition (1872–76) was a joint Royal
Society and Royal Naval mission to circumnavigate the globe aiming
at oceanographic research. *HMS Challenger* only briefly entered
Antarctic waters, but was the first steam ship to cross the Antarctic
Circle, reaching 66.67° South 78.37° E on 16 February 1874. The
rocks that were dredged from the floor of the Southern Ocean
provided the first firm evidence that there might be a great Southern
Continental land mass. The expedition is also credited with the first
photographs ever taken of Antarctic Icebergs. (sources: McGonigal
and Woodworth (2001) p. 412 and Headland (2009) p. 201. See also
Report of The Scientific Results of the Exploring Voyage of H.M.S.
Challenger *during the years 1873–76*. John Murray, who supervised
its publication, described the report as 'the greatest advance in the
knowledge of our planet since the celebrated discoveries of the
fifteenth and sixteenth centuries'. The expedition among many other
discoveries, catalogued over 4,000 previously unknown species.

14 Professor Sir Charles Wyville Thomson (1830 –1882), was an
eminent oceanographer with a particular interest in the biology of
the oceans. He was the son of a surgeon working for the British
East India Company. Educated at Merchiston Castle School in
Edinburgh and the University of Edinburgh, in 1851 he became
a lecturer in botany at the University of Aberdeen, and two years
later was appointed Professor of Natural History in Queen's
College, Cork. He then went to the Queen's University of Belfast,
first as Professor of Mineralogy and Geology and later as Professor
of Natural History. In 1870 he became Professor of Natural
History at the University of Edinburgh. In 1868 and 1869 he

persuaded the Royal Navy to lend him two ships to undertake deep
sea dredging to gain a better understanding of life down to a depth
of 1200m. He published his results in *The Depths of the Sea* in
1873. By the time it appeared, however, he had already embarked
on a far greater adventure because in 1870 the Royal Navy agreed
that he could specially modify *HMS Challenger*, for scientific
purposes and use it to explore aspects of the marine environment
never before explored. Thomson was knighted on his return. He is
remembered in a stained glass window in St Michael's Church in
Linlithgow, and the Wyville-Thomson Ridge in the North Atlantic
Ocean is named after him. The NASA Space Shuttle Challenger was
named after *HMS Challenger*. Source: http://www.undiscovered-
scotland.co.uk/usbiography/t/charleswyvillethomson.html

15 Sir John Murray (1841–1914) – Founder Of Modern
    Oceanography – was born in Canada of Scottish descent, Murray
    came to Scotland to be educated and eventually entered Edinburgh
    University, ostensibly to study medicine. Instead he joined a whaler
    as surgeon for a seven-month voyage to the Arctic. Murray took no
    examinations and on his return studied as he pleased, in particular
    zoology and geology. In 1872 he was appointed as an assistant
    scientist on the *Challenger* Expedition (1872–6) under the leadership
    of Wyville Thomson. On his return to Edinburgh he was employed
    at the Treasury-sponsored *Challenger* Commission. This work
    was conducted in the Natural History Department until Wyville
    Thomson's death in 1882, one consequence of which was that the
    official connection of the *Challenger* Commission with Edinburgh
    University ended. But from 1882–4 Murray managed to continue
    research on the *Challenger* collection, sometimes at his own expense.
    In 1883, he set up the Edinburgh Marine Laboratory at Granton, the
    first of its kind in Britain. This laboratory was moved to Millport

in 1894 to become the Scottish Marine Station, the forerunner of
the Scottish Marine Biological Association (SMBA) and the Scottish
Association for Marine Science (SAMS). Throughout this time,
Edinburgh through Murray had retained its dominant position
at the head of the oceanographic community. During this time
Murray became a friend of kings (Norway), princes (Monaco)
and the common man. The contribution of Murray's research in
oceanography is immense. Besides coining the name 'oceanography',
Murray is noted today as the founder of modern oceanography.
The year 1914 was catastrophic for the oceanographic community;
Murray was killed by a motor car as he crossed Frederick Street,
Edinburgh Source: http://www.eeo.ed.ac.uk/public/JohnMurray.html.
He came to disagree with Sir Clements Markham about the aims
of Antarctic exploration. As a consequence he became a strong and
influential supporter of Bruce's expedition to Antarctica in 1902

16 Entry requirements for Edinburgh were the same as for London,
    The Calendar 1887–8

17 *Class Tickets and Certificates* Special Collections, University of
    Edinburgh Library, 1647/ 47/5

18 Special Collections, University of Edinburgh, *Attendance General*
    1647/46/5

19 Special Collections, University of Edinburgh, *Class Tickets and
    Certificates* 1647/46/5

20 Sir John Arthur Thomson (1861–1933) was a Scottish naturalist
    whose clearly written books on biology and attempts to correlate
    science and religion led to wider public awareness of progress in the
    biological sciences. A professor of natural history at the University
    of Aberdeen (1899–1930), Thomson concentrated his research on
    soft corals. He collaborated with the biologist Sir Patrick Geddes in

writing several popular books. He was knighted in 1930. Source:
https://www.britannica.com/biography/John-Arthur-Thomson

21 William Gordon Burn Murdoch (1862–1939) was a Scottish
painter, travel writer and explorer. Murdoch travelled widely,
visiting India, the Arctic and the Antarctic. He was a keen musician
and is said to be the first person to have played the bagpipes in
the Antarctic. He could also claim that he was the first 'Artist in
Residence' in the Antarctic. He published several travel books. A
cape in the South Orkneys is named in his honour. He studied law
at Edinburgh University, but then went to study art in Antwerp
and Paris. He had a lifelong friendship with William Spiers Bruce,
helping Bruce by lending him money and later with organising
a number of projects including the Scottish National Antarctic
Expedition in 1902–04 and the Scottish Spitsbergen Syndicate
which was intended to commercially exploit, as well as chart, the
island of Spitzbergen. In 1905 he travelled with the Prince and
Princess of Wales on their visit to India. In 1906 he was made a
fellow of the Royal Scottish Geographical Society, and he remained
an active member. The Society owns a collection of his work,
including a large oil painting in its board room. Burn Murdoch
died in 1939 in Edinburgh. He and his wife had lived at Arthur
Lodge, where they entertained visitors, including Roald Amundsen
and Robert Falcon Scott. Source: https://www.revolvy.com/main/
index.php?s=William%20Gordon%20Burn%20Murdoch

22 Rudmose Brown, R. N. (1923), *A Naturalist at The Poles*. Seeley,
Service and Co, London p. 24

23 Speak, P. (2003), *William Speirs Bruce, Polar Explorer and Scottish
Nationalist*, Edinburgh, National Museums of Scotland, p. 25

24 Special Collections University of Edinburgh, 1646/46/5

2 *The First Visit to Antarctica, the Dundee Expedition on* Balaena

1 Bruce, W. S. *The Antarctic*, National Museum of Scotland, Box1, File1

2 Gray, J. (1874), Pamphlet, *Report On The New Whaling Grounds of the Southern Seas*. This is reported to have first been circulated in Aberdeen in 1874. It was then reprinted in Aberdeen in 1874, in the periodical of the Royal Society of Victoria in Melbourne in 1887 and again in Peterhead in Scotland in 1891. (Source: Tønnessen, J. N. & A. O. Johnsen (1982), *The History of Modern Whaling*, Hurst & Company, London, p.148)

3 Benjamin Leigh Smith (1821–1913). Leigh Smith (a cousin of Florence Nightingale) made many expeditions to the Arctic regions; on his fifth, his especially adapted ship, the *Eira*, was stranded on a rock and subsequently crushed between icebergs off Cape Flora (Franz Josef Land). The crew was stranded for ten months, survived the Arctic winter, and subsequently set sail in boats with sails made from tablecloths. They were rescued off the coast of Russia. Remarkably, it appears that the *Eira* has now been located, after over 120 years, and at a depth of sixty feet, off Northbrook Island. (The *Times*, Oct. 10 2017, p. 17)

4 Carl A. Larsen (1860–1924) was a Norwegian whaling pioneer and Antarctic explorer. He was Captain of the *Jason* in 1892/3. He made the first discovery of fossils in Antarctica in 1893 and was the first to ski there (on the Ice Shelf named after him). He was Captain of the *Antarctic* during the Swedish National Antarctic Expedition of 1902–04, which included an enforced winter on Paulet Island after the ship was crushed. The ship's cat was kept alive throughout this enforced stay on Paulet Island, resulting in Larsen receiving a medal from the *Sociedad Argentina Protectera de los Animales* ! He was the first to appreciate the opportunities

for whaling using modern techniques in the Southern Ocean and was the first to establish a whaling station in South Georgia, he is regarded as founder of the Antarctic whaling industry.

5 Ernst Haeckel (1834–1919), biologist, naturalist, philosopher, physician, artist

6 Mill, H. R. (1951), *An Autobiography*, Longmans & Green, London, p. 138

7 Burn Murdock W. G. (1894), *From Edinburgh to the Antarctic*, Longmans & Green, Edinburgh, p. 21

8 *ibid*

9 Burn Murdoch, W. G. (1894), *From Edinburgh to the Antarctic*, Longmans & Green, Edinburgh, pp. 79–81

10 Bruce, W. S. *The Antarctic*, National Museum of Scotland, Box1, File 1

11 Burn Murdoch, W. G. (1894), *From Edinburgh to the Antarctic*, Longmans & Green, Edinburgh, p. 140

12 Burn Murdoch, W. G. (1894), *From Edinburgh to the Antarctic*, Longmans & Green, Edinburgh, p. 140

13 Bruce, W. S. *The Antarctic*, National Museum of Scotland, Box1, File 1

14 Burn Murdoch W. G. (1894), *From Edinburgh to the Antarctic*, Longmans & Green, Edinburgh, p. 187

15 Burn Murdoch W. G. (1894), *From Edinburgh to the Antarctic*, Longmans & Green, Edinburgh, p. 170

16 Burn Murdoch W. G. (1894), *From Edinburgh to the Antarctic*, Longmans & Green, Edinburgh, p. 203

17 Bruce, W. S. *The Antarctic*, National Museum of Scotland, Box1, File 1

18 Burn Murdoch W. G. (1894), *From Edinburgh to the Antarctic*, Longmans & Green, Edinburgh, p. 216

19 Special Collections, University of Edinburgh, *Recent Antarctic Explorations*, 1649/77/3

20 Rudmose Brown, R. N. (1923), *A Naturalist at the Poles*. Seeley Service and Co. London, p. 51

21 Bruce, W. S. Special Collections, University of Edinburgh, *Recent Antarctic Explorations*, 1649/77/3

22 Bruce, W. S. (1900), *The Antarctica: An account of the Dundee Whaling Expedition*, National Museum of Scotland. Box1. File 1:1–27

23 Rudmose Brown, R. N. (1923), *A Naturalist at the Poles*. Seeley, Service and Co. London, p. 54

24 Rudmose Brown, R. N. (1923), *A Naturalist at the Poles*. Seeley, Service and Co. London, p. 56

25 *ibid*

26 Bruce, W. S. *Letter to Hugh Robert Mill*, SPRI 100/131/3;D

27 The penguin was found years later in the Scottish National Museum, plus its £5 price tag.

28 Bruce, W. S. *Letter to Hugh Robert Mill*, SPRI 100/131/2;D

29 Swinney, G. N. (2001), *Some new perspectives on the life of William Speirs Bruce (1867–1921)*, Edinburgh, Archives of Natural History. 28 (3) 285–311

30 Bruce, W. S. (1900). '*The Antarctica: An account of the Dundee Whaling Expedition*', National Museum of Scotland, Box1. File No1. p 1–27. He noted Sea Leopard, Weddell, Ross and Crabeater seals

31 Metamorphic rock: rocks that have been transformed after being subjected to high heat and pressure which causes physical and chemical changes, e.g. marble/slate.

32 Sedimentary rock: formed by the accumulation of sediment, in this case in the sea, e.g. sandstone

33 Bruce, W. S. *Meteorological remarks by W. S Bruce on board the Balaena 1892–93*, SPRI MS 101/2;D

34 Burn Murdoch, W. G. (1894), *From Edinburgh to the Antarctic*, Edinburgh, Longmans & Green, p. 355

35 Special Collections, University of Edinburgh, *Recent Antarctic Explorations*, 1649/77/3

36 Murray, J. (1984), *The Renewal of Antarctic Exploration*, The Geographical Journal, No 1, Vol. 111, p. 1–40

37 Burn Murdoch, W. G. (1894), *From Edinburgh to the Antarctic*, Longmans & Green, Edinburgh,

38 Southwell, T. (1895), *Natural Science* Vol. VI, No. 30. pp. 97–107

39 Burn Murdoch, W. G. (1894), *From Edinburgh to the Antarctic*, Longmans & Green, Edinburgh, p. 19

40 Bruce, W. S. *Letter to Editor of Natural Science*, Special Collections Edinburgh Library, 1467/47/5

41 Keighren. J. M. (2003), *A Scott in the Antarctic. The Reception and Commemoration of William Speirs Bruce*, The University of Edinburgh School of Geosciences Institute of Geography, Edinburgh. p. 59

42 Special Collections, University of Edinburgh, 1646/46/5

43 Rudmose Brown, R. N. (1923), *A Naturalist at the Poles*, Seeley Service and Co., London pp 295–97

44 Speak, P. (2003), *William Speirs Bruce, Polar Explorer and Scottish Nationalist*, National Museums of Scotland, Edinburgh, p. 22

45 Statement of Probate, registered in the Principle Probate Registry of His Majesty's High Court of Justice, 5 October 1926, some 4 years after William Speirs Bruce had died. Dr Bruce's will, signed and witnessed, was dated 15 September 1925

3 *The Ben Nevis Observatory*

1 Limelight was a means of illumination in the nineteenth century in which quicklime (calcium oxide) is heated by a flame, producing an

intense white light used for such things as illuminating a stage, or 'illustrations' for projecting images (from photos etc.) onto a screen.

2   Rudmose Brown, R. N. (1923), *A Naturalist at the Poles*: Seeley, London, Service and Co., p. 59

3   *ibid*

4   Bruce, W. S. *Letter to Robert Mill. (1893)*, SPRI; 100/13/3;D

5   Keighren. J. M. (2003), *A Scott in the Antarctic. The Reception and Commemoration of William Speirs Bruce*, The University of Edinburgh School of Geosciences Institute of Geography, Edinburgh, p. 122

6   The National Archives, Colonial Office file CO 78/87 (CO 13891) Letter from William Speirs Bruce to the Governor of the Falkland Islands dated 5 August 1893

7   The National Archives, Colonial Office file CO 78/87 Falkland Islands Public Offices, Misc & Individuals 1893 (CO 13891), handwritten minuting and draft letter to go to Bruce refusing help.

8   Sir Clements Robert Markham KCB FRS (1830 –1916) was an English geographer, explorer, and writer. He was secretary of the Royal Geographical Society (RGS) between 1863 and 1888 and became the Society's president in 1893, serving in that capacity until 1905. Markham started his professional life as a Royal Naval cadet and midshipman, during which time he went to the Arctic with *HMS Assistance* in one of the many searches for the lost expedition of Sir John Franklin. Later, he was a geographer in the India Office and was responsible for the collection of cinchona plants from their native Peruvian forests, and their transplantation in India. By this means the Indian government acquired a home source from which quinine could be extracted. Markham also served as geographer to Sir Robert Napier's Abyssinian expeditionary force, and was present in 1868 at the fall of Magdala. Markham's RGS presidency saw the revival at

the end of the 19th century of British interest in Antarctic exploration after a 50-year interval. He had strong and determined ideas about how the National Antarctic Expedition should be organised, and fought hard to ensure that it was run primarily as a naval enterprise, under Scott's command. To do this he overrode hostility and opposition from much of the scientific community. In the years following the expedition he continued to champion Scott's career, to the extent of disregarding or disparaging the achievements of other contemporary explorers. All his life Markham was a constant traveller and a prolific writer, his works including histories, travel accounts and biographies. He authored many papers and reports for the RGS, and did much editing and translation work for the Hakluyt Society, of which he also became president. He received public and academic honours, and was recognised as a major influence on the discipline of geography, although it was acknowledged that much of his work was based on enthusiasm rather than scholarship. Among the geographical features bearing his name is Antarctica's Mount Markham, named after him by Scott in 1902. He died in his bed having set fire to it with a candle. Source: https://en.wikipedia.org/wiki/Clements_Markham

9 *Report of the British Association for the Advancement of Science Annual Meeting* (1894), pp. 358–9

10 Scottish Geographical Magazine (1894), *Report on Antarctic exploration*, 10, p. 47

11 John Scott Keltie, FRGS, FRS, LL.D. (1840–1927), Geographer and Secretary of the Royal Geographical Society

12 Rudmose Brown, R. N. (1923), *A Naturalist at the Poles*: Seeley, London, Service and Co., p. 59

13 Parliamentary Papers 1920, 34

14 Bruce, W. S. *Letter to Robert Mill*, SPRI, 100/13/3; D

15 Bruce, W. S. Special Collections, University of Edinburgh, Application to Raffles 1647/47/11

16 Robert Cockburn Mossman (1870–1940). Mossman was a self-taught meteorologist, cutting his observing teeth at the Ben Nevis observatory, and also spending a year alone in 1901–02 in a hut high on Glen Nevis, making a series of comparative observations. He later joined the Scottish National Antarctic Expedition and led the wintering party for the second year. He took part in the search for Charcot on the Argentine vessel the *Uruguay*, visiting Grahamland. He then spent 6 years in the Argentine Meteorological Office in Buenos Aires under the direction of W G Davis. He returned to the UK, but then spent most of the rest of his career in Argentina in a variety of roles in the Argentine Met Service. He received the Keith Prize of the Royal Society of Edinburgh in 1918 and also the Gold Medal of the RSGS. He died in Buenos Aires in 1940 (Source: *Nature*, Obituaries, 1940, No 3698, p359)

17 Roy, M. (2013), *The Weathermen of Ben Nevis 1883–1904*, The Royal Society of Edinburgh RSE@Lochaber

18 Angus Rankin (1862 – after 1925). Meteorologist, Ben Nevis and subsequently chief forecaster for Argentina. He died in Cordoba.

19 Bruce, W. S. letter to Rankin, A. *Ben Nevis*. Special Collections University of Edinburgh, 1647/46/4

20 Rankin A. letter to Bruce, *Ben Nevis*. Special Collections, University of Edinburgh, 1647/46/4

21 Bruce, W. S. (1911), *Polar Exploration*, Williams & Norgate, London, p. 192

22 Bruce, W. S. *Letter to Hugh Robert Mill*, SPRI, 100/13/6;D

23 Swinney, G. N. *Some new perspectives on the life of William Speirs Bruce, with a preliminary catalogue of the Bruce Collection of manuscripts held at the University of Edinburgh*. Archives of

Natural History, 285–311, Bruce, W. S., Copy of letter to Arnold, dated 1 Jan 1895 (in error for 1896), in unnumbered notebook Edinburgh University Library Gen 1650.

24 In this claim he was more than 80 years too late. The first people recorded to have set foot on the Continent were the crew of the *Cecilia*, captained by John Davis who landed in the vicinity of Hughes Bay on the Antarctic Peninsula on 7 February 1821. In the ship's log Davis noted 'I think this to be a continent' (Stackpole, E. A., 1955, *The voyage of the Huron and the Huntress: The American Sealers and the Discovery of the Continent of Antarctica*, Connecticut Printers Inc. Hartford)

25 Speak, P. (2003), *William Speirs Bruce, Polar Explorer and Scottish Nationalist*, National Museums of Scotland, Edinburgh, p. 45

26 Archibald Geikie (1836–1924), Scottish geologist and writer. In 1881 he was appointed Director-General of the Geological Survey of the UK and Director of the Museum of Practical Geology. He was a founder member of the Royal Scottish Geographical Society in 1884.

27 Charles Thomson Rees Wilson (1869–1959), Scottish physicist and meteorologist. He was awarded the Nobel Prize in 1927 for his invention of the cloud chamber.

28 William Morris Davis (1850–1934), geographer, geologist and meteorologist.

4 The Jackson–Harmsworth Expedition to Franz Josef Land

1 Alfred Harmsworth, 1st Viscount Northcliffe (1865–1922), newspaper proprietor and owner of tabloid journals

2 Robert E Peary (1856–1929). Peary was an American naval officer (rising to the rank of Rear Admiral) and polar explorer. He claimed to have reached the geographic North Pole in 1909, and this was

widely accepted at the time over the rival claims of Frederick
Cook. But it is becoming accepted that though Peary may have got
to within 60 miles of the pole, it was actually the British explorer
Wally Herbert who was first to reach the Pole 60 years later, when
he dog sledged across the Arctic from Alaska to Spitsbergen.

3 Special Collections, University of Edinburgh, *The Jackson Harmsworth
   expedition 1897, Memorandum from Harmsworth*, 1647/46/4

4 Jackson, F. G. (1935), *The Lure of Unknown Lands*, London, Bell
   and Sons, p. 97

5 *The Times*, 10 July 1894

6 Rudmose Brown, R. N. (1923), *A Naturalist at the Poles*: Seeley,
   Service and Co., London, p. 71

7 Mill, H. R. (1951), *An Autobiography*, Longmans & Green,
   London, p. 139

8 Robert Neil Rudmose Brown (1879–1957) was educated at Dulwich
   College (where he and Shackleton may well have overlapped), at the
   University of Aberdeen and the University of Montpellier. He was
   by training a botanist with a strong inclination towards field study.
   He was an assistant professor of botany at University College from
   1900 to 1902, but then joined Bruce's expedition to Antarctica, being
   awarded the Gold Medal of the RSGS for his part in the expedition.
   He then worked at the Scottish Oceanographical Laboratory, as
   well as visiting Burma on behalf of the Indian Government to
   report on oyster fisheries. He became the Head of the newly created
   Department of Geography at the University of Sheffield in 1908.
   He played a major role in several (1909, 1914, 1919) of Bruce's
   expeditions to Spitsbergen and was deeply involved as a shareholder
   in the Scottish Spitsbergen Syndicate. He had a lifelong passion for
   the Polar Regions and was a very loyal colleague and supporter
   of Bruce. In 1931 a chair in Geography was created at Sheffield

to which Rudmose Brown was appointed. He held this chair until his retirement in 1945. He was seconded to Admiralty Intelligence during WW1, and also in WW2, for the latter work he was awarded the insignia of Commander of the Order of Prince Olav, by King Haakon of Norway. Source: *Nature*, 1957 V179, pp610–611

9 Rudmose Brown, R. N. (1923), *A Naturalist At The Poles*. Seeley, Service and Co., London, p. 66

10 Henry Fisher, Curator Nottingham University College Museum

11 Albert Armitage (1864–1943). Lieutenant Royal Naval Reserve, Navigator & Second-in-command, *Discovery* expedition

12 Reginald Koettlitz (1860–1916). He trained as doctor in Guy's Hospital, London. Physician and geologist on Jackson-Harmsworth Expedition, and on Scott's first expedition as the doctor in charge.

13 Named after the Earl of Northbrook, President of the Royal Geographical Society 1890–1893

14 David Wilton (1863 –1940). Assistant zoologist on the Franz Josef Expedition and a member of the *Scotia* expedition

15 Bruce, W. S. *Letter to H. R. Mill, 1896–99*, SPRI 1325/7/2; D

16 *ibid*

17 Rudmose Brown, R. N. (1923), *A Naturalist At The Poles*. Seeley, Service and Co London, p. 68

18 Fridtjof Nansen (1861–1930) was an explorer, scientist, diplomat, humanitarian, and Nobel Peace Prize laureate. In his youth he was a champion skier and ice skater. He led the team that made the first crossing of the Greenland interior in 1888, and won international fame after reaching a record northern latitude of 86°14'N during the *Fram* expedition of 1893–96. He studied zoology at the Royal Frederick University in Christiania and later worked as a curator at the University Museum of Bergen where his research earned him a

doctorate. Nansen spoke out for the ending of Norway's union with Sweden in 1905, and was instrumental in persuading Prince Carl of Denmark to accept the throne of the newly independent Norway. Between 1906 and 1908 he was the Norwegian representative in London, where he helped negotiate the Integrity Treaty that guaranteed Norway's independent status. In the final decade of his life, Nansen devoted himself primarily to the League of Nations, following his appointment in 1921 as the League's High Commissioner for Refugees. In 1922 he was awarded the Nobel Peace Prize for his work on behalf of the displaced victims of the First World War and related conflicts. After his sudden death in 1930 the League established the Nansen International Office for Refugees to ensure that his work continued. This office received the Nobel Peace Prize in 1938. (source: https://en.wikipedia.org/wiki/Fridtjof_Nansen)

19 Hjaimar Johanson (1867–1913). He went with Nansen to reach a Farthest North record and with Amundsen on the successful South Pole expedition of 1910–1912, though he was not one of the party to reach the pole

20 The *Fram*. She was designed by the Scottish-Norwegian shipwright Colin Archer specifically to survive being trapped in the ice. She had a rounded hull so that ice pressure would cause her to rise up out of the ice. She was used by Nansen for his famous Arctic expedition of 1893–96 when she was intentionally beset in the Arctic Ice and allowed to drift as the ice drifted. She was also the ship used by Amundsen for his South Polar expedition of 1910–12

21 Nansen, F. *Farthest North, The Voyage and Exploration of the Fram 1893–96* (1897), London, Archibald Constable and Company, Vol II, p. 112

22 The Geographical Journal (1944), *Obituary*, Vol. 104, p. 69, The Royal Geographical Society, Stanton Ltd

23 Jackson, F. G. (1935), *The Lure of Unknown Lands*, London, Bell and Sons, p. 165

24 Jackson, F. G. (1899), *1000 Days in the Arctic*, V. II, Harper & Brothers, London, p. 62

25 Bruce, W. S. *Letters to H. R. Mill 1896–99*, SPRI,1325/7/3; D

26 Special Collections, Edinburgh University of Edinburgh, *Diary W. S. Bruce. April 1897*, 1646/39/3

27 Koettlitz, R. (1906), *Scurvy and Antiscorbutics*, Guy's Hospital Gazette, p. 152

28 Jackson, F. G. (1935), *The Lure of Unknown Lands*, London, Bell and Sons, p. 109

29 If seal liver was eaten this would have been Harp Seal

30 Jackson, F. G. (1935), *The Lure of Unknown Lands*, London, Bell and Sons, p. 129

31 Riffenburgh, B. (2004), *Nimrod*, Bloomsbury, p. 78 (paperback edition)

32 Bruce, W. S. *Letters to H. R. Mill 1896–99*, SPRI, MS 1325/7/1-11; D

33 The name by which indigenous Inuit inhabitants of the Arctic were known at this time

34 Special Collections, University of Edinburgh 1647/44/4/1b

35 W. S. Bruce Papers, *1896–1897 the Jackson Harmsworth Expedition*, National Museum of Scotland. Box 2 File 5

36 Jackson, F. G. (1899), *1000 Days in the Arctic*, V. II, Harper & Brothers, London. p. 314

37 Bruce, W. S. *Letters to H. R. Mill 1896–99*, SPRI,1325/7/1-11; D

38 Jackson, F. *Leader's report*, SPRI 287/29; D

39 Jackson, F. *Original maps and charts 1893–1897*, SPRI 419/1-7; MSM

40 Bruce, W. S. National Museum of Scotland, Box 2, File 11

41 Jackson Harmsworth Expedition. 1897 Special Collections, University of Edinburgh 1647/46/4a

42 William Eagle Clarke (1853–1938). He was Curator of Leeds Museum 1884–1888 then moved to Natural History Department of Royal Scottish Museum in 1888 Where he was Keeper, 1906–1921

43 Speak, P. (2003), *William Speirs Bruce, Polar Explorer and Scottish Nationalist*, National Museums of Scotland, Edinburgh, p. 51

44 Special Collections, University of Edinburgh *Lt Col Bailey to W. S. Bruce 1647/46/5*

5 *Novaya Zemlya, the Barents Sea and Spitsbergen*

1 Andrew Coats (1852–1930). He was a member of the textile company, J&P Coats Ltd, manufacturers of Paisley. The family founded the Coats Observatory in Paisley for Meteorological work.

2 Mill, H. R. (1951), A *Biography*, Longmans & Green, London, p. 141

3 Bruce, W. S. *Letter to H. R. Mill*, SPRI 1325/7/5: D

4 Albert, Prince of Monaco (1848–1922). As a young man he served in the Spanish Navy, and then in the French Navy, where during the Franco-Prussian war of 1870 he was awarded the Legion of Honour. The prince devoted much of his life to science, particularly oceanography. He had a succession of four specially designed research yachts (including the *Princesse Alice* which was the second to be commissioned) and made many research expeditions to the North Atlantic and the Arctic. He also founded the Oceanographic Museum of Monaco. (source: https://en.wikipedia.org/wiki/Albert_I,_Prince_of_Monaco)

5 Bruce, W. S. *Letters to H. R. Mill*, SPRI 1325/7/1-11; D

6 Bruce, W. S. (1898), *Blencathra*. National Museum of Scotland, Box 2, File. 22

7   Equipment Accounts, *Blencathra*. National Museum of Scotland, Box 2, File 23

8   Bruce, W. S. *Letters to H. R. Mill* SPRI, 1325/7/5; D

9   Rudmose Brown, R. N. (1923), *A Naturalist At The Poles*. Seeley, Service and Co., London, p. 80

10 The Grey Phalarope breeds in the Arctic areas and winters around the African and South American coasts. It has a black cap (males more streaked than females), a yellow bill with black tip and a red underside.

11 Svalbard archipelago. Approximately midway between Norway and the North Pole, Islands in the group vary from 74° to 81° N. latitude

12 Bear Island. Southernmost Island of the Svalbard Archipelago. In the Western Barents Sea

13 Wiche Island. Discovered 1617 by an expedition of the Muscovy Company and named after a member of the Company

14 Bruce, W. S. *Letter to H. R. Mill*. SPRI,100/13/3; D

15 Bruce, W. S. *The Coats Antarctic Expedition*, The National Museum of Scotland, Box 2, File 22

16 Knight Commander of the Order of the Bath, 1898

17 Bruce, W. S. *Letter to H. R. Mill*, SPRI,1325,7/8; D

18 In 1885, Prince Albert I of Monaco decided to create a marine biology laboratory in the Principality. In 1889, his scientific collections were presented in the pavilion of Monaco at the Universal Expo in Paris and generated immense interest. The Prince therefore decided to create an Oceanographic Museum. The first stone is laid on 25 April 1899 but the official opening inauguration did not take place until 29 March 1910. Both his Oceanographic Institute and the Museum continue to operate. (source: http://www.institut-ocean.org/)

19 Jules Richard. (1863–1956), was the first director of the Musée Océanographique de Monaco, filling that post from 1900 to 1945.

20 John Young Buchanan (1844–1925). Chemist and Oceanographer. He was the Chemist on *The Challenger* Expedition

21 Karl Brandt (1854–1931), Professor of Zoology at Kiel. In 1880s made a series of cruises that showed the ubiquity and uniqueness of plankton species.

22 Rudmose Brown, R. N. (1923), *A Naturalist At The Poles*. Seeley, Service and Co., London, p. 84

23 Kaiser Wilhelm II (1859–1941), Emperor, German Empire and Prussia, 1888 to 1918

24 Empress Auguste Viktoria of Schleswig-Holstein (1858–1921)

25 Bruce, W. S. *Spitsbergen 1898 and 1899: Voyages with the HSH Prince of Monaco* National Museum of Scotland, Box 3, File 22

26 Named after Charles, second son of King James I of England. He became King Charles I.

27 Bruce, W. S. *Spitsbergen 1898 and 1899: Voyages with the HSH Prince of Monaco* National Museum of Scotland, Box 10, file 109

28 Bruce, W. S. *Spitsbergen 1898 and 1899: Voyages with the HSH Prince of Monaco* National Museum of Scotland, Box 3, File 22

29 Bruce, W. S. *Spitsbergen 1898 and1899: Voyages with HSH The Prince of Monaco* National Museum of Scotland, Box 10, File 109

30 Bruce, W. S *Spitsbergen 1898 and 1899: Voyages with HSH The Prince of Monaco*. National Museum of Scotland Box 3, File 29

31 The Swedish Government expedition had its headquarters at Treurenberg

32 Bruce, W. S. *Spitsbergen 1898 and 1899: Voyages with the HSH Prince of Monaco* National Museum of Scotland Box 10, File 109

33 Bruce, W. S. *Letter to H. R. Mill*, SPRI, 1325/7/10; D

34 Bruce, W. S. *Letter to H. R. Mill*, SPRI, 1325/7/11; D

6 *Preparations for the Scotia Expedition*

1   In 1707, on 22 October (2 November, by the modern calendar),
    Admiral Sir Cloudesley Shovell's flagship, HMS *Association*,
    struck rocks near the Isles of Scilly. *Association* went down in
    three or four minutes. None of the 800 men that were on board
    survived. It was largely as a result of this disaster that the Board
    of the Admiralty instituted a competition for a more precise
    method to determine longitude.

2   John Murray edited the fifty volumes of the *Challenger* results and
    wrote seven himself

3   Murray, J. (1894), *The Renewal of Antarctic Exploration*, The
    Geographical Journal. No.1, Vol. 111, pp 1–40

4   Markham, C. *Personal Journal, 27 November 1893*, CRM/1/15,
    RGS (with IGB) Archive

5   Markham, C. *Personal Journal, 8 August 1893*, CRM/1/15, RGS
    (with IGB) Archive

6   Alexander Buchan (1829–1907), meteorologist, oceanographer
    and botanist. He established the weather map as a basic for
    weather forecasting.

7   Bartholomew, J. C. (1860–1920). A founder member of the RSGS
    with James Geikie and Agnes Livingstone Bruce (the daughter of
    David Livingstone and no relation to William Speirs). He came
    from a distinguished family of cartographers (grandson of the
    founder of the map maker John Bartholomew Ltd) and is credited
    as having named the Continent of Antarctica in 1890

8   Rudmose Brown, R. N. (1923), *A Naturalist At The Poles*. Seeley,
    Service and Co., London, p. 93

9   Keighren, I. M. (2003), *A Scott in the Antarctic. The reception and
    Commemoration of William Speirs Bruce*, University of Edinburgh
    School of Geosciences Institute of Geography. Edinburgh, p. 92

10 Georg Newmayer (1826–1909), Polar explorer and scientist. A proponent for international cooperation for meteorology and scientific observations.

11 Keltie, J. S. & H. R. Mill (1986), *Report of the Sixth International Geographical Congress: Held in London, 1895*. London. Vol. 6. Murray J.

12 Bruce, W. S. (1985), *The Proposed Scientific and Commercial Expedition to the Antarctic 1896–1898*. RSGS: Archives Series 3593, Box 1

13 Sven Foyn (1809–1894). Norwegian whaler and shipping magnate. He invented the grenade harpoon gun that exploded on impact with whales.

14 John Henrik Bull (1844–1930), Norwegian pioneer of Antarctic exploration

15 Communication from Robert Burton, Antarctic writer, 2016

16 Burn Murdoch, W. G. (1894), *From Edinburgh to the Antarctic*, Longmans & Green, Edinburgh, p 253

17 Buchanan, J. *Letter to William Speirs Bruce*, SPRI, 101/26/1: D

18 The Royal Society, London, Box 547/8

19 Fowler, M. *Letter from R.S. to R.S.G.S (14/11/1899)*, RSGS Archive Series 3593 Box 1

20 Bruce, W. S. *Letters between Bruce and Sir Clements Markham, 1899–1901*, SPRI, MS 441/16

21 Edinburgh University Library, Special Collections 1651/101/5

22 Bruce, W. S. *Letters between Bruce and Sir Clements Markham, 1899–1901*, SPRI, MS 441/16; D

23 Bruce, W. S. Royal Scottish Geographical Society, Archives Series, 3593, Box 1

24 RGS (with IBG) Archive, Mill H. R. *Daily Jottings*, 23 March 1900, GB402HRM – the Hugh Robert Mill collection,

25 Bruce, W. S. *Letters between Bruce and Sir Clements Markham, 1899–1901*, SPRI, MS 441/16;D

26 Bruce, W. S. *Letters between Bruce and Sir Clements Markham, 1899–1901*, SPRI, MS 441/16; D

27 SPRI Archive, Bruce, William S MS441/7D letter from Bruce to PM Price, dated 24 August 1917 SPRI 44 1/7;D

28 Bruce, W. S. *Letters between Bruce and Sir Clements Markham, 1899–1901*, SPRI, MS 441/16; D

29 Rudmose Brown, R. N. (1923), *A Naturalist At The Poles*. Seeley, Service and Co., London. p. 98

30 Bruce, William S. *Letters between Bruce and Sir Clements Markham, 1899–1901*, SPRI, MS441/16; D

31 Mill, H. R. (1951), *An Autobiography*, London, Longman; p. 147

32 RGS (with IBG) Archive, Mill, H. R. *Daily Jottings*, 28 March 1900, GB402HRM – the Hugh Robert Mill collection

33 Jessie Mackenzie Bruce (1870–1942). She was born in Nigg, a community on the east coast of Scotland

34 Bruce, W. S. *Letter to Hugh Robert Mill*. SPRI MS 100/131/7; D

35 Bruce, W. S. to Prince Albert of Monaco.1900–1920 Musée de Monaco, Dossier 288

36 Buchanan, J. *Letter to William Speirs Bruce*, SPRI, 101/26/2: D

37 Marriage Certificate *Scotland's People*, Scotlandspeople.gov.uk Statutory Marriages 078/1 1901, Bruce William S.

38 Census data from 1901 Census. This is at odds with what Peter Speak states. He gives their address in 1902 as 2 Milton Road, it is not clear from where his information came. Speak, P. (2003), *William Speirs Bruce, Polar Explorer and Scottish Nationalist*, Edinburgh, National Museums of Scotland, p. 60

39 Speak, P (2003), *William Speirs Bruce, Polar Explorer and Scottish Nationalist*, p. 75, NMS Publishing, Edinburgh

40 RGS (with IBG), Letter from Bruce to Markham dated November 20 1902. File CB7/Bruce, W. S.

41 A review of Markham's personal Journals held in the RGS (with IBG) Archive from 1900 to 1912 failed to find any entries referring to Bruce or the SNAE.

42 For example Buchanan sent Bruce £30 in January and £30 in July 1901, a further £20 in 1902, followed by £30 in August1910 and £10 in January 1911

43 Census data for the family household for 1901 and 1911 show that there were no resident domestic staff on the days of the census, *Scotland's People*, Scotlandspeople.gov.uk

7 *The Scotia Expedition*

1 John Buchanan sent £100 to be entirely at Bruce's disposal. SPRI 101/26/5; D

2 Special Collections, University of Edinburgh, 1651/101/12

3 The Prince of Monaco gave deep-sea appliances. Other donations included a thermometer, a hydrometer, a theodolite and a telescope.

4 This quote is attributed to Bruce, but the authors have been unable to track down its original source. The sentiments are however recorded by Bruce in: Bruce, W. S. (1911), *Polar Exploration*, Williams & Norgate, London, p. 236.

5 Bruce, W. S. (1902), *The Scottish National Antarctic Expedition*, Geographical Journal, V20, No 4, pp. 438–440

6 Bruce, W. S. (1902), *The Scottish National Antarctic Expedition*, Geographical Journal, V20, No 4, p. 439

7 George Lennox Watson (1851–1904). He started the first yacht design office that was dedicated to small boats.

8 Rudmose Brown, R. N. (1923). *A Naturalist at the Poles*, Seeley, Service and Co., p. 104

9   Bruce, W. S. *General Articles*, National Museum of Scotland Box
    3, File 29

10 Bruce, W. S. *Letter to High Robert Mill*, SPRI, 100/131/1/10/; D

11 Keighren, I. M. (2003), *A Scott in the Antarctic the reception and
    Commemoration of William Speirs Bruce*, University of Edinburgh
    School of Geosciences Institute of Geography; Edinburgh, p. 135

12 Rudmose Brown, *Notebook*, SPRI 356/4:BJ

13 Rudmose Brown, R. N. (1923), *A Naturalist at the Poles*, Seeley,
    Service and Co; p. 116

14 Rudmose Brown, R. N. (1923), *A Naturalist at the Poles*, Seeley,
    Service and Co; p. 117

15 Rudmose Brown, R. N., J. H. H. Pirie & R. C. Mossman (1978
    edition of the original published in 1906), *The Voyage of the
    Scotia*, Hurst & Co. London p. 13

16 Rudmose Brown, R. N., J. H. H. Pirie & R. C. Mossman (1978
    edition of the original published in 1906), *The Voyage of the
    Scotia*, Hurst & Co, London p. 24

17 *The Scotsman*, 23 October 1902

18 Bruce, W. S. (1903), *The 'Scotia' Voyage to the Falkland Islands*,
    Scottish Geographical Magazine, p. 169–183

19 Bruce, W. S. *Manuscript Journal*, SPRI, 101/3;BJ

20 This is now known not to be unusual. Pack ice is commonly
    encountered to the north of the South Orkneys throughout the
    summer.

21 Bruce, W. S. *Log of the* Scotia, N.M.S; 5/02/1903

22 The usual way to penetrate the Weddell Sea nowadays is to sail
    east to nearly the Greenwich meridian, then turn South, skirting
    the edge of the Weddell Sea gyre (a system of rotating currents
    particularly those involved with large wind movements), hoping to
    encounter open water (the 'shore lead') between the pack ice and

the shore that often appears along the coast of the Weddell Sea
and allows a South Westerly passage into the Weddell.

23 Rudmose Brown R. N., J. H. H. Pirie & R. C. Mossman (1978
edition of the original published in 1906), *The Voyage of the
Scotia*, C. Hurst & Co, London p. 69

24 Bruce, W. S. (1992), *Log of the* Scotia *Expedition 1902–4*, Ed.
Peter Speak, Edinburgh University Press Edinburgh, p. 77

25 *ibid*

26 These days, ships can hold position to a very high degree of
accuracy by using GPS coupled to a sophisticated autopilot
driving both the main engine and thrusters at the bow and stern.

27 The temperature increased towards the Equator to 81.6°F. It fell
sharply beyond 25°S latitude, dropping 20° between 28 December
1902 and 3 January 1903.

28 Made so that whichever side of the equipment was uppermost the
trawl remained functional

29 W. S. Bruce Papers. *Meteorological Observations*. National
Museum of Scotland, Box 8, File 100

30 Mossman, R. C. (1910), *The present position of Antarctic
meteorology*. Quarterly Journal of the Royal Meteorological
Society, 36(156) pp. 361–374

31 Bruce, W. S. *Log of the* Scotia *Expedition 1902–4*, Ed. Peter
Speak, Edinburgh University Press, Edinburgh, p. 79

32 This condition is known as a 'white out'. It occurs when there is an
even but complete cloud cover over a snow surface. Light bounces
back and forward between surface and cloud to create illumination
from all directions, thus removing all shadow and hence, contrast
or definition in the snow surface, but visibility can be perfect,
in that a coloured rock feature miles away will be visible, but a

crevasse a few feet away will be invisible. A complete white-out is like being trapped inside a table tennis ball. It is very disorienting.

33 Bruce, W. S. (1992), *Log of the* Scotia *Expedition 1902–4*, Ed. Peter Speak, Edinburgh University Press, Edinburgh, p. 115

34 Bruce, W. S. *Extracts from Journal*, SPRI, 101/4;BJ

35 Rudmose Brown, R. N., J. H. H. Pirie & R. C. Mossman (1978 edition of the original published in 1906), *The Voyage of the Scotia*, Hurst & Co. London p. 78

36 Rudmose Brown, R. N, J. H. H. Pirie & R. C. Mossman (1978 edition of the original published in 1906), *The Voyage of the Scotia*, Hurst & Co. London p. 109

37 Rudmose Brown, R. N. (1923), *A Naturalist at the Poles*, Seeley, Service and Co., p. 143

38 The ten-legged 'Sea Spider' is a *Pentanymphon antarcticum*, a type of primitive marine arthropod. Found commonly amongst the World's oceans, but grows to massive size due to a phenomenon known as 'polar gigantism'. This is believed to be linked to the high oxygen content held in the cold water in which they live

39 Rudmose Brown, R. N. (1923). *A Naturalist at the Poles*, Seeley, Service and Co., p. 148

40 Bruce, W. S. (1992), *Log of the* Scotia *Expedition 1902–4*, Ed. Peter Speak, Edinburgh University Press, Edinburgh, p. 133

41 Speak, P. (2003), *William Speirs Bruce, Polar Explorer and Scottish Nationalist*, National Museums of Scotland Publishing, p. 84

42 The remains of the stone work of Ormond House are still visible though the building has largely collapsed.

43 Bruce, W. S. *Biology and Bird Notes*, National Museum of Scotland Box 5 File 54

44 Rudmose Brown, R. N., J. H. H. Pirie & R. C. Mossman (1978 edition of the original published in 1906), *The Voyage of the* Scotia, Hurst & Co. London p. 169

45 *Podocarpus* was in fact, a common species in the flora of Antarctica during the Cretaceous period around 100 million years ago. But this was not known in the early 1900s and the presence of *Podocarpus* was taken as providing new information of wind carriage from South America.

46 Ferrier J. G. *Letter to Bruce*, SPRI.101/40/1;D

47 Special Collections University of Edinburgh, *South Orkneys and Argentina* 1646/24/14

48 Rudmose Brown, R. N. (1923). *A Naturalist at the Poles*, Seeley, Service and Co; p. 166

49 *El Gladiator*, 8 January 1904

50 Walter G Davis (1851–1919). Davis an American, trained as an engineer. He became a renowned Meteorologist and the Director of the Argentine Meteorological Office from 1885 to his retirement in 1915

51 William Henry Doveton Haggard (1846–1926), First Minister to Argentina from 1902 to 1906. At that time the Foreign Office did not consider the Buenos Aires legation important enough to warrant ambassadorial rank.

52 Dudeney, J. R. & D. H. Walton (2011), *From Scotia to 'Operation Tabarin': developing British policy for Antarctica*, Polar Record DOI: 10.1017/S0032247411000520

53 The National Archives, Foreign Office file, FO 118/264, Letter from Admiralty to Undersecretary of State, Foreign Office, 26 March 1904

54 Bruce, W. S. (1992), *Log of the* Scotia *Expedition* 1902–4, Ed. Peter Speak, Edinburgh University Press, Edinburgh, p. 205

55 The National Archives, Colonial Office file CO78/109 (30162),
    South Orkneys

56 The National Archives Colonial Office file CO537/2465,
    Memorandum from J Barton dated 17 November 1947

57 Headland, R. K. (2009), *A Chronology of Antarctic Exploration*,
    Quaritch, London. Entry 557, p. 133

58 To be internationally accepted a territorial claim needed to progress
    through three stages to be 'perfected'. The raising of a flag on a piece
    of territory provided an 'inchoate' claim, which unless followed
    up would lapse after an ill-defined time. To perfect the claim the
    claimant nation would have to recognise the claim be enacting some
    form of legislation recognised as valid in international law, and then
    take steps to demonstrate that it was administering the territory.

59 Dudeney, J. R. & D. H. Walton (2011), *From Scotia to 'Operation
    Tabarin': developing British policy for Antarctica*, Polar Record;
    DOI: 10.1017/S0032247411000520

60 Keighren, I. M. (2003), *A Scott in the Antarctic the reception and
    Commemoration of William Speirs Bruce*, University of Edinburgh
    School of Geosciences Institute of Geography. Edinburgh, p. 151

61 Acuña, H. (2015), Diario *Del Estafeta*, Ushuaia, Ojosvista
    Pubilcaciones

62 Bruce, W. S. (1992), *Log of the* Scotia *Expedition 1902–4*,
    Ed. Peter Speak, Edinburgh University Press, Edinburgh, p. 216

63 Rudmose Brown, R. N. (1923). *A Naturalist at the Poles*, Seeley,
    Service and Co., p. 176

64 Bruce, W. S. (1992), *Log of the* Scotia *Expedition 1902–4*,
    Ed. Peter Speak, Edinburgh University Press, Edinburgh, p. 219

65 At this position she was over a feature now known as the 'Scotia Rise'
    close to the Stancomb-Wills Icestream and a significant 'land' feature
    now known as the Lydden Ice Rise, where the shelf ice is grounded.

66 Murray, J. (1903), The Renewal of Antarctic Exploration: *The Geographical Journal*: 3:1–43

67 Bruce, W. S. to J. Bartholomew, SPRI, 1550; D

68 *ibid*

69 Rudmose Brown, R. N. (1923). *A Naturalist at the Poles*, Seeley, Service and Co., p. 212

70 Confirmation from Mike Robinson, BA Hons. Chief Executive RSGS

71 Rudmose Brown, R. N., J. H. H. Pirie & R. C. Mossman (1978 edition of the original published in 1906), *The Voyage of the Scotia*, Hurst & Co. London p. 313. It is interesting to note that Burn Murdoch seems to imply in Rudmose Brown's biography of Bruce (Rudmose Brown, R. N. (1923), *A Naturalist At The Poles*. Seeley Service and Co., London, p. 269), that the text Edward VII sent also contained the enigmatic comment '…alas and alack-a–day! Our regalia on the shelf, and the red flag instead of the Lion Rampant in Glasgow Streets! Are you surprised that with no one on the bridge the crew try to take charge!' This could be interpreted as a Royal hint relating to the expedition's persistent emphasis on its Scottish nature. It seems unlikely however that the King would have actually sent such a public text.

72 The RSGS President, Sir John Murray, presented the medal to Bruce at Millport, on Great Cumbrae in the Firth of Clyde, on his return from the Antarctic.

8 *The Scottish Oceanographical Laboratory*

1 Rudmose Brown, R. N. (1923), *A Naturalist at The Poles*. Seeley, Service and Co., London.1923, p. 250

2 Keighren. I. M. (2003), *A Scott in the Antarctic. The Reception and Commemoration of William Speirs Bruce*, The University of Edinburgh School of Geosciences Institute of Geography, Edinburgh, p. 168

3   Rudmose Brown, R. N. (1923), *A Naturalist at The Poles*. Seeley, Service and Co., London. p. 215

4   Keighren. I. M. (2003), *A Scott in the Antarctic. The Reception and Commemoration of William Speirs Bruce*, The University of Edinburgh School of Geosciences Institute of Geography, Edinburgh, p. 94

5   Bruce, W. S. National Museum of Scotland, Box NMS, Supplementary information

6   Bruce, W. S. *Letter to Rudmose Brown*, SPRI, 356/46/62;D

7   Bruce, W. S. *Letter to Rudmose Brown*, SPRI, 356/46/114:D

8   Rudmose Brown, R. N., J. H. H. Pirie & R. C. Mossman (1978 edition of the original published in 1906), *The Voyage of the Scotia*, London, C. Hurst and Co.

9   Rudmose Brown, R. N., J. H. H. Pirie & R. C. Mossman (1978 edition of the original published in 1906), *The Voyage of the Scotia*, London, C. Hurst and Co, p. vii

10 The *Athenaeum*, No 4122, Oct.27, 1906 p 516

11 Huntford, R. (1985), *Shackleton*, Hodder & Stoughton, p. 459

12 Andrew Murray (1849–1942), 1st Viscount Dunedin. He was a Politician and Judge. In 1907 he was Lord Justice General and Lord President of the Court of Session.

13 Keighren. I. M. (2003), *A Scott in the Antarctic. The Reception and Commemoration of William Speirs Bruce*, The University of Edinburgh School of Geosciences Institute of Geography, Edinburgh, p. 98

14 Bruce, W. S. *Letter to Rudmose Brown* SPRI, 356/46/24; D

15 *Scotia* returned to sealing and whaling off East Greenland but was laid up in 1910 due to declining catches. She then became part of an international ice patrol that monitored ice conditions in the North Atlantic after the sinking of *Titanic*, which was established later in the year. In World War 1 she was sold to the Hudson's Bay Company,

which chartered her to the French government. On January 1916, while carrying coal and ammunition from Bristol to Bordeaux, she caught fire and was beached on Sully Island in the Bristol Channel. She burned for more than ten days and became a total wreck

16 Rudmose Brown, R. N. (1923), *A Naturalist At The Poles*, Seeley Service and Co., London, asserts this on p. 252, but the Carnegie Trust UK was not established until 1913. However, there was and still is a Carnegie Dunfermline Trust, which was established in 1903 to do good works in Carnegie's town of birth. It may be that it was this precursor that gave Bruce help.

17 Bruce, W. S. *Letter to Rudmose Brown*, SPRI.356/46/106; D
The application had to be from a Scottish graduate, resident in Scotland. It was made by Rudmose Brown from Aberdeen.

18 Rudmose Brown, R. N. (1923), *A Naturalist At The Poles*, Seeley Service and Co., London, p 239

19 Bruce, W. S. *Letter to H. R. Mill*, SPRI, 100/13/16;D

20 Rudmose Brown, R. N. (1923), *A Naturalist At The Poles*, Seeley Service and Co., London, p. 240

21 Bruce, W. S. *Letters to Robert Neil Rudmose Brown*, SPRI,356/46/10

22 The National Archives, Treasury file T1/11679 *Grants to Scottish National Antarctic Expedition 1914*. Treasury 21596, 25 October 1909

23 Bruce, W. S. *Letter to Hugh Robert Mill*, SPRI, 100/13/18;D

24 *Nature*, Vol. 82 13/1/1910 'Notes', p. 315

25 Rudmose Brown, *Letter to Ferrier*, SPRI, 101/19/2; 2. It is worth noting that Shackleton's *Endurance* expedition could hardly be labelled as 'English' since only just over half of the team were English by birth, the rest coming from Scotland (3), Ireland (4), Wales (1), Australia (1), New Zealand (2), India (1) and North America (1).

26 *The Field, Travel and Colonisation,* 5/1/1910 p. 80

27 *ibid*

28 Keighren. I. M. (2003), *A Scott in the Antarctic. The Reception and Commemoration of William Speirs Bruce,* The University of Edinburgh School of Geosciences Institute of Geography, Edinburgh, p. 105

29 Personal communication Mrs Moira Watson (née Bruce), born 1930, Mrs Watson emigrated to Canada in 1967.

30 The National Archives, Treasury file T1/11679 *Grants to Scottish National Antarctic Expedition 1914.* Letter from James Ferrier (secretary of the *Scotia* Expedition) to Prime Minister Asquith, dated 27 November 1909.

31 David Lloyd George (1863–1945), Chancellor of the Exchequer 1908–1915, later Prime Minister

32 Charles Edward Price (1857–1934), Liberal Member of Parliament Edinburgh Central 1906–1918

33 The National Archives, Treasury file T1/11679 *Grants to Scottish National Antarctic Expedition 1914,* Letter from Lord Pentland to the Chancellor of the Exchequer (Lloyd George) dated 4 March 1910

34 John Sinclair (1860–1925), 1st Baron Pentland. He was a Scottish Liberal Politician and held the post Secretary of State for Scotland from 1905 to 1912.

35 Keighren. I. M. (2003), *A Scott in the Antarctic. The Reception and Commemoration of William Speirs Bruce,* The University of Edinburgh School of Geosciences Institute of Geography. Edinburgh, p. 106

36 Rudmose Brown, R. N. (1923), *A Naturalist at The Poles* Seeley, Service and Co., London. p. 253

37 The National Archives, Treasury file T1/11679 *Grants to Scottish National Antarctic Expedition 1914*. Treasury 16880, 21 January 1911 and 15982, 21 August 1911

38 Copies of the finished editions were sent to, amongst others: Nordenskjold. Drygalski, Cardot, Charcot, Shackleton, Scott, Sir John Murray.

39 Bruce, W. S. *Letter to Robert Neil Rudmose Brown*, SPRI 356/46/21:D

40 Eagle Clarke, W. (1905.1906 & 1907), The *Ibis*, Eighth series, vol. v. April 1905, pp. 247–268. Eighth series vol. vi Jan 1906. pp 145–187, Ninth Series vol. 1, April 1907. pp 325–348

41 Dudeney, J. R. & J. Sheail (2014), *William Speirs Bruce and the Polar Medal: myth and reality*, *The Polar Journal* DOI: 10.1080/2154896X.2014.913915

42 Documents consulted include: The National Archives, The Archives of the Royal Geographical Society (with IBG) and the Royal Archives at Windsor.

43 Bruce, W. S. (1911), *Polar Exploration*, Williams & Norgate, London

44 Amanuensis is defined by the Oxford Concise Dictionary as 'a literary assistant'

45 Ferrier, J. *Letter to Bruce, W. S.* SPRI 100/40/39; D

46 Bruce, W. S. *Letter to Robert Neil Rudmose Brown*, 356/46/21; D

47 Rudmose Brow, R. N. *Letter to Bruce*, SPRI, 101/19/37; D

48 Bruce, W. S. *Letters to Robert Neil Rudmose Brown*, SPRI, 356/46/23; D

49 Bruce, W. S. *Letters to Robert Neil Rudmose Brown*, SPRI, 356/46/31; D

50 Rudmose Brown, R. N. *Letter to Bruce*, SPRI 101/19/31; D

51 Rudmose Brown, R. N. *Letter to Bruce*, SPRI 101/19/29; D

52 Bruce, W. S. *Letter to Rudmose Brown*, SPRI 356/46/16; D

53 Rudmose Brown, R. N. *Letter to Bruce*, SPRI 101/19/42; D

54 Rudmose Brown, R. N. (1923), *A Naturalist At The Poles* Seeley Service and Co, London, p. 260

55 Mossman, R. *Letter to H R Mill* SPRI 100/81/10;D

56 Personal communication, Mrs Moira Watson, June 2016

57 Bruce, W. S. *Letter to Rudmose Brown* SPRI 356/46/59;D

58 *ibid*

59 Bruce, W. S. *Letter to T. H. Gillespie*. Special Collections University of Edinburgh 1674/42/11. The Zoo was the brainchild of Thomas Gillespie. Bruce wanted an aquarium because the aquarium in New York attracted two million visitors/annum – he did not support the development of either a research institution or a laboratory.

60 The National Archives, Colonial Office file CO78/127 (26677) August 1913, *Dr W. S. Bruce*

61 Bruce, W. S. *Letter to Rudmose Brown* SPRI 356/46/58:D

62 By this time they appear to have set up home in South Morton Street, which leads off Joppa Road. Peter Speak (2003, p. 60) gives their dates there as 1906 to 1919, the 1911 Census certainly places them there in 1911. This house was given the name 'Antarctica', according to Speak in 1907, and the name was transferred to the Joppa Road house subsequently.

63 Personal communication, Mrs Moira Watson née Bruce, June 2016

64 The National Archives, Treasury file T1/11679 Grants to Scottish National Antarctic Expedition, letter dated 23 January 1914 from Treasury to Ferrier

65 Bruce, W. S. *Letter to Rudmose Brown* SPRI, 356/46/114;D

66 Bruce, W. S. *Letter to Rudmose Brown*, SPRI, 356/46/115; D

67 SNAE *Application to the Lords Commissioners of His Majesty's Treasury*, RGS, CB8 1911–1920

68 Ramsay MacDonald (1855–1937). Labour MP 1906, First Labour Prime Minister, 1924

69 Bruce, W. S. *Letter to Rudmose Brown* SPRI 356/46/111;D

70 Bruce, W. S. *Letter to Lord Curzon*, 20 April 1914 RGS, CB8, 1911–1920

71 Heath, T. L. *Letter to the Secretary of the SNAE*, 6 April 1914 RGS, CB8 1911–1918

72 The *Glasgow Herald*, Friday 17 April 1914

73 Bruce, W. S. *Letter to Rudmose Brown* SPRI 356/46/114: D

9 *The Impact of the First World War on Bruce*

1 Bruce, W. S. *Letter to R. N. Rudmose Brown*, SPRI, 356/46/123

2 Rudmose Brown, R. N. (1923), *A Naturalist at The Poles*. Seeley, Service and Co, London. p. 284

3 Bruce, W. S. *Letters to Rudmose Brown* SPRI 356/46/; D

4 *ibid*

5 MacKellar, C. D. *Letter to Bruce*, SPRI, 356/96; D

6 *ibid*

7 Bruce, W. S. *Letter to C. D. MacKellar*, SPRI, 356/96; D

8 Shackleton was bound by an exclusive contract to the Daily Chronicle which by this time was funding the expenses of the dependents of the expedition, and also raising the alarm as to the need for a rescue mission. (Dudeney J. R., J. Sheail & D. W. H. Walton, 2014)

9 Bruce, W. S. *Letter to R. H. Boyle*. SPRI, 1606;D

10 Dudeney J. R., J. Sheail & D. W. H. Walton (2014), *The British Government, Ernest Shackleton, and the rescue of the Imperial Trans-Antarctic Expedition*, Polar Record, DOI:10.1017/ S0032247414000631

11 Bruce, W. S. Letter to Rudmose Brown dated 6 May 1916, SPRI MS356/46/143

12 Bruce, W. S. *Letter to Rudmose Brown* SPRI 356/46/121;D

13 Bruce, W. S. *Letter to Rudmose Brown* SPRI 356/46/174;D

14 Rudmose Brown, R. N. *Letter to Bruce*, W. S, SPRI, 101/19/22:D

15 Bruce, W. S. *Letter to Rudmose Brown* SPRI 356/46/176;D

16 Bruce, W. S. *Letter to Rudmose Brown* SPRI 356/46/174:D

17 Bruce, W. S. *Letter to Rudmose Brown* SPRI 356/46/193;D.
   The River Tweed runs along the border between Scotland and
   Northern England.

18 Darnley, E. R. (1875–1944), He joined the Colonial Office as a
   Second Class Clerk in 1898. He retired as an Assistant Secretary
   in 1933. He was deeply involved in the genesis of the Southern
   whaling industry and the territorial claim to the Dependencies.

19 The National Archives, Colonial Office File CO 78/144 (55321),
   Letter from Admiralty to Colonial Office dated 9 November 1917

20 The National Archives, Colonial Office file CO 78/152 (62457)
   letter dated 19 December 1919.

21 The Royal Scottish Museum received books, sealskins (five species
   including male, female and one baby seal), birds, eggs and fish. All
   the museums received specimens, Perth and Dundee received seal
   skeletons after the first complete set had been sent to Edinburgh
   Museum. The Royal Scottish Geographical Museum received
   birds (duplicates could be sold and the proceeds put towards a
   publication fund).

22 Volume V, Zoology was published in 1909 (33/6d in cloth
   £1.1shilling in paper) Volume VI Zoology, 1912 (thirty shillings in
   cloth). Volume 111 Botany, 1913 (price 23 shillings/6p, in cloth!).
   Volume 11 Ornithology 1913 (eleven shillings. with no logo
   on the frontispiece) Volume 1V Zoology, 1915 (fifty shillings),
   Volume VII Zoology Invertebrates 1920 (fifty shillings)

23 Speak, P. (2003), *William Speirs Bruce, Polar Explorer and Scottish Nationalist*, National Museums of Scotland, Edinburgh, p. 100

24 RGS (with IBG) Archives, Scott Keltie, *Letter to Bruce*, dated 11 November 1913. CB8 1911–1918

25 RGS (with IBG) Archives, Bruce, W. S., *Letter to Keltie*, dated 17 November 1913CB8 1911–1918

10 *The Arctic: The Scottish Spitsbergen Syndicate*

1   Robert Fotherby (died 1648), He made a number of whaling voyages to Spitsbergen, 1613–1615.

2   Posthumus, H. (1624), *Purchas his Pilgrimes, Contayning a History of the World, in Sea Voyages, & Lande Travells, By Englishmen and Others*, Vol. xiv p. 65

3   Rudmose Brown, R. N. *Letter to Bruce*. SPRI MS 101/19/47:D

4   Bruce, W. S. (1908), *The Exploration of Prince Charles Foreland 1906–1907*, The Geographical Journal, London. pp 139–150

5   *ibid*

6   Jonas Poole (1566–1612) was an English explorer and sealer. He was important in the establishment of the Arctic whaling trade.

7   Bruce, W. S. (1908), *The Exploration of Prince Charles Foreland 1906–1907*, The Geographical Journal, London. pp 139–150

8   Bruce, W. S (1907), National Museum of Scotland, Box 10 File 112

9   Burn Murdoch, W. G. (1907), National Museum of Scotland, Box10 File 116

10 Bruce, W. S. (1908), *The Exploration of Prince Charles Foreland 1906–1907* The Geographical Journal, London. pp 139–150 and National Museum of Scotland, Box10 File115

11 Briggs, H. *Report*, Heriot-Watt College, Edinburgh, National Museum of Scotland, Box10, File 115

12 The quality of coal is determined by age, temperature and proportion of inorganic matter. Personal communication, 2016, David J Large, Head of Department, Chemical and Environmental Engineering, Faculty of Engineering, University of Nottingham.

13 Cadell, H. M. *Letter to Bruce*, National Museum of Scotland Box 10. File 119

14 Distance in nautical miles: Norway 350, Bergen to Ice fjord 1300, London 1750

15 Scottish Spitsbergen Syndicate Subscription Slip, National Museum of Scotland Box 11 File. 143

16 Kruse, F. (2013), *Frozen Assets*, Circumpolar Studies Vol.9, Arctic Centre, University of Groningen, p. 333

17 W. S. Bruce Papers, *Letter to Bruce from Paul Rottenburg*, National Museum of Scotland, Box 11 File. 136

18 Certificate of incorporation (1909), The Scottish Spitsbergen Syndicate Ltd, BT2/7201/1 National Museum of Scotland

19 The directors were Paul Rottenburg, Charles Hanson Urmston, John Henry Davidson, Thomas Barnby Whitson and Paterson (initials unknown)

20 Certificate of incorporation (1909) The Scottish Spitsbergen Syndicate Ltd BT2/7201/1 National Museum of Scotland

21 Kruse, F. (2013), *Frozen Assets*, Circumpolar Studies Vol.9 Arctic Centre, University of Groningen, p. 333

22 Luis Charles Bernacchi (1876–1942) was born of Italian parents in Belgium, but was educated in Tasmania. He trained in astronomy at Melbourne University and developed a passion for Antarctica. He took part as the physicist in Carsten Borchgrevink's *Southern Cross* expedition, which wintered at Cape Adare at the turn of the century. He went again to Antarctica as physicist with Scott's *Discovery* expedition (1901–1904).

23 The National Archives, Colonial Office Files CO78/114 (29910) *Dr Bruce's appeal for Lease of Sandwich Islands*, and CO 78/115 (18172 and 20612) *Lease of the South Sandwich Group*

24 The National Archives, Colonial Office File CO78/114 *Falkland Islands Governor 1909* Report by Carl Larsen to the Governor of the Falkland Islands,

25 John Mathieson (1855–1945), surveyor, cartographer and Gaelic scholar

26 Barents Island and Barents Land are the same. A German map from of 1914 shows Barent's Land as Barents Island. A map of Spitsbergen dated 1758 does not show Barents Island as separate from the main island. This earlier map 'Suivant les Hollandois' was drawn from Barents' information. The area that was Barents Island was called Nieu Vreisland, presumably Barents did not discover the channel between the islands.

27 Edward Grey (1862–1933), 1st Viscount Grey of Fallodon, Foreign Secretary from 1905 to 1916, the longest continuous occupation of that post before or since.

28 Kruse, F. (2013), *Frozen Assets*. Circumpolar Studies Vol.9 Arctic Centre, University of Groningen, p. 345

29 Speak, P. (2003), *William Speirs Bruce, Polar Explorer and Scottish Nationalist*, Edinburgh, p. 105

30 SPRI 311 1-6 ER 20/9/09

31 Rudmose Brown, R. N. (1912), *The Commercial Development of Spitsbergen*, Scottish Geographical Magazine, Vol.28, no 11, pp. 561–571

32 Kruse, F. (2013), *Frozen Assets*, Circumpolar Studies Vol.9 Arctic Centre, University of Groningen, p. 337

33 Bruce, W. S. *Letter to Rudmose Brown*, SPRI, 356/46/13

34 Bruce, W. S. *Letter to Rudmose Brown*, National Museum of Scotland, Box 19 File 118

35 Rudmose Brown, *Letter to Bruce*, SPRI 101/19/47; D

36 Rudmose Brown, *Letter to Bruce*, SPRI 101/19/52; D

37 Bruce, W. S. *Letter to Robert Neil Rudmose Brown*, SPRI, 356/46/14

38 John Foster Stackhouse (1864–1915), English. Described as an explorer though no significant explorations were achieved. Died on the *Lusitania* when she was destroyed by a German warship.

39 Burn Murdoch, V. *Letter to Bruce*. SPRI, 101/64/4; D

40 Bruce, W. S. *Letter to Rudmose Brown, R. N.* SPRI, MS 101/87/1-7; D

41 Bruce, W. S. *Letter to Rudmose Brown*, National Museum of Scotland Box 10. File 133

42 Rudmose Brown, R. N. *Letter to Bruce*, SPRI, 101/19/41; D

43 Rudmose Brown, R. N. *Letter to Bruce*, SPRI, 101/19/48; D

44 Markham, C. (1912), Geographic Magazine, MS 356/46/1-295 D p. 17

45 Bruce, W. S. *Letter to Robert Neil Rudmose Brown* 10/6/12, 356/46/28; D

46 *ibid*

47 *ibid*

48 Bruce, W. S. *Letter to Robert Neil Rudmose Brown* 12/6/12. 356/46/29; D

49 Rudmose Brown, R. N. *Letter to Bruce*, SPRI 101/19/50:D

50 The Scottish Geographic Magazine (1912), Volume 28 pp. 579–583

51 Entry from Sir Clements Markham's Personal Journal, April 9 to 12 1912. Royal Geographical Society – with IBG, CRM/53. The reference to the "gadfly" is somewhat obscure, but possibly relates to Amundsen. "Shackles" is presumably Shackleton.

52 Bruce, W. S. *Letter to R. N. Rudmose Brown*, SPRI, 356/46/35;D

53 *ibid*

54 Bruce, W. S. *Letter to Charles Price* 16/9/12/ National Museum of Scotland, Box11, File 134

55 Bruce, W. S. *Letter to Scott Keltie*, RGS CB8 1911–1918

56 Norway developed a particular interest in Spitsbergen after she had achieved independence from Sweden in 1905, when the Prince of Denmark became King Haakon VII of Norway.

57 Bruce, W. S. *Letter the Right Hon The Earl of Norton*, SPRI,356/46/22;D

58 *ibid*

59 Keltie, J. S. *Letter to Bruce, W. S.* SPRI, 356/46/39;D

60 Kruse, F. (2013), *Frozen Assets*, Circumpolar Studies Vol.9, Arctic Centre, University of Groningen, p. 347

61 Bruce, W. S. *Letter to Keltie*, RGS, CB8 1911–1920 (5 October 1914)

62 Bruce, W. S. *Letter to Keltie*, 5/10/13/RGS CB8 1911–1920

63 Bruce, W. S. *Letter to R. N. Rudmose Brown*, SPRI,356/46/67;D

64 Bruce, W. S. *Letter to R. N. Rudmose Brown*, SPRI,356/46/124;D

65 *ibid*

66 'Nature' Notes, Vol. 97, Macmillan and Co. p. 449

67 Arthur Robert Hicks (1873–1946), astronomer, geographer

68 Arthur Balfour (1848–1930), Prime Minister 1902–1905 Foreign Secretary 1916

69 Letter to President RGS, 22/12/16, RGS CB8 1911–20, Annexation of Spitsbergen

70 In 1997 Norway established a 200-nautical-mile exclusive economic zone around Svalbard. In 2010, she agreed a boundary between the Svalbard and Novaya Zemlya archipelagos with Russia.

71 Report by Herbert Ponting (1870–1935), who was the camera artist on Scott's *Terra Nova* expedition and who visited Spitsbergen with the Northern Exploration Company

72 SPRI Archive, MS356/95CP *Scottish Spitsbergen Syndicate, Miscellaneous Correspondence*, Letter from J V Burn Murdoch to Aitkin, dated 21 September 1918

73 SPRI Archive, MS356/95CP *Scottish Spitsbergen Syndicate, Miscellaneous Correspondence*, Letter from Bruce to Hanney dated 26 September 1918

74 SPRI Archive, MS356/95CP *Scottish Spitsbergen Syndicate, Miscellaneous Correspondence*, Letter from Bruce to Rudmose Brown dated 15 October 1918

75 Certificate of Incorporation (1919), Scottish Spitzbergen Syndicate, NAS02024 BT2-10219, National Archives of Scotland, Edinburgh

76 Bruce, W. S. *Letter to A. Arthur*, National Museum of Scotland, Box 10 File 114

77 Speak, P. (2003), *William Speirs Bruce, Polar Explorer and Scottish Nationalist*, Edinburgh, p. 115

78 The gypsum was said to be of exceptionally fine quality. Norway and Sweden had imported between them about 28,000 tons in 1913

79 *Information regarding the Hire of Sloop*, National Museum of Scotland Box12 File 155

80 These were drawn from Scottish universities, Geographic and Geological Societies, the Royal Society of Edinburgh, the Institute of Mining and Metallurgy and the Institute of Civil Engineering.

81 Scottish Spitsbergen Syndicate, Report *from Skinningrove Iron Co.* SPRI MS 311/88;ER Arctic

82 Wilton, D. W. *Letter to W. S. Bruce* National Museum of Scotland, Box11. File 142. Coal prices: Black Sea, 6 copeiks/lb.7sh10, 1/2d/ ton along western frontier and ports of Baltic Sea 11copeiks/ lb.1sh11d, 3/4d/ton. Ports of White Sea, Free: Coke prices: Black Sea, 9 copeiks/lb. 11sh10d/ton. Western Frontier, 21/4copeiks/lb: Russian consumption was: State Railway, 222.506.000 lbs: Private Railways, 97,979,000 lbs: Coal lines, 2, 448,000 lbs. Total 322,932,000

83 RGS (with IBG) Archive, CB81911–1920. Aitken, A., Letter to Arthur Robert Hinks, dated 12 October 20.

84 David Livingstone Centenary Medal. Established 1913 by the Hispanic Society of America and awarded for outstanding public service in which geography has played an important part, either by exploration, by administration, or in other directions. Awarded to Bruce for his work in the Southern Ocean

85 Frank Debenham (1883–1965), Emeritus Professor of Geography, Cambridge. He was a member of Scott's second expedition, one of three geologists. He served in the infantry during WW1. He was co-founder and the first Director of the Scott Polar Research Institute

11 *Bruce's Final Illness and Death: Reflections on His Life*

1 Statutory Deaths 685/15 0058: Deaths in the District of Liberton in the City of Edinburgh, p. 20

2 *Obituary: William Speirs Bruce, LL.D* The Geographical Journal, Vol.58. No.6 December 1921

3 490 shares in SSS £312,7s, 6d; 400 shares in name of The Commercial Bank of Scotland £255; Deposit Receipt with City of Edinburgh in name of Whitson/ Methuen for W. S. Bruce, £713,4s; 2 policies with North British & Mercantile Co. Ltd on life of WS Bruce £1,000 & £1,169, 7s 10d; 3000 National War Bonds (1928), £2996

4   Will by William Speirs Bruce. National Records of Scotland, SC70/4/555 Registered 8/11/1921 p. 230

5   Speak, P. (2003), *William Speirs Bruce Polar Explorer and Scottish Nationalist*, National Museums of Scotland, Edinburgh, p. 62

6   Will by William Speirs Bruce. National Records of Scotland, SC70/4/555 Registered 8/11/1921 p. 229

7   Speak, P. (2003), *William Speirs Bruce Polar Explorer and Scottish Nationalist*, National Museums of Scotland, Edinburgh, p. 62

8   Will by William Speirs Bruce. National Records of Scotland, SC70/4/555 Registered 8/11/1921, p 229

9   Will by William Speirs Bruce. National Records of Scotland, SC70/4/555 Registered 8/11/1921, p. 230

10 Mossman R. *The South Orkneys observatory* SPRI 356/74/5

11 The National Archives, Foreign Office file, FO 118/265 (*General correspondence of British Embassy, Argentina*), *Letter from Haggard to Marquess of Lansdowne on Scottish National Antarctic Expedition*, dated 5 Jan 1904.

12 The National Archives, Colonial Office file CO78/109 (30162), *South Orkneys*

13 Rudmose Brown, R. N. *Letter to Mill*, SPRI 100/15/2:D

14 Rudmose Brown, R. N. (1923), *A Naturalist At The Poles*, Seeley Service and Co., London, pp. 295–297

15 Rudmose Brown, R. N. *Letter to Mill*, SPRI 100/15/6:D

16 *ibid*

17 Rudmose Brown, R. N. (1923), *A Naturalist At The Poles* Seeley Service and Co, London, p. 260

18 Mossman, R. *Letter to H R Mill* SPRI 100/81/10;D

19 Lewy Bodies. Aggregates of protein that develop inside nerve endings in some forms of dementia

20 Dudeney, J. R. & D. W. H. Walton (2011), From "Scotia" to "Operation Tabarin" – Developing British Policy for Antarctica, Polar Record, DOI: 10.1017/S0032247411000520

21 People with autism regularly make great achievements in specific fields

22 The Patron's Medal and the Founder's Medals are awarded by the Royal Geographical Society to those who have made an exceptional contribution to exploration and geography. The medal was made by Wyon of Langham Chambers, London and bears the bas-relief image by Allan Wyon (H. M. Engraver of Seals) of King Edward VII (then patron of the Royal Geographical Society) on the obverse, and a classical female figure by W. Wyon on the reverse. It was "adjudged for eminence in Natural History" to William Speirs Bruce LLD, 1911–12, 1912–13

23 The Neill Medal was first awarded in 1859, as the result of a bequest in 1851 from the late Dr Patrick Neill, a distinguished Scottish naturalist. It is still awarded every three years for a work or publication by a Scottish naturalist, preferably based in Scotland, on some branch of natural history.

24 Prof. David Mackenzie Munro MBE, BSc, PhD, FRGS, FRSA, FSAScot

Appendix 1: Captain Thomas Robertson, 1855–1918

1 *Scottish Geographical Magazine*, Vol. 35, ISS. 4, 1919

2 Scott Polar Research Institute archives, Bruce, William S.MS441/7D

Appendix 2: Excerpts from The Log of the Scotia by William Speirs Bruce

1 Bruce, W. S. (1992), *The Log of the* Scotia, Edited by Peter Speak. Edinburgh University Press.

Appendix 3: *Plans for a Trans-Antarctic Journey*

1   The *Times* of London, April 8 1908, p. 7

2   *The Scotsman*, 17 November 1909

3   The National Archives, Treasury file T1/11679 Grants to Scottish National Antarctic Expedition 1914

4   *ibid*

5   *The Scotsman*, 10 January 1910, p. 10

6   *ibid*

7   *The Scotsman*, 11 January 1910

8   *The Scotsman*, 13 January 1910

9   Royal Geographical Society (with IBG) CB7/Bruce, W. S.

10 *ibid*

11 *ibid*

12 *ibid*

13 *ibid*

14 From Speak, P. 2003, p.118–119

15 *The Scotsman*, 18 March 1910

16 The National Archives, Treasury file T1-11679, Grants to Scottish National Antarctic Expedition 1914

Appendix 4: *Bruce and the Polar Medal*

1   The National Archives, Treasury file T1-11396 British Antarctic Expedition 1907, letter from the Admiralty to the Treasury dated 9 August 1909

2   The National Archives, Treasury file T1-11396 British Antarctic Expedition 1907, draft letter to be sent to Admiralty

3   Letter dated 23 November 1909 to Ferrier, SPRI Archive MS/101/20/1–18

4   Letter dated 24 November 1909 to Ferrier, SPRI Archive
    MS/101/20/1–18

5   The National Records Office of Scotland, Scottish Office file HH
    1–1943

6   *ibid*

7   Speak, P. (2003), *William Speirs Bruce Polar Explorer and Scottish
    Nationalist*, National Museums of Scotland, Edinburgh, p. 128

8   The National Archives, Admiralty file ADM 1/8367/21, *Polar
    Medals Scottish Antarctic Expedition 1914*

9   The National Archives, Treasury file number T 1/11599, *Award of
    Polar Medal 1914*

10 The National Archives, Admiralty file ADM 1/8367/21 *Polar
    Medals Scottish Antarctic Expedition 1914*

11 *ibid*

12 The National Archives, Treasury file number T 1/11599, *Award of
    Polar Medal 1914*

13 The National Archives, Admiralty file ADM 1/8367/21 *Polar
    Medals Scottish Antarctic Expedition 1914*

14 *ibid*

Appendix 5: Attempt by Bruce to Lease the South Sandwich Islands

1   The National Archives, Colonial Office File CO78/114 *Dr Bruce's
    appeal for Lease of Sandwich Islands, Report by Captain C A
    Larson on an exploring expedition round part of South Georgia
    and to the Sandwich Islands*

2   The National Archives, Colonial Office File CO78/114 *Dr Bruce's
    appeal for Lease of Sandwich Islands,* Letter from the Governor
    to the Colonial Office

3 The National Archives, Colonial Office File CO78/115 (18172 and 20612) *Lease of the South Sandwich Group*, Letter from Bruce to the Colonial Office

4 The National Archives, Colonial Office File CO78/115 (18172 and 20612) *Lease of the South Sandwich Group*, Draft of a letter from Colonial Office to Bruce

5 The National Archives, Colonial Office File CO78/115 (18172 and 20612) *Lease of the South Sandwich Group*, Letter from Bruce to Colonial Office

6 The National Archives, Colonial Office File CO78/115 (18172 and 20612) *Lease of the South Sandwich Group*, file note dated 23 June 1909

7 The National Archives, Colonial Office File CO78/115 (18172 and 20612) *Lease of the South Sandwich Group*, draft letter to Bruce

8 The National Archives, Colonial Office File CO78/114 (29910) *Dr Bruce's Application for lease of Sandwich Islands* File note dated 7 September 1909

9 The National Archives, Colonial Office File CO78/114 (29910) *Dr Bruce's Application for lease of Sandwich Islands* Draft of a letter to be sent to Bruce.

Appendix 6: Bruce and the Patron's Medal

1 Royal Geographical Society (with IBG) Council Minutes/Vol 8 p. 146

Appendix 7: An Insight into Bruce's Character

1 Royal Geographical Society (with IBG), CB7/Bruce, W. S., Letter to Sir George Goldie dated 7 October 1907

2 *Geographical Journal*, Volume XXXI, 1908, p 685

3 Royal Geographical Society (with IBG), CB7/Bruce, W. S., Letter to The Secretary of the RGS dated 19 November 1908

4 Royal Geographical Society (with IBG), CB7/Bruce, W. S., Letter to Bruce dated 20 November 1908

5 Royal Geographical Society (with IBG), CB7/Bruce, W. S., Letter to Bruce dated 23 November 1908

6 Royal Geographical Society (with IBG), CB7/Bruce, W. S., Letter to The Secretary of the RGS dated 25 November 1908

7 Royal Geographical Society (with IBG), CB7/Bruce, W. S., Letter to Major Lachlan Forbes dated 27 November 1908

8 Royal Geographical Society (with IBG), CB7/Bruce, W. S., Letter From Lachlan Forbes to Secretary of the RGS dated 30 November 1908

BIBLIOGRAPHY

Bruce, W. S. (1902), *The Scottish National Antarctic Expedition*,
Geographical Journal, vol. 20, no. 4, pp.438–440

Bruce, W. S. (1903), *The* Scotia *Voyage to the Falkland Islands*, Scottish
Geographical Magazine, vol. 19, no. 4, pp.169–183

Bruce, W. S. (1908), *Scotland and the Antarctic*, 'Scotia', 2

Bruce, W. S. (1908), *The Exploration of Prince Charles Foreland*
1906–1907, The Geographical Journal, London, pp.139–150

Bruce, W. S. (1911), *Polar Exploration*, Williams & Norgate, London

Bruce, W. S. (1992), *Log of the* Scotia, *1902–4*, ed. Peter Speak,
Edinburgh University Press, Edinburgh

Burn Murdock, W. G. (1894), *From Edinburgh to the Antarctic*,
Longmans & Green, Edinburgh

Dudeney, J. R. & D. H. Walton (2011), *From* Scotia *to 'Operation*
Tabarin': developing British policy for Antarctica, Polar Record,
DOI: 10.1017/S0032247411000520

Dudeney, J. R. & J. Sheail (2014), *William Speirs Bruce and the*
Polar Medal: Myth and Reality, The Polar Journal, DOI:
10.1080/2154896X.2014.913915

Dudeney J. R., J. Sheail & D. W. H. Walton (2014), *The British Government, Ernest Shackleton, and the rescue of the Imperial Trans-Antarctic Expedition*, Polar Record, DOI:10.1017/S0032247414000631

Headland, R. K. (2009), *A Chronology of Antarctic Exploration*, Quaritch, London

Huntford, R. (1985), *Shackleton*, Hodder & Stoughton, London

Jackson, F. G. (1935), *The Lure of Unknown Lands*, Bell and Sons, London

Jackson, F. G. (1899), *1000 Days in the Arctic*, Vol. II, Harper & Brothers, London

Keighren. J. M. (2003), *A Scot in the Antarctic. The Reception and Commemoration of William Speirs Bruce*, The University of Edinburgh School of Geosciences Institute of Geography, Edinburgh

Keltie, J. S. & H. R. Mill (1896), *Report of the Sixth International Geographical Congress: Held in London, 1895*. Vol. 6, London

Koettlitz, R. (1906), *Scurvy and Antiscorbutics*, Guy's Hospital Gazette

Kruse, F. (2013), *Frozen Assets*, Circumpolar Studies, Vol. 9, Arctic Centre, University of Groningen

McGonigal, D. & L. Woodworth (2003), *Antarctica, The Complete Story*, 2003, Francis Lincoln, London

Mill, H. R. (1951), *An Autobiography*, Longmans, Green, & Co., London

Mossman, R. C. (1910), *The present position of Antarctic meteorology*, Quarterly Journal of the Royal Meteorological Society, vol. 36, no. 156, pp.361–74

Murray, J. (1894), *The Renewal of Antarctic Exploration*, The Geographical Journal, vol. 111, no. 1

Murray, J. (1903), *The Renewal of Antarctic Exploration*, The Geographical Journal, vol. 3, pp.1–43

Nansen, F. (1897), *Farthest North, The Voyage and Exploration of the Fram 1893–96*, Archibald Constable and Company, London

Posthumus, H. (1624), *Purchas his Pilgrimes, Contayning a History of the World, in Sea Voyages, & Lande Travells, By Englishmen and Others*, vol. xiv

Riffenburgh, B. (2004), *Nimrod*, Bloomsbury, London

Roy, M. (2013), *The Weathermen of Ben Nevis 1883–1904*, The Royal Society of Edinburgh, RSE@Lochaber

Rudmose Brown, R. N. (1923), *A Naturalist at the Poles*, Seeley, Service and Co., London

Rudmose Brown, R. N., J. H. H. Pirie & R. C. Mossman (1906), *The Voyage of the Scotia* (1978 edition), C. Hurst & Co., London.

Speak, P. (2003), *William Speirs Bruce, Polar Explorer and Scottish Nationalist*, National Museums of Scotland, Edinburgh

Swinney, G. N. (2001), *Some new perspectives on the life of William Speirs Bruce (1867–1921)*, Edinburgh, Archives of Natural History, vol. 28, no. 3

Tønnessen, J. N. & A. O. Johnsen (1982), *The History of Modern Whaling*, Hurst & Company London

INDEX

Also available from Amberley Publishing

THE NORTHWEST PASSAGE OVERLAND

THE EPIC JOURNEY THAT HELPED CREATE CANADA

E. C. COLEMAN

Available from all good bookshops or to order direct
Please call **01453–847–800**
www.amberley-books.com